Schi

ZABAR'S Deli BOOK

By Susan Katz

With Murray Klein, Saul Zabar,
and Stanley Zabar

Illustrated and designed by Push Pin Studios
under the direction of Seymour Chwast

Hawthorn Books
A division of Elsevier-Dutton
New York

‖ "When I die and go to heaven, I
hope the Zabar's up there is as
good as the one down here." ‖
    Neil Simon

ZABAR'S DELI BOOK

Designed by Push Pin Studios
Illustrated by Seymour Chwast,
Richard Mantel & Haruo Miyauchi
Production : Terry Berkowitz

Library of Congress Catalog Card Number : 79–84935
ISBN : 0–8015–9200–3
1 2 3 4 5 6 7 8 9 10

Contents

ONLY AT

Zabar's

"It's like going to a small European country for the price of a cab ride."
Pat Collins and Joe Raposa

■ At the height of the Watergate scandal, midnight meetings in the prosecutor's office temporarily broke up while someone raced to the airport to pick up a Zabar's care package from the New York shuttle—bagels, lox, and scallion cream cheese—what else?

■ A young man and a young woman locked eyes over the pastrami, and it was love at the meat counter. They were married and lived happily ever after. A true story—even if no one remembers their names!

■ Isaac Stern, the renowned violinist, is a long-time Zabar's customer, with a Zabar's charge account (a privilege only a couple of hundred regulars have). He went into the store one day, filled his basket, and insisted on paying cash. He abashedly explained that his wife had put him on a very strict diet, and he didn't want her to know he was cheating.

■ Woody Allen, writing about women some years ago in *The New York Times*, described one of his paramours as having "skin like satin, or should I say like the finest of Zabar's Novy."

■ In *The Sunshine Boys*, Dick Benjamin toted a Zabar's shopping bag around with him throughout the movie.

■ *The Cook's Catalogue* called Zabar's "New York City's answer to Fauchon," Paris' enormous and high-quality gourmet supermarket. Zabar's disagrees. "We're better."

■ More than 30 percent of Zabar's customers every week are first-timers. And if they can't come back in person, they order by mail or harass friends into bringing them care packages.

Zabar's. A "gourmet and epicurean emporium," they call it; but it is much more than that.

Smaller than the average apartment in the kaleidoscopic Upper West Side neighborhood in which it resides, Zabar's satisfies the more than a million people —over 20,000 a week—who willingly spend nine million dollars a year on everything from cutting boards to caviar.

It is its very own sound-and-light show, and as you walk in the door, it all hits you at once. The overall view is spectacular.

On the right, just behind the cash registers, is a densely packed wall of bread, rolls, bagels, croissants, brioches. Incredible shapes; even more incredible aromas. On the left, a window full of fresh pasta in assorted shapes and sizes; beer and ale—30 kinds—follow; then the choicest, freshest, tastiest produce.

Look up for a moment. Glistening copper pots and utensils hang suspended from every free inch of the ceiling, broken only occasionally by a braid of red onions or snowy-white garlic. Look down. The floor is stacked with salad spinners and vegetable steamers, food processors and juice extractors. And anything else that will fit.

Move on. You aren't yet five feet into the store.

Just past the bread, still on the right, a universe of mustards and almost every variety of packaged tea to reach the U.S. shores. On the opposite wall, almost hidden, a freezer full of ice cream, frozen yogurt, and frozen desserts.

The next 30 feet—the heart of Zabar's—are truly an assault on the senses. The fish department is on the left, a mouth-watering seduction of more than two dozen varieties of smoked and pickled fish—salmon, lox, sturgeon, carp, whitefish, herring, eels, brook trout, and more—plus salads, pickles, olives, and of course, caviar. Behind it, truffles, dried mushrooms, dried fruits, and nuts. In New York, it's collectively called "appetizing," this mélange of wonderful aromas, tastes, and textures.

This is almost, but not quite, outdone by the deli department, directly opposite. Here, 423 different meats, wursts, salamis, sausages, more salads, pâtés, sitting or hanging in glorious profusion.

Next, the cheeses. Beginning where the fish counter ends, hundreds of varieties of cheese, from every corner of the world, sharp and mild, hard and soft, cow, sheep, goat, high-fat, low-fat, low salt, creamy white to intensely veined with blue. On the other side, hundreds of jars, bottles, boxes, and tins of imported wonders—the hottest chili sauce in the world; the lightest, nuttiest French salad oils; honeys; jams; crackers; vinegars. A whole marketplace of gourmet foods tucked into an amazingly small space.

Above you, still more things hang from the ceiling or are piled high on shelves—everything from soup ladles to nutcrackers, bagel cutters to wicker baskets.

Toward the back of the store, cakes and cookies galore—sweets to the sweet—and nuts. A dairy case, on the left, with milk, butter, cream, yogurt—the usual. And the unusual, too : *crème fraiche*, for example, that heavy, sweet, slightly nutty matured cream that is the essence of French cuisine; and really fresh eggs, single-yolk and double-yolk; the purest French butter.

Dried herbs and spices on the right, in all the colors of the rainbow, all the nuances of the culinary world.

At the very rear, coffee and tea. Wooden barrels hold 15 varieties of specially selected and freshly roasted coffee beans. Buy them whole, or Zabar's will grind them to order. A dozen blends of loose tea, in airtight containers, are surrounded by everything you'll ever need to brew tea properly—teapots, kettles, strainers, infusers, even canisters to keep it in. And the back wall. A bazaarlike arrangement of coffee-makers and grinders, mugs, filters, espresso machines, *chotchkas* for the coffee lover, which literally spill over onto the floor and nearby shelves.

There's even more. Something you've missed perhaps, or something brand-new, jammed into a nook or cranny.

The people are all part of it. Crowding into the already filled aisles, deftly avoiding elbows and shopping baskets, looking either determined or confused, but always slightly disbelieving. You think you know just what you want, but it's easy to be distracted by, well, everything.

On weekends, Zabar's is literally wall-to-wall people (although the store is open seven days a week, 365 days a year). And the double- and triple-parked cars in front of the store are like a blockade. It scares away some would-be shoppers.

Nevertheless, most people more than just put up with the crowds at Zabar's; they make weekend shopping a habit. Some even like the crowds. If you have to have fresh bagels and lox with your *New York Times* on Sunday morning, you have to grin and bear it.

Art Garfunkel and Joel Grey do. Mimi Sheraton doesn't. Barbra Streisand, Lauren Bacall, Shelley Winters, and Faye Dunaway do. Mikhail Baryshnikov and John Lennon don't. Dore Schary used to; so did Jacob Javits. Grin and bear it, that is.

The list of celebrity shoppers reads like a *Who's Who* of Broadway, Hollywood, and TVland. Woody Allen, Abe Burrows, Leonard Bernstein, Lee Grant. Half the TV soap-opera world. Most of Broadway's current stars. Raul Julia, Joseph Papp, Lee Strasberg, Anne Jackson and Eli Wallach, Mitch Miller, Beverly Sills, Martin Balsam, Dick Cavett, Isaac Stern, Allen Funt, Harry Belafonte, Teddy Kennedy. Almost anyone at all.

They go to Zabar's for coffee, bread, smoked salmon, whatever, and they stand in line like everyone else. They get no special treatment; they fight the crowds, wait their turns, and are pretty much unbothered by the rest of the customers. Once in a while, someone asks for an autograph, but quietly, without fuss. Everyone is so intent on just being there that celebrity faces blend with the salamis.

The biggest—and loudest—laments come from Zabar's regulars who leave New York City for the glamour and glitter of the West Coast and can't find a decent piece of lox anywhere. Peter Nero. Mel Brooks. Neil Simon. They have to rely on care packages from friends and pleas to traveling acquaintances to "please stop at Zabar's on the way to the airport," to pick up a little of this and a little of that. Zabar's is good about packing its best for traveling : dry ice, special bags, superprotective wrapping. Still, nothing ever arrives quite whole. Bits and pieces of things have a funny way of disappearing somewhere between JFK and LAX.

THE PARTNERS

What makes Zabar's Zabar's is not just the wondrous concentration of foods and housewares, or the amalgam of enticing aromas that bombard the unsuspecting, or even the crowds and the lack of space and the learning to put up with them. It's the three men who run it. The partners. Saul Zabar. Stanley Zabar.

APPETIZERS

25°° MINIMUM
PURCHASE FOR

ZAB

FREE PA

not any more." That, of course, doesn't mean he's not working. His days usually start with the sun. As the chief taster, he's in Brooklyn sampling coffee at least two days a week, and in Brooklyn or Queens watching out for his fish the rest of the time. That is, when he isn't checking out a shipment of Brie or fooling around with the salads in the store's kitchen. Or taking apart an espresso machine.

He knows intimately every fish that Zabar's sells, and every coffee bean has passed through his hands several times. He can change the proportions of a salad recipe a dozen times in a day until he's completely satisfied that it's exactly as it should be. It isn't unusual to find an old favorite at the appetizing counter missing if Saul hasn't got the lemon juice in correct proportion to the sugar. His head chef, Louie, is as finicky as Saul.

Yet, Saul admits, when he's home, he's not quite the tyrant of the taste buds. He'll make coffee Melitta, which is easiest; his favorite dinner is whitefish salad or kippered salmon salad with some lettuce and tomato on the side. In the midst of roasting thousands of pounds of coffee at the plant, he'll break for a lunch of canned salmon, bread, and tomatoes and relish it with enthusiasm that belies the fact that almost everything he tastes for Zabar's—be it coffee, fish, cheese, or salad—he never swallows.

By the time he stumbles back to the store late in the afternoon, the jaunty, predawn Saul is about wiped out. But he can't resist, as he passes the appetizing counter on his way to the office, the urge to pop a piece

Murray Klein. Three totally different personalities, usually in conflict. Murray Klein loves a good fight, and he's had several. Saul avoids them. Stanley is the buffer.

There's a highly volatile interaction going on there, totally dependent on its very precariousness. Without the tension, the acutely competitive spirit that drives them all to their respective extremes, there would be no Zabar's as it is. The three are often on a collision course; but when they stand together, Zabar's is unshakable.

SAUL

Saul Zabar, with almost-white hair (he's only 51) and darting, quick eyes, is a compact, active man, always in motion. He looks as if he might just have come off a squash court, and he might have. He's a relaxed athlete who plays hard, but for the fun of it. When it comes to the store, however, the fun and games stop. He's exacting, impatient, a stickler for perfection. He is also the full-time Zabar who probably spends the least time in the store.

"I'm sort of semiretired," he says, grinning. "I used to be here until eleven P.M. or midnight, but

of smoked sturgeon into his mouth or to try a spoonful of whitefish salad. Just checking. Always checking. He'd like to do the same as he saunters by the deli counter, but he doesn't. That's Stanley's province, and Saul never would dare butt in.

STANLEY

Since the age of eleven, Stanley Zabar has been part of Zabar's. As a teen-ager he worked in the store on weekends, then worked full time, and then part-time again, somehow managing an extensive education. His list of degrees is impressive: besides his LL.D. from Brooklyn Law School, he has an L.L.M. in Taxation and Finance from New York University and did undergraduate work at Wharton and N.Y.U. in accounting. He is, indeed, the learned partner, and he retains a sort of scholarly air. He's not as flamboyantly outgoing as his older brother, nor as stern-faced and patriarchal as Murray Klein. He's somewhere in the easy-does-it middle; the voice of reason and compromise.

In the seven years Stanley has given to the store, he has made some remarkable changes, in his own subtle, effective manner. He upped the profits of the meat department quite significantly. He introduced so many new deli features that even he has lost count, and he

decided, quite rightly, that if Murray Klein could hang housewares from the ceiling, he could hang salamis.

Stanley is the one who plows through the mountains of paperwork that cross his desk every day. There's an office staff, naturally, but it's Stanley who knows precisely what has been ordered, when, and from whom; what needs immediate attention and what can wait—in general, what's happening at Zabar's.

"My role," he claims modestly, "is peacemaker and financial advisor. In general, I stay out of Saul and Murray's way."

Well, yes, that's true. They all stay out of one another's way. All may be in the store at the same time (at least one of them always is), but rarely in the same place. So things are lively.

Stanley says it's all because of Murray Klein and his never-ending supply of new ideas and merchandising concepts that keeps them all going. "There's a constant need to prevent boredom, especially with Murray, who is always fighting for something new."

MURRAY

To most of Zabar's customers, Murray Klein *is* Zabar's. He's the most visible partner, the most voluble. He's the one you yell at and even occasionally thank. He's the one who yells back, who knows when the Jamaica Blue Mountain is due to arrive and how much chopped liver to buy for a party of 20.

He is all energy, constantly on the go. From the

13

minute he opens the door at six each morning—sometimes earlier—Murray Klein and Zabar's are indefatigable. When he isn't checking the bread delivery, he may be stocking the shelves with new merchandise or sweeping the floor. Nothing is beneath him, and he won't ask his employees to do anything that he wouldn't—and doesn't—do himself.

Klein has been known to smile, but rarely. His demeanor is no-nonsense steel. He takes Zabar's seriously.

"I'm a proletarian at heart," he explains. "Standing around watching the money come in doesn't do anything for me. I'm happy only when I'm doing, changing, twisting things around. By nature, I'm a drifter. I don't like to stay in one place. But here it's always different, it stimulates me."

If anyone makes things stimulating, he does. His eyes are constantly circling the store, watching what goes on in every corner. He knows instinctively when something's about to go wrong, and he catches it before it has a chance to happen. That's a trick he learned early in life, you realize; a vital quickness that makes Murray Klein so alive.

He was born in the Ukraine in 1923, not a very good year for Russian Jews. By the time he was 15, he was making the kinds of instant life-and-death decisions that were often more dangerous than enterprising. He came to this country in 1950 and went to work at the Zabar's on West 110th Street. But the manager didn't like foreigners, and Murray lasted about a week. He got another job easily. But something about Zabar's had gotten to him. He was at the West 96th Street store within a year and eventually managed it.

Like a gypsy, though, he had wanderlust, and when the five-and-ten next door offered him a partnership, he took it. For a while. Once again, he wanted out, and he opened his own housewares store. He drove the neighborhood merchants crazy for three years with his unheard-of tactics. If the store across the street sold something for a dollar, Murray Klein put it in his window for 79 cents. Stanley Zabar was impressed. He convinced Murray to come back to Zabar's. It would be temporary, "just to see." Three years later, he was a full partner.

Zabar's has been in a state of constant flux under Murray's charge, and although he says he's ready to get out and move to the country, that's not about to happen. Not as long as there is a change to be made, a fight to be fought, a principle to uphold.

"As a Jew, I was knocked around all my life," he says. "I was always told I was nothing. I came out with an inferiority complex, and so I have to prove to myself every day that I'm good." He is.

Just look at the people who work for him. They love him. Zabar's personnel is like a little United Nations. Nine or ten nationalities are represented. Leslie, the front manager, is Haitian; Louie, the chef, is Chinese; Boris is Russian. There are Puerto Ricans, Germans, Dominicans, Americans, Filipinos, Poles, and an Irish colleen at the check-out counter. A little bit of everything. Without them, Murray Klein says,

there would be no Zabar's.

Most of them are loyal, long-termers, who don't ever seem to quit. ''Of course,'' Murray explains, ''they get paid very well, with a lot of benefits. And they work very hard. But that's to our advantage. When you have to change people all the time, it costs you money in the long run, and it's not good for business.''

The salaries are good. And Zabar's employees eat as much of anything they want during working hours. What more could you ask?

Murray's only complaint is that it's hard to find young people who want to make Zabar's a career. They'd rather work in offices. Of course, the reason could be the sick-leave policy. ''Unless they're dead, I don't want anyone to call in sick,'' Murray says.

There is an office, too, up a flight of stairs so narrow that the boxes of merchandise lining their sides barely leave room for an average-size person to climb them. Then you have to fight your way through piles of tea bags and coffeepots, a copying machine, three desks, and several closed-circuit television sets to get to the two women who seem to be the only ones who can make order out of the chaos.

Pearl and Joy Watman, a mother-daughter team, preside over the business end of Zabar's with unflappable presence. The phones in the office are always ringing. Someone always has a question or needs an old invoice or a new packing slip. They alone know exactly where every little piece of paper is, under what pile of bills or beside what sheaf of orders. It is largely because of the Watmans that Zabar's policy of prompt payment of bills—usually within a week—is carried out.

They are truly remarkable. Like everything else at Zabar's, they have to be.

THE WAY WE WERE

It wasn't always quite this way.

There have been Zabar's' on the Upper West Side of Manhattan ever since Louis Zabar and his wife, Lillian, opened their first neighborhood appetizing and cheese store in the 1930s. In less than a decade, there were four supermarket/deli/appetizing stores with the Zabar name, from 80th Street to 110th Street.

When Louis Zabar died in 1950, he left the stores to his wife and three sons, Saul, Stanley, and Eli. They sold all except the 80th Street store at 2245 Broadway. Stanley and Eli went off to college, and Saul became the only full-time Zabar at Zabar's. He did a lot of modernizing here and there, but nothing big. It was relatively simple, though. The cheeses were mostly American, even the Brie; very little was imported. All this started to change in the early 1960s.

Saul began adding imported delicacies, starting with cookies, sweets, and crackers. By 1965, when Murray Klein became a partner, there was not only a new emphasis in the store, but a new breed of customer—discriminating, exacting, worldly; drawn to this new ''gourmet and epicurean emporium'' by foods they could get nowhere else.

What Saul did for the food, Murray Klein did for the ambience of the store. He shifted entire departments from one end of the place to another; built up the housewares inventory; used the ceiling as it had never been used before. He hired, fired, instructed, educated, and trained the personnel. His unflagging energy was contagious; all of Zabar's bustled with it.

By 1972, when Stanley Zabar decided to minimize his law practice and become the third full-time partner, Zabar's was almost complete. Stanley's dramatic overhaul of the meat and produce departments was the crowning glory. In addition, his head for figures and detail made him a natural to take over much of the paperwork. He was, and is, meticulous about record keeping, and with his business and legal training, he revitalized the general business systems into sharply efficient, productive arrangements.

Eli and his mother sold their shares of the store to his brothers and Murray Klein. He opened E.A.T., an Upper East Side shop filled with his own food fantasies. It's similar to Zabar's, but different.

It has occurred to many people over the years that a Zabar's would be welcome and successful anywhere. You'll never see that happen. ''There are no clones of Zabar's,'' Saul says for them all. ''And there won't be any. It requires all our energy to run one Zabar's.''

ZABAR'S BEST-SELLER LIST

1. BRIE 1,000 pounds a week
2. COFFEE 6,000 pounds a week
3. RYE BREAD 3,000 loaves a week
4. TEXAS BARBECUE 2,000 pounds a week
5. SMOKED SALMON 1,000 pounds a week (plus another 200 pounds of Scotch and Norwegian salmon)
6. PICKLED HERRING 3 barrelfuls, about 2,500 filets, a week
7. CROISSANTS AND BRIOCHE 10,000 a week
8. SANYO FOOD PROCESSORS 1,000 a month
9. JARLSBERG CHEESE 1,200 pounds a week (12,000 pounds of all cheeses combined are sold each week)
10. LOX about 130 pounds a week sliced; another 200 pounds pickled

Fish

Twenty-three years ago I walked into Zabar's and asked for a pound of sturgeon. When I asked for a pound, the clerk, in a contemptuous sneer, said, "That's seven ninety-six a pound."

Being embarrassed by his contempt, I retorted, "Seven hundred ninety-six dollars a pound?"

"No," he said, being more reasonable. "Seven dollars and ninety-six cents a pound."

A long silence ensued, during which time his stare fixed mine in deadlock. Finally, relenting, he very humanly asked, "What do you want—a pound?"

Walter Matthau

To many people, Zabar's is the appetizing department, a 30-foot-long extravaganza of smoked and cured fish, salads, pickles, and olives—especially fish. All this bewitches and bewilders the uninitiated, delights and excites the cognoscenti. Here is the only way to start Sunday, feed friends, or turn a fast dinner into an instant gourmet feast.

It's more than lox and Nova, of course, and whitefish and sturgeon—the staples of every good, old-fashioned appetizing counter—it's special Old-Country favorites, imported from Europe; exotic delicacies from exotic places; unusual treats from all over the world. From smoked eels to pickled herring, it's a fish fancier's dream come true.

Zabar's customers go to any lengths to get their fish, even if that means waiting in the longest lines in the store, holding the highest number from the ticket machine, or putting up with the maddening crowds hellbent on the same errand. On weekends, it's a mob scene: minks mingling with muskrats; uniformed chauffeurs standing in line next to blue-jeaned West Side sybarites. Yet surprisingly enough, the fish department is not the biggest moneymaker in the store, and the smoked salmon, despite its popularity, is the least profitable item sold there.

Who could guess?

Not the stylishly dressed matron who innocently asks the counterman, "You have any sturgeon?"

"Does a bank have money?" answers Harry Reiter, a seven-year veteran of Zabar's appetizing counter. It's his stock retort to a rather silly question.

"I don't want any dry fish," the lady says.

"Taste this," Harry offers. "Is this dry?" He slices off a sliver of the most expensive fish on the counter and serves it on the tip of his knife.

"Too dry. Give me from a different piece," the customer insists.

Harry does. "We aim to please," and the countermen never stop trying. Never mind that it's Sunday and many people are waiting for their "Next" call. Harry lets her taste sturgeon from a couple of sides kept in refrigerated compartments under the counter. They are all exactly the same, not only from the same smokehouse, but smoked and bought the same day. Each is as fresh and succulently moist as the next; Saul Zabar has made sure of that.

"Here's special for you." Harry winks as he slices. "A perfect piece of sturgeon."

"Not bad," the customer allows, seemingly satisfied at last.

It's a game. She and Harry go through the same charade all the time, and the scenario rarely changes. She waits, giving up her place in line several times, until Harry is free, just as so many customers wait for him, or for Sam Cohen or any of the others. All are practiced magicians who can cut lox paper thin with their eyes closed; at the same time, performers and professionals, equally skilled and knowledgeable. Yet every customer has his favorite, who can be depended on to come up with the "best of the best" always. It's a terrific way to run a store.

Also, the smoked fish happens to be the best there is.

Why it's the best—the freshest, juiciest, moistest—is mainly due to the indefatigable Saul Zabar. He is picky, picky, picky. Absolutely everything passes through his hands—not to mention in front of his eyes and nose—at least once, usually three or four times. His own taste preferences guide him unerringly to the finest fish available anywhere.

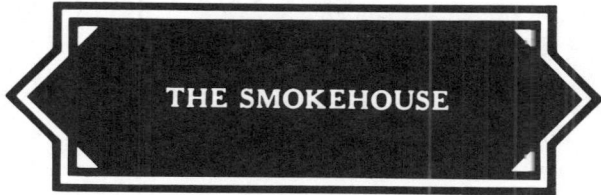

THE SMOKEHOUSE

There were, not too long ago, a few dozen fish smokers in Brooklyn and Queens. Now there are perhaps six.

The Rego Smoked Fish Company is one of them. On a sunny afternoon, Rego's building doesn't look any different from the other's in the Middle Village, Queens, neighborhood. On the same block, near the tracks of the Long Island Railroad, are a ribbon factory, a garage, and a warehouse.

If you expect to smell fish, you won't, at least not until you get inside the combination smokehouse and retail shop. Rego boasts customers from all over, including the most difficult to please, Saul Zabar.

Rego is not Zabar's only supplier of smoked fish, but it is one of the few who allow Saul to hand pick, and sometimes manhandle, each piece of fish. Rego smokes fish to his specific requirements.

Conrad Spizz owns and runs Rego, as he has for 30 years. He's a veritable font of facts, figures, and folklore. He learned his business working for a smokehouse in Brooklyn when he was a teenager and delivered fish to, among other places, one of the Zabar's stores.

The small smoked-fish business is not long for this world, according to Connie. He used to dry three tons of kapchunka—salt-cured whitefish—a year; now, if he does 1,000 pounds, it's a lot. When Rego started in 1949, it produced about 30,000 pounds of smoked fish a week. It is down to about a fifth of that today. However, the larger smokehouses are doing more business than ever.

There are many reasons for the decline of the small smokehouse. There are fewer fish; tastes are changing; the old-time, steady customers are dying out; and the "new generation" is not eating smoked fish. But this isn't stopping Rego altogether. The company will endure.

In New York, fish is very lightly smoked, a different method and a different taste from anywhere else. Irish smoked salmon is a whole different ballgame, for example, heavily smoked and dryish; Scotch salmon is another special case (see page 29). In Los Angeles,

smokehouses use their own formulas for brining and smoking, and even the wood is different (which may be why so many expatriate New Yorkers swear they can't find in California smoked fish that tastes anything like Zabar's).

"We have basically two kinds of smoke, hot and cold," Connie explains. "With all fish, we cure or brine before drying, cooking, and smoking. Nova Scotia salmon is cold-smoked. If you put it in a hot oven, it would be soup in three minutes."

Cold-smoked fish are hung fairly high above a low fire and smoked at temperatures between 70° and 80°F. for hours, days, or even weeks. Huge fans circulate the air and smoke, and the entire operation is watched with eagle eyes.

Hot-smoking is sometimes called kippering. The fish are hung closer to the fire, where they are cooked, partially or totally, before smoking is begun. A quantity of wood shavings and excelsior is fired; then all the air is forced out of the oven, so that the flame goes out and only the smoke remains. Chubs, whitefish, kippered salmon, sable, and sturgeon are all processed this way.

Obviously, they're not all done at the same time. Kippered salmon is cooked at a much higher temperature than are chubs and whitefish and is smoked carefully to make sure it doesn't become too dark or too dry. Chubs need at least three fires to be smoked to the right texture and color. Sable and sturgeon get less intense heat.

Rego does most of its smoking on Tuesday and Wednesday, so its wholesale customers can buy for the weekend. The fish seldom gets to be even a week old, since stores don't buy more than they need, and Connie Spizz doesn't smoke more than he can sell. Zabar's might buy from two or three smokes a week, to guarantee that the customers always get the freshest product possible.

With Saul Zabar, Connie Spizz has a very special relationship. It's as much a friendship as a business arrangement, and they're as likely to spend hours reminiscing and trading "fish stories" as buying and selling fish.

"Saul Zabar doesn't come here to buy fish," Connie Spizz cracks, "he comes here to consort with me."

When Saul approaches a smokehouse—Rego or any other—he's like a soldier prepared for battle, with unsinking determination to defend his honor and reputation.

There aren't many places that will let Saul take over whenever he walks in. But he's found those that will, and he picks and chooses more carefully than a bargain hunter looking for a designer-label dress on a Lower East Side pushcart. But for the privileges he gets, he pays dearly. Most volume purchasers receive a discount for buying in large amounts. Saul doesn't even ask. He's prepared to pay more for the golden opportunity to examine each and every piece of fish.

"When are you doing the kippered salmon?" he

BRINE: A solution of salt and water, and sometimes brown sugar, in which cleaned and gutted fish are soaked for various amounts of time, to add flavor.

PICKLE: At one time, this meant essentially the same as brine: a salt or vinegar solution in which fish are marinated, to flavor and preserve them. Today, pickle means a solution specifically made of vinegar, sugar, and spices.

The brining or pickling process does three basic things to and for the fish: The salt or vinegar draws out fluids from the fish (most fish are between 70 to 80 percent water), firming the flesh; helps preserve the fish while it is being smoked or cured; adds flavor, which is further accented by the smoking process.

CURE: To preserve by the process of brining or pickling. Surprisingly, the methods and recipes used today are almost identical with those of the early Romans. Refrigeration, however, has lessened the need for the preservation function of curing; it's now done mostly for taste.

DRY CURE: An alternative to brining or pickling. Salt and other flavorings are rubbed directly into the fish, to draw out their water and add flavor. The fish form their own brine as their water is extracted and mixes with the salt and flavorings. Dry-curing is used especially for fish with a high fat content.

COLD SMOKING: Smoking at temperatures no higher than 70 to 80°F. for extended periods of time, to impart a light, smoky flavor to the fish and dry them out a bit. Finnan haddie and smoked salmon are cold-smoked.

HOT-SMOKING: Smoking at temperatures from 110 to 250°F. for much shorter time periods than cold-smoking. Fish are partially or totally cooked at the highest temperatures. Kippered salmon, whitefish, chubs, etc., are smoked this way.

Both smoking processes give the fish their basic flavor, firm their flesh, and finish the curing so the fish are ready to eat. For cold-smoking, fish are placed in large ovens, overnight or longer, with huge fans to circulate the smoke. The hot-smoking method is much more intense: A fire is built up, then smothered, and the door to the oven is closed, to let the smoke envelop the fish.

The wood used for smoking fires can add a definite flavor dimension to the fish. Applewood and other fruitwoods impart their own fruityness; hickory, oak, mesquite, and so on, impart a more woodsy, smoky taste and aroma.

asks. "I'll be back." Saul likes kippered salmon slightly undercooked, and that's the way the Rego smokehouse gives it to him. Most people prefer it a little drier, smoked a little longer. Saul doesn't, and here he gets it the way he likes it—which is why he's here.

He buys thousands of pounds of fish each week, and the fish must be perfect. He'll visit two or three smokehouses until he finds exactly what he wants, tasting, smelling, poking, and prodding. It's not a frivolous exercise; it's serious business.

THE SMOKING SECTION

Fish by fish, Zabar's is a cornucopia brimming with temptations, a dazzling, confusing, glorious array of goodies not only for fish lovers, but also for those who would like to be.

STURGEON: The supreme taste treat. Expensive because it's hard to come by, it's the status symbol of the smoked-fish counter; like caviar, sturgeon can turn any gathering into a prestigious affair.

The blue-white diamond of them all is the lake sturgeon, a fish whose numbers are decreasing rapidly, making it even more in demand. The very best come from the Canadian lakes, and that's the kind you'll find at Zabar's. Rich, fat, coarse-fleshed—almost flaky. Some say sturgeon tastes more like chicken than like fish. The texture is similar, and it even looks a little like plump, juicy breast meat.

Murray Klein claims that sturgeon has a very distinctive taste, impossible to forget once you've tried it. This is in large part because of the processing, which adds special flavors to the already tasty fish. First, they are soaked in a mild brine and then lightly smoked for about four hours high above a low fire; the fire is then built up, and the fish are quickly and intensely smoked.

How do you eat sturgeon? The best way is the simplest. Succulent slices, accompanied, perhaps, by rings of Bermuda onion, a sprinkle of freshly ground black pepper, a splash of lemon juice. But who's to say you can't layer slices on a bagel or a piece of pumpernickel along with cream cheese, onions or tomato, or with sweet butter and Swiss cheese? A quarter of a pound of sturgeon makes three nice slices, maybe four (it's not sliced superthin, as salmon is), enough for a like number of sandwiches or two pretty and plentiful platefuls.

SABLE: Some call this "poor man's sturgeon," although it's an entirely different fish, a Pacific Ocean denizen, caught mostly off Alaska, British Columbia, and Washington State.

It's an American saltwater fish with a firm, white, flaky texture. It has a full, definite, flavor all its own, and many people prefer it to sturgeon for just that reason.

Like sturgeon, most sable is sold smoked. It's wet-cured first, then smoked over a low fire for several hours before the temperature and the smoke are increased to give it a final, smoky boost.

Sable is much less expensive than sturgeon because it's so much more available. It's sold in two ways: sliced from slabs by the pound and, at slightly lower prices, chunks, which measure about three by six inches and weigh up to about a pound. There's no difference in the fish; if you buy the whole chunk you just have to slice it yourself. Either way, it's deliciously unfishy and melts in your mouth. Eat it as you do sturgeon, or for a real treat, heat it under the broiler or in a steamer, and serve it with melted butter and parsley. A quarter of a pound goes far, as it easily makes two to four servings.

WHITEFISH: These are wonderful. Plump, juicy, from the Great Lakes, they are smoked slowly until their skins are golden and shimmery and their flesh is firm, but sweet and full. They are as beautiful to look at as they are delectable and tasty—not fishy—on the tongue. Whitefish at Zabar's are sold by the pound, by the piece, or by the whole fish. There is nothing quite

HOME IS WHERE THE HEARTH IS

Can you smoke fish at home? Yes, and with good, if not excellent, results. But you must be committed. Many smokers, some portable, are available in department stores, hardware stores, sporting-goods shops, and through mail-order sources. They are electric or charcoal fired and are more than adequate for home use (they must be used outdoors or in a very-well-ventilated garage).

If your kitchen is large enough, you can have a smoke oven built in at moderate cost. Or, if you've a mind to, you can build your own outdoor smoker, using relatively available materials—old wheelbarrows and heavy-duty aluminum foil, refrigerators, cartons, barrels, and so on. In libraries and bookstores, there are several how-to books on home smoking, with complete directions. Do be aware, however, that it will take much experimenting and probably quite a few failures to reach perfection, and home smoking will never duplicate the flavor and style or the incredible variety of appetizing-counter smoked-fish products.

so exquisite on a buffet table as a whole, golden white-fish that Zabar's experts have boned, sliced, and put back into its skin, garnished with tomato wedges, onion rings, coleslaw, and olives. Whitefish makes a terrific sandwich with almost any bread, spread with cream cheese or sweet butter.

A whole fish can run between two and eight pounds; half a pound is enough for two plates or four sandwiches.

CHUBS: Look like small whitefish, but are a different kettle of fish. They're small lake herring, caught in deeper waters than whitefish, and usually weigh well under a pound. A perfect meal for one, a chub is fat and delicious, with a scrumptiously smoky taste and smell. Chubs and whitefish are similar in taste—sweet and delectable—and flaky/firm. They are eaten the same way, but chubs are bought whole. If you're squeamish about looking at a fish with its head still attached, ask for it to be removed. Some people believe that the meat around the head is the sweetest; it's also the boniest.

Removing the backbone from chubs and whitefish frees the fish from other bones, so there's no need to worry about finding little ones in every mouthful. The fattiest part of both fish is the skin, which is not eaten, but can be gnawed to get at the best morsels.

CARP: With their bright, crusty paprika coating, carp are juicy and subtle, with a unique taste that belies their humble origin. Carp are fat and firm, with coarse flesh that takes to smoking particularly well. They are a favorite at every appetizing counter. (Fresh carp are essential to great gefilte fish.)

Like most smoked fish, carp goes particularly well with onions, tomatoes, cucumbers, and coleslaw; great on a bagel or bialy (a flattened, doughy, chewy roll with a thumb-print hole in the middle, sprinkled with onions), thinly sliced bread, or all by itself. A quarter of a pound will make two hefty sandwiches or four daintier ones. It's usually sliced fairly thick to give full flavor with each bite.

SALMON, BAKED (or KIPPERED): It is cooked while it's being smoked, to give it a perfect blend of flavors. It's especially moist and tender at Zabar's, slightly pink and juicy, but firm and chewy. It is delicious—like the the white meat of chicken, delicate, not at all salty and quite difficult to describe save to say that smiles are common after the first mouthful. Cold, creamy potato salad is its best mate, along with fresh challah—the traditional Jewish eggy yeast bread that welcomes the Sabbath—or rolls and butter.

KIPPERS: One of those things Zabar's goes to special lengths to provide its customers. The best kippers reputedly come from Scotland, and that's where Zabar's gets them, flown in fresh each week. Frozen kippers from Canada are the next best thing (Zabar's does carry some canned kippers, but they're not the same). Fresh kippers, although more expensive,

kipper per person, unless they're really small; then allow two.

MACKEREL: Firm and oily. They may come from the Northeast Atlantic or from waters as far south as Brazil. Mackerel are salt-water fish, caught in nets, smoked over a low fire, then quickly over hotter and denser heat, to give them their smoky flavor and glistening skins. According to Murray Klein, smoked mackerel is particularly enjoyed by his special customers, mostly older Europeans who relish not only the taste, but the memories of the Old Country that eating the mackerel calls to mind.

SPRATS: A special favorite of Zabar's German clientele. They are small herring, 5 to 7 inches long, and are hot-smoked for about two hours, until they are golden-brown on the outside. They are imported from Holland and Germany, and their delicate, smoky flavor and rich, full taste make them a perfect accompaniment to scrambled eggs or a green salad.

TROUT, RAINBOW BROOK: Flown to New York from the cold, rapid waters of Idaho. They are pliant and sweet, about 10 to 12 inches long, usually weigh 8 ounces or less, and have a superb, lightly smoked flavor. Trout used to be a seasonal delicacy, but fish-breeding farms, such as the excellent ones in Idaho, make them available all year. Some people claim that hatchery trout are not quite as flavorful as those that fight the fast currents of mountain streams; but the smoked trout at Zabar's are as lusty a delicacy as you can find. With eggs or salad or by themselves, they are terrific. They are bony, so care should be taken when eating them.

HERRING: Another favorite with Zabar's European customers. They are nice, fat fish, fairly heavily smoked, so they have a distinct smoky aroma and flavor.

EELS: Long, thin, and black, eels are a rare delight. They have always been considered a delicacy in Europe and Scandinavia and are fast becoming quite popular in this country. They have a naturally full flavor that is greatly enhanced by the curing process (a brine heavily spiced), and the smoking (long and light), which make them deliciously tangy and chewy. Serve them for lunch, surrounded by lettuce, radishes, tomatoes, black and green olives, celery, pimiento, cucumber, and hard-cooked eggs. Sprinkle everything with a little basil, and pass a bowl of mayonnaise.

KAPCHUNKA: Murray Klein says the younger generation just doesn't appreciate this. But the older folks, especially Eastern Europeans, certainly know what good is. Kapchunka is Russian-style dried whitefish, not smoked, but with a smoky taste, very chewy, and a bit salty. The only way to eat it, Mr. Klein says, is to cut off a chunk and chew it, with maybe a piece of corn bread (European, not Southern-style) or rye and a glass of icy-cold vodka. Cut into tidbits, though, it makes a good and unusual addition to an hors-d'oeuvres tray or salad platter.

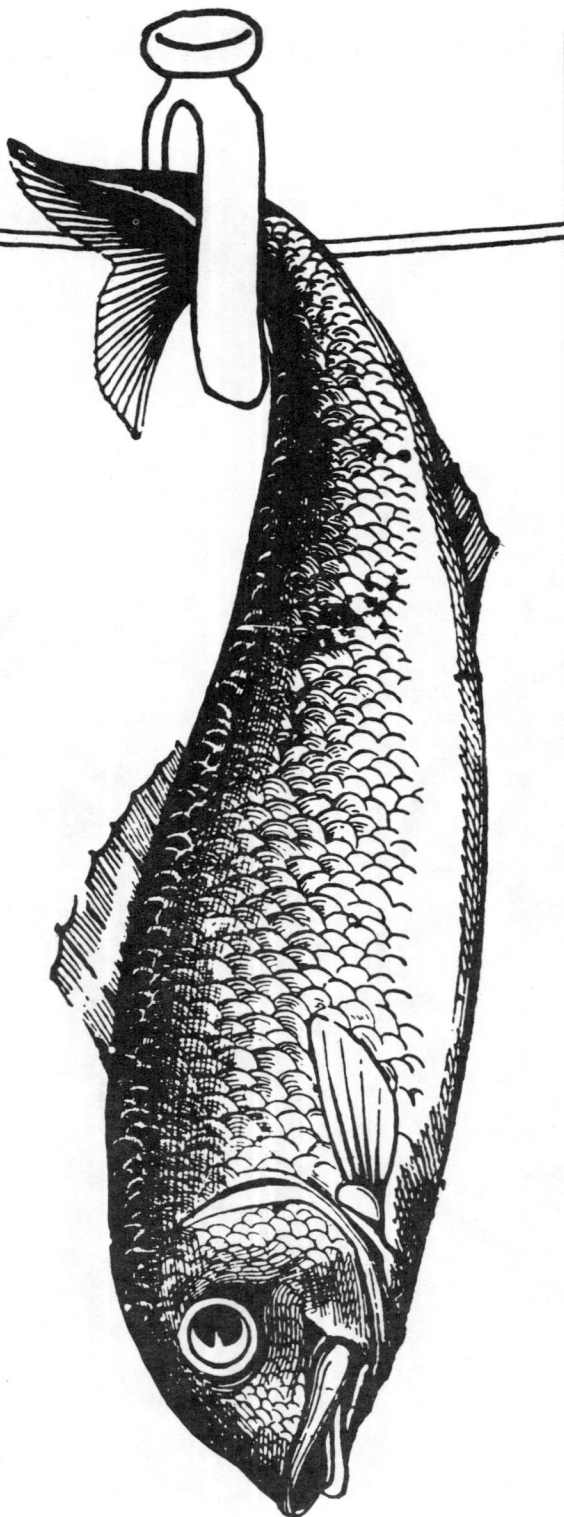

are far superior in taste and texture to the frozen ones, which are more heavily salted and smoked and tend to lose some of their distinctiveness in the freezing process.

Kippers are actually herring that have been split, salted, and smoked. They're small—under a pound—and fat. They can be eaten as is or quickly fried or broiled and served with scrambled eggs, for an English-style breakfast beyond compare. Figure on one

The true star of Zabar's appetizing department is undisputedly the salmon. Smoked, baked, poached, gravad lax, Nova Scotia, Scotch, Norwegian, pickled, the shimmering slabs of fish sit proudly in all their glory, waiting to be expertly sliced and eagerly consumed.

SCOTCH AND NORWEGIAN SALMON: Flown directly to Zabar's from Scotland, fresh, whole, delectable sides of it and vacuum-sealed gift packs, ready for shipping.

BAKED SALMON: This is what other kippered fish aspire to be—moist, tender, delicious.

NOVA SCOTIA: Gaspé salmon is the finest money can buy. It has very little salt, very subtle flavor, and comes from the icy waters of eastern Canada. Western (Pacific) salmon is similar.

LOX: Salty, inexpensive, a perennial favorite. It's the best to be found anywhere.

PICKLED LOX: A treat for those who never thought lox could put on airs and carry it off. In cream sauce or the traditional Zabar's clear sauce, it's truly unique.

Saul Zabar's touch has helped establish the reputation of the appetizing department. It's everywhere, except for the two following salmon specialties, which are out of his hands and in the very capable ones of his brother Stanley.

GRAVAD LAX: Swedish-style marinated salmon is pressed under a weight for several days in a zesty combination of herbs and spices. It has a fresh, delicate flavor, mellow and exotic, and when it's sliced thinly and topped with mustard-dill sauce, it's a rare treat.

POACHED SALMON: This is Stanley's second pièce de résistance. It's cooked in a subtle, exquisite light court bouillon, then carefully chilled. Served with its traditional accompaniments, green sauce and cucumber salad, it's the ultimate in elegance.

Stanley and his wife, Judy, were in Europe and kept hearing wonderful things about gravad lax and how delicious it was. When they finally tasted it, the dill-flavored salmon was every bit as good as its reputation—and not too difficult to make, they discovered. Armed with an original Swedish recipe, they started experimenting as soon as they were home.

"We bought two or three salmon," Stanley says, and "marinated them for twenty-four hours, as the recipe called for, then forty-eight, then seventy-two. We changed the spicing until it tasted the way we thought it should. When we were satisfied, we started buying salmon just for gravad lax and making it once a week. Now we sell about one to two hundred pounds weekly."

As long as they were buying salmon, and selling salmon poachers, too, there was no reason not to try their hands at poached salmon. They developed a poaching stock—it's called court bouillon and is basically fish stock, wine, and seasonings—in which they gently simmer the salmon (on a rack in the poacher). Poached salmon is one of the most popular items at the fish counter.

"We buy better salmon," explains Stanley, "and control the production, so we can sell an excellent product at a fairly low price. Our stock is retained and added to every few days, so we have one of the most valuable and delicious poaching stocks around."

Both salmon delicacies are directed at Zabar's younger customers who are looking for variety and quick, noncook foods of gourmet quality and instant edibility. It's fast food with a difference—well-prepared, delicious, and most assuredly not junk.

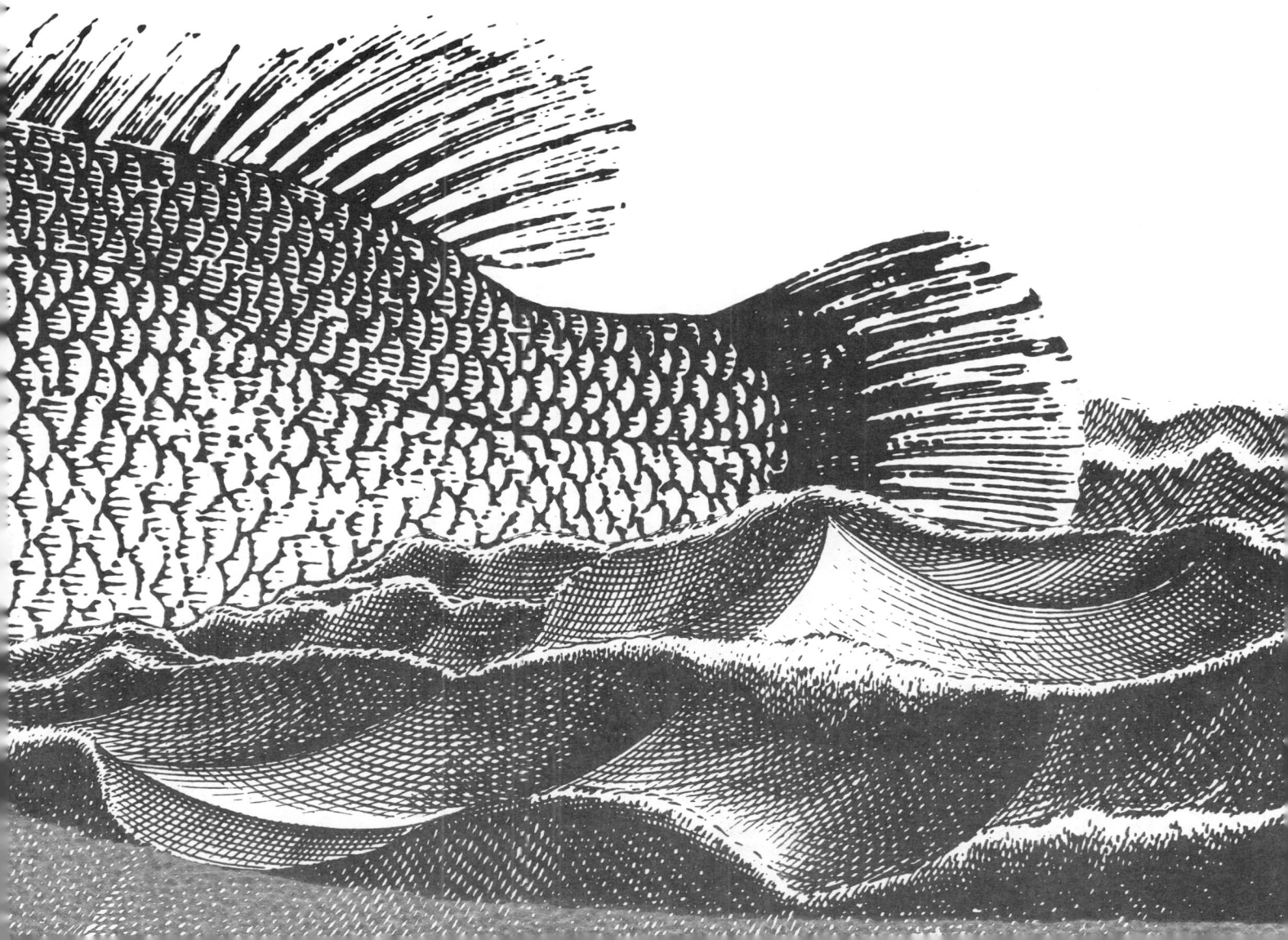

LOTSA LOX—
IT AIN'T WHAT IT
USED TO BE

The difference between *lox* and *Nova Scotia salmon* isn't just in the taste, but in the smoking. Nova always is. Lox, only sometimes.

It's confusing, to be sure. Years ago, when heavily salted salmon from Alaska arrived in New York, it had to be soaked to get rid of the salt. It was probably even lightly smoked to give it some taste. It was called lox, from the Swedish *lax* or the German *lachs* or the Yiddish *laks*—all names for salmon. Since about 1945, however, lox is merely soaked, not smoked.

Nova Scotia salmon used to come only from Nova Scotia. Now it can come from almost anywhere along the Atlantic—Newfoundland, Scotland, Scandinavia, Iceland, the Gaspé Peninsula—but mostly from the Pacific. (At Zabar's, the finest Nova Scotia salmon comes from Canada's Gaspé.) It is smoked in New York—almost no salmon is smoked in Canada for export to the United States—after it has been lightly rubbed with salt and brown sugar or brined in a light salt-and-brown sugar solution. Then it's cold-smoked so that it doesn't cook, and it has only the most delicate of flavors from the type of wood used—hickory, oak, or fruitwood.

In general, when you ask for *Nova*, you get unsalty smoked salmon, no matter where the fish was caught. But there's often a tremendous difference in taste and price from store to store.

For New Yorkers, that's less of a problem because of the city's truth-in-labeling law. Only smoked salmon from Atlantic or Eastern fish can legally be called Nova Scotia salmon. Made from Pacific Ocean salmon, it may be called Nova, Novy, or Western Novy, but not Nova Scotia salmon, and while this can be delicious and very tasty, it just doesn't compare with the real thing.

Zabar's, naturally, has the very best of both. But unless you specifically ask for Nova Scotia salmon, you'll probably get Western Novy (it's clearly marked as such at the counter), which is less expensive and not quite as delicate in taste. If you've never eaten anything else, it will be almost impossible to tell from the real thing.

A little bit of Nova Scotia salmon goes a long way. Two ounces (ask for an eighth of a pound) may not sound like much, but it's enough for four bagels with cream cheese. The same amount, served as you might Scotch salmon—sliced thinly and accompanied by chopped or sliced onion, capers, ground black pepper, and lemon juice—makes a nice appetizer for two.

Back to lox. At Zabar's, you can get the finest *belly lox*, from the belly, the fattest part of the salmon. It's a bit more expensive than lox not from the belly, because it is particularly succulent—the choicest lox you can buy.

Both belly and regular lox come entirely from Western or Pacific Ocean salmon, and that's perfectly fine. Fresh sides of salmon are put into 100% salt brine. The fish are left in their initial salt brine for two weeks or more, then washed and packed in fresh brine for another few weeks. They should be in the salt solution for a minimum of two months before being offered for sale. Lox is definitely salty, which is why many people prefer the more subtle Nova Scotia salmon.

The first things most people think of when they hear the word lox are bagels and cream cheese, and why not? That's a perfect blend of flavors, and the sourish tang of the cream cheese nicely offsets the saltiness of the lox. Millions of people have grown up believing that bagels and lox are the only foods allowed on the breakfast table on Sunday mornings. Little do they know that lox makes an outrageous omelet (see page 31), a terrific dip for raw vegetables or crackers (see

LOX-AND-ONION
QUICHE

1 pound onions, minced
4 tablespoons butter
1 tablespoon flour
2 eggs
Salt and freshly ground black pepper,
  to taste
Pinch nutmeg
2/3 cup heavy cream
1/8 pound lox, diced
1/2 cup grated Swiss cheese
8-inch pie shell, partially baked

Preheat oven to 375° F.

In a skillet, over low heat, sauté onion in 3 tablespoons butter until onion is very soft and golden (this may take a while, so be patient). Add flour, stirring gently, and cook 3 minutes. Set aside.

Combine eggs, salt, pepper, nutmeg, and cream; beat well. Add lox, sautéed onions, and 1/4 cup cheese; mix until blended. Pour into pie shell; sprinkle with remaining 1/4 cup cheese, and dot with remaining 1 tablespoon butter.

Place quiche on cookie sheet, and bake 25 to 30 minutes, or until nicely browned and puffed up.

·Serves 4 as a main dish, 8 as an appetizer.

page 31), and a very special quiche (see page 28).

Pickled, or marinated, lox is a specialty of the house at Zabar's. The lox is freshened by being rinsed thoroughly in icy-cold water. Then it is covered with a brine made of vinegar, water, spices—sugar, cloves, peppercorns, bay leaves, and mustard seed—and sliced onion. The length of time the lox pickles is at least two weeks, with two changes of brine. Zabar's also offers pickled lox in cream sauce, made by adding sour cream sauce to the pickled lox. No matter how it's prepared, it's delicious, salty, sweet, tangy, and at the same time, slightly sour. It's perfect as an hors d'oeuvre or with salad and bread and butter.

SCOTCH SALMON

Scotch salmon is similar to the very finest Nova Scotia salmon, but nothing at all like lox. It's in a class by itself, smoked differently, sliced differently, and eaten differently.

At Buckingham Palace, a slice of Scotch salmon covers an entire plate of royal dinnerware, and it's frequently served as a first course. At Zabar's, the imported Scotch salmon are every bit as tasty. They're flown in weekly from smokehouses in Scotland and are sliced to order. They can be shipped fresh, frozen, or vacuum-sealed. Zabar's are fresh.

The differences between Scotch salmon and its American cousins are many. First, it's more expensive; it is imported, after all.

Scotch salmon is a lovely, rosy-pink color (lox is more coral). The salmon are first dry-cured, rather than brined, then smoked slowly over smouldering wood in a cold-smoke process. (Lox, remember, is not smoked at all.)

Scotch salmon is firm, easy to slice, has a smoky, mildly salty taste. Its delicate, savory flavor is at its best when the salmon is a bit colder than room temperature. The trick to truly appreciating the flavor is having the salmon cut so thin you can almost see through it—although it loses none of its natural shiny pinkness. (Because it is so firm, it can be sliced much thinner than Nova Scotia salmon or lox.) Serve it with a squeeze of fresh lemon juice, perhaps a garnish of chopped capers, chopped onion, and freshly ground black pepper, thinly sliced black bread or imported flatbread (such as FinnCrisp), and sweet butter. Some

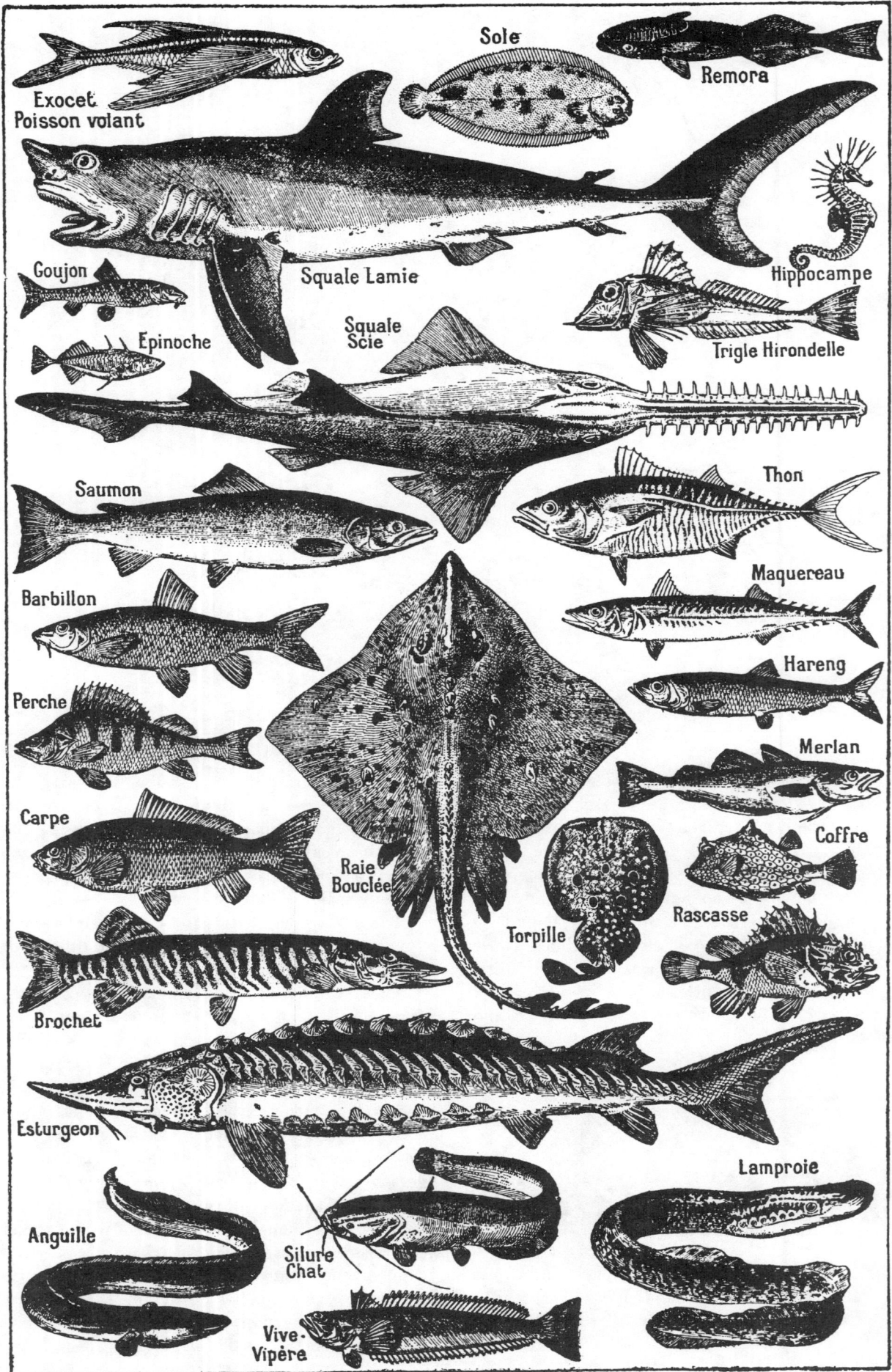

Exocet
Poisson volant

Sole

Remora

Squale Lamie

Hippocampe

Goujon

Squale
Scie

Trigle Hirondelle

Epinoche

Thon

Saumon

Maquereau

Barbillon

Hareng

Perche

Merlan

Carpe

Coffre

Raie
Bouclée

Rascasse

Torpille

Brochet

Esturgeon

Lamproie

Anguille

Silure
Chat

Vive
Vipère

LOX, NO BAGEL

¼ *pound lox*
Dash freshly ground black pepper
½ *teaspoon capers*
⅓ *cup cream cheese, softened*

Mix all ingredients in the blender until smooth.

Makes about ¾ cup.

If you buy lox trimmings, this will be a lot cheaper, and just as delicious—and no one will ever know. It's a great spread for pumpernickel, good as a dip for raw vegetables.

gourmets insist that fine Scotch salmon needs only a bit of lemon juice; anything else would be a criminal offense.

Although Scotch salmon is expensive, a little goes a long way when served as an appetizer or first course. Just a quarter of a pound provides six thin slices, and two per person is the perfect way to start a meal.

How to win friends and influence people: Buy whole sides of Scotch salmon, about two to two and a quarter pounds, vacuum-sealed and specially packed for shipping. Zabar's packages them in a smashing box, and a side is the perfect gift for the gourmet who has almost everything. Zabar's Scotch salmon made Christmas very merry for thousands of people, and it has been added to the store's year-round mail-order catalog. Scotch salmon is elegant, unusual, and just what someone's always wanted!

HERRING

Among Zabar's 7,000 food and kitchenware items, the herring is particularly well represented—in more than 20 ways. This isn't surprising when you consider that herring has always been the most important fish in the curing industry.

There are, it is said, over 200 recipes just for pickling herring, many of them of German origin. But today almost everyone pickles herring, and Zabar's offers the best of them: from Norway, Sweden, Denmark, Holland, and Germany, of course.

Depending on the sauce it's in, pickled herring can be sweet, tart, spicy, creamy, winy, sour, almost anything. Each pickler has his own recipe, and recipes usually are passed down from generation to generation.

Zabar's is no exception. From its own kitchen come *schmaltz herring*, filets or whole fish, regular or extra-large size, pickled in the old-fashioned way with vinegar, sugar, pickling spices, and water. The walk-in refrigerator is crammed with barrels of herring in various stages of pickling, and Saul is constantly poking around and sampling the pickle to make sure it has enough vinegar or spice.

Salt herring (fish that have been cured in salt and held in storage) and *milt herring* (male herring caught just before mating) are also pickled at Zabar's.

The pride of Zabar's own, however, is *herring in cream sauce*. Usually, sour cream is added. Chock-full of sliced onion (the best part), it is at once sweet and tangy, mildly spicy, and makes a great snack, appetizer, or whole meal. It's made from whole filets and cut into one- to two-inch pieces on request. It's in such demand that it's prepacked in half- and one-pound containers for the weekend.

What Zabar's doesn't make is stocked in jars or tins from the people who do it best.

Old-fashioned *pickled herring*, in regular sauce, is made by Zabar's. For the cocktail set, there are bite-size pieces of filets, mildly spiced, marinated, or in a dill sauce. Just add a toothpick. *Matjes herring* are packed, either whole filets or chunks, in sour sauce or in a sweet wine sauce. They are particularly nice with plain boiled potatoes sprinkled with chives and topped with a healthy dollop of cold, creamy sour cream.

Herring tidbits from Norway come in four sauces: dill, ketchup, wine, and lemon. With plain crackers, they're perfect hors d'oeuvres. Tidbits from Sweden and Holland come in wine sauce, and from Sweden, too, come Matjes-herring filets in spiced sauce. *Party snacks* in wine sauce and *herring salad* packed by one of New York's finest companies are right next to the

JAY'S "LEO"

"Leo" is the short-order cook's term for that old-fashioned favorite, lox and eggs and onions. Jay added the green peppers.

About 4 tablespoons unsalted butter or
  margarine
¾ *cup coarsely chopped onion*
½ *cup coarsely chopped green pepper*
4 *eggs, lightly beaten with 2 tablespoons*
  water
½ *cup diced lox (⅛ lb.)*

Melt butter or margarine in skillet or omelet pan, sauté onion and pepper until onion is almost golden. Add eggs; stir gently until they are half-cooked. Stir in lox; cook until eggs are set.

Serves 2.

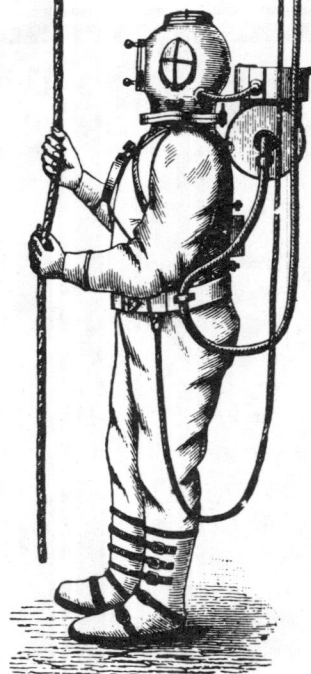

Bismarck herring (boned and fileted, but with the sides still joined), pickled in vinegar and spices. *Roll-mops* (Bismarck-herring filets rolled around dill pickles, pickled onions, or gherkins) are packed in a spiced vinegar sauce. (These consummate party snacks are easy to make. Top pickled herring filets with pickles, gherkins, onions, or capers, and roll them up. A toothpick holds them together. Marinate in the refrigerator for about two weeks in a sauce made of wine vinegar, salt, lemon peel, sliced onion, peppercorns, and mustard seeds.)

Finally, there are *herring in aspic,* a particularly pretty German delicacy.

All the herring varieties make terrific hors d'oeuvres. Eating them requires no more than a toothpick or a party fork, since most of them are in bite-size pieces.

Of course, you don't have to wait for a party. Try any of these herring varieties for lunch or supper. No muss, no fuss, no bother.

CAVIAR— THE EMPRESS OF STURGEON

The deluxe gourmet can't live without his caviar, and why should he? At Zabar's, he can indulge himself with the very best or balance his budget with something a little less exclusive.

Caviar is simply the roe of a fish, ideally sturgeon, salted and processed. That, of course, is about as accurate as saying that ice cream is just a frozen dairy product.

Caviar is one of the world's most expensive foods (truffles are close behind). At well over $250 a pound for the freshest Iranian Malossol Beluga caviar, it's not exactly for the hamburger-helper crowd. There are less costly caviars, but once you've tasted the best, there's no going back.

"Caviar is rare," says Zabar's resident expert, Sam Cohen. "It comes from fish that live in the Black and Caspian Seas. A lot of fish give caviar, but the beluga gives the best and the largest and the tastiest caviar in the world."

It can be jet-black or golden-yellow; gray, dark brown, and nearly every color in between. The color has little to do with how good it is; the quality, experts say, really depends on how much salt the eggs are packed in, and how delicately they are handled during packing and shipping. Careless handling results in smashed eggs, not whole and distinct—the very qualities that make caviar so prized. One should be able to feel each individual egg on the tongue.

According to Zabar's, the large, grayish eggs of the beluga are the *non plus ultra,* followed by the smaller

FRIED HERRING

The best accompaniments to fried herring are plain boiled potatoes and fresh, thickly sliced rye bread.

2 schmaltz-herring filets
Flour for light dredging
¼ to ⅓ cup matzoh meal; or ¼ to
⅓ cup mixture, to taste, flour and
bread crumbs
1 egg
2 tablespoons milk
Butter or margarine

Soak filets in water overnight (to get rid of the salt); change water once. They may be left whole or cut into pieces.

Put dredging flour and matzoh meal or flour-and-breadcrumb mixture on separate, shallow plates. Beat egg and milk together lightly. Dip herring into flour; shake off excess; then dip into egg-milk mixture and finally into matzoh meal or flour-and-bread crumb mixture. Let coated pieces stand about 5 minutes, to set. Then sauté in butter or margarine until brown on both sides—about 10 minutes in all. *Serves 2.*

eggs of the sevruga sturgeon (only $130 for 14 ounces). If you love caviar a great deal, Zabar's will gladly sell you either kind in its original one- or two-kilo tin. Zabar's also packs the caviar in two-ounce jars and pretty much every size in between.

Zabar's fresh caviar is as it should be: smooth, shiny, translucently gray. It has almost no smell and tastes only slightly of salt. It is never bitter, and on the tongue, it's firm and distinguishable—each egg perfect and distinct, never a mass of mush. (The designation Malossol, by the way, is not a type of caviar; it simply means lightly salted.)

To serve it correctly, set the dish of caviar in cracked ice in a larger bowl (caviar, especially fresh caviar, is very perishable and should never be held at temperatures above 38°F.) and accompany it with freshly made toast and icy-cold champagne or vodka. Connoisseurs scoff at any other garnishes, such as chopped hard-cooked egg, onion, or parsley, but they admit that a splash of lemon juice is acceptable. Always serve caviar in glass, wood, or even plastic, never metal. The salt acting on a metal dish would add an unpleasantly metallic taste.

CAVIAR FOR THE MASSES

Other fish besides sturgeon supply roe, and far less expensively. But as Murray Klein says, "Either you

THE HERRING.

buy good caviar—beluga—or bad caviar—lumpfish. How bad can caviar be? Go to a Jewish wedding, you'll see." Lumpfish caviar sells for about $10 a pound. It comes, not surprisingly, from the lumpfish, caught in Icelandic waters. It doesn't taste anything like beluga or sevruga, and in fact, it is pasteurized, preserved, and artificially colored (the eggs' natural color is an unappetizing tan; black food coloring is added to make the roe more attractive). Lumpfish caviar is much too salty to serve plain; but mixed with sour cream or cream cheese, it is a delicious canapé spread. *Whitefish caviar* from Canada or the Great Lakes is similar in taste and is served the same way.

Fresh salmon caviar, red and shiny, is sold loose at Zabar's. It makes a good dip or spread when mixed with sour cream, and since it's not too salty, stands quite nicely on its own. (It's also available pasteurized and vacuum-packed in glass jars.) Try salmon caviar in an omelet; vacuum-packed in jars. Use your

NOVA MOUSSE

¼ pound Nova Scotia salmon, diced or
shredded
1 tablespoon lemon juice
Salt and freshly ground black pepper to
taste
½ cup heavy cream, whipped

Gently fold salmon, lemon juice, salt, and pepper into whipped cream. Chill until ready to serve (at least 2 hours).

To do this the lazy way, put everything into the blender or food processor, and blend until smooth and creamy. It won't be quite as solid, but it will be every bit as good.
Makes about ¾ cup.

STRETCHING CAVIAR THREE WAYS

You can get away with using less-expensive caviar by mixing it with other ingredients to cut the saltiness. Lumpfish, salmon, or any other caviar can be used in the first two recipes. All make good spreads for crackers or toast.

ONE

½ cup heavy cream, whipped
¼ cup caviar
2 tablespoons finely chopped onion

Mix all ingredients, and chill. Salmon caviar looks particularly pretty in this.
Makes about 1 cup.

TWO

2 slices French or Italian bread
3 tablespoons caviar
½ cup salad oil
Juice of 2 lemons

Trim crusts from bread. Soak in water; squeeze out. In a large bowl, beat caviar and bread slices (you can use an electric mixer or blender) until smooth. Gradually add oil alternately with lemon juice. Beat until thick and smooth, adding a few drops of water if necessary.
Makes about ¾ cup.

THREE

¼ cup salmon caviar
¼ pound scallion cream cheese, softened
1 cup sour cream
1 teaspoon lemon juice

Blend all ingredients, and chill. This is good as a dip for raw vegetables.
Makes about 1½ cups.

favorite omelet recipe and technique, and when the eggs are just about set, spread about two tablespoons of caviar on one side, and fold. Delicious!

The caviar story continues. *Pressed caviar,* which may be Russian or Iranian, fresh or pasteurized, is like jam; it has almost no grain and is made of the smallest, softest eggs pressed out during grading. At one time, it was literally scraped from the bottom of the barrel, compressed into a solid mass by the weight of the roe on top of it. Today it's packed that way purposely.

Pasteurized caviar is quite salty, and because of the salt, keeps very well. It can be eaten alone or mixed into spreads. *Tarama* is roe from carp or cod; it's the Greek version of caviar. It's always mixed

with other ingredients (see page 36).

There's an old Russian folk saying that if you eat caviar during the holidays, the new year will be rich and beautiful. That's as good a reason to try it as any.

WHO MADE THE SALAD?

One of the nicest things about the appetizing counter at Zabar's is the positively splendiferous array of salads lined up and waiting to be sampled. Whitefish, baked salmon, chopped herring, and potato salad, coleslaw, and more.

Nearly all are made in Zabar's tiny kitchen, a space to surely make any cook shudder, but is surprisingly functional. Here herrings are gutted, fileted, and set to pickle. Lox is pickled; celery is chopped; eggs, shrimp, chicken, whitefish, lobster, vegetables, mayonnaise, spices wait expectantly, ready to be mixed into one of Saul Zabar's magical compositions.

This work is done late at night or very early in the morning, when the store is empty except for Louie, the chief chef, and the sounds of the chopping knife thwacking against the polyethylene cutting boards. Saul checks the salads while they're being made, before they're set out, and even once or twice during the day if he's around. He's an endless putterer, and if a salad isn't right to him, he fiddles with the ingredients until it is. Or he throws it out and starts again.

Each and every salad is made with the same prime ingredients that are sold separately at the appetizing and produce counters. They are not made with leftovers or trimmings (lox trimmings, the ends of the fish that can't be sliced neatly, are sold to anyone who wants them; they're fine for omelets or noncompany meals).

And what a bunch of salads to choose from! The *whitefish* and *baked salmon salads* are smooth and creamy, almost spreadable. The finely flaked fish is mixed with celery, mayonnaise, lemon juice, and blended to a thick, even smoothness. The whitefish salad is white, naturally; the baked-salmon, a delicate pink. They are fine for lunch, spread on rolls or bread or bagels, or scooped into hard-cooked-egg whites, or heaped on crackers.

Herring salad, or chopped herring, is an all-time favorite and decidedly different at every appetizing counter that offers it. Saul Zabar's recipe seems to be the best in town, and his customers keep coming back for more. Slightly sweet, slightly tart, smooth but with a definite crunch, it begins with pickled herring in wine sauce and goes on to include celery, salt, onion, green pepper, a touch of mayonnaise, and Saul's careful blending technique.

Alaskan king crabmeat makes an irresistibly tempt-

CAVIAR

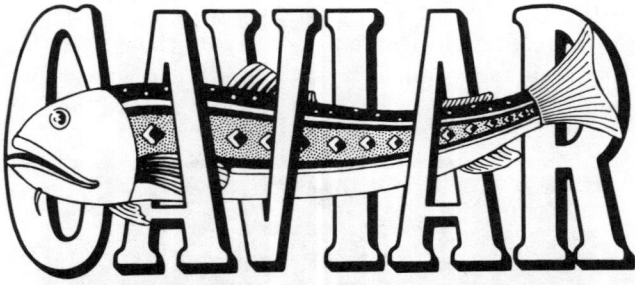

TARAMASALATA (FISH-ROE SALAD)

As a dip for raw vegetables or crackers, or on toast points or French bread for canapés, this will easily serve 15 to 20 people. It's never missing from a plate of *meza*, Greek for tidbits to whet the appetite. For variety, you can add a clove of garlic, finely minced, a few chopped parsley sprigs, 2 or 3 tablespoons sour cream (this will mellow the taste even more).

The Greeks drink Retsina—a wine that tastes somewhere between turpentine and alcohol—with Taramasalata, but any dry red wine should be fine.

5 slices Italian or French bread
1 8-ounce jar tarama
1 medium onion, grated
1 cup olive oil
Juice of 3 lemons (½ cup)

Trim crusts from bread. Soak slices in water; then squeeze dry.

In a large bowl, mix tarama and onion. Gradually add about ¼ cup olive oil, beating well until smooth and pastelike. Beat in the bread slices alternately with lemon juice and remaining olive oil. Keep beating until smooth, creamy, and salmon-colored. Chill until ready to serve.
Makes about 3 cups.

ing salad. Just a quarter of a pound, plus some lettuce and tomato, bread and butter makes a scrumptious lunch. The *lobster salad* is made with chunks of langostino lobster; you can pick them out easily and taste and savor each one. *Shrimp salad* is made with good-sized shrimp, immediately identifiable as shrimp, not some mysterious filling. These salads are not so overwhelmed by mayonnaise and celery that the eater is hard pressed to figure out exactly what's in them, and are not so overblended they're like mush. They're chewy, chunky, distinctive, and delicious. Great for lunch, terrific as sandwiches, and very very nice on black bread or crackers for canapés.

Egg salad, tuna salad, chicken salad, and *chopped*

liver, while perhaps not so exotic, nevertheless rate the same careful preparation and top-quality ingredients as does everything else. They lend themselves to an infinite variety of creative salad platters, hors d'oeuvres, tomato surprises, and the like.

Zabar's also offers a special *Greek salad*, a combination of cabbage, green peppers, carrots, onions, and salt herring in a sweet-sour dressing. It's topped with chewy chunks of Matjes herring (without the herring, it's sold as *Health Salad*). An instant and tasty lunch.

The fish counter is also the place to get your whipped cream cheese, plain or with scallions, all made in Zabar's kitchen. No bagel is complete without it; even croissants generously spread with cream cheese take on new dimensions! *Potato salad* and *coleslaw* are here, of course, and a delicately sweet *cucumber salad*.

Pickles, olives, and pickled tomatoes and peppers are possible and probable accompaniments for smoked fish and salads. They're also available at the deli counter and will be discussed in greater detail in chapter 3.

One other special delicacy will charm your palate: *gefilte fish*. If you didn't have a gefilte-fish-making grandmother, there's probably a good reason. Besides being a typically Eastern European specialty, it's also a time-consuming, laborious project, requiring more time, patience, and effort than most people—even grandmothers—are willing to give it.

Gefilte fish is made by finely grinding together several firm-fleshed, fresh, white-meat fish—such as carp, pike, and whitefish—with onions, eggs, seasonings, cracker or matzoh meal, then shaping the mixture into balls, loaves, or patties and simmering them in a rich fish stock. Gefilte fish can be eaten hot or cold, but always with a dollop of sinus-clearing horseradish and a slice of cooked carrot on top. It makes a perfect appetizer or hors d'oeuvre, light, tasty, and unusual; or serve it warmed, with boiled potatoes, as a main dish. Gefilte fish has a definite nonfishy taste. If you want to make your own—or persuade your grandmother to make it—see page 37.

ROLLMOPS

Per herring filet, use 1 teaspoon chopped shallots, 1 teaspoon chopped gherkin or sour pickle, ½ teaspoon chopped capers, and a dab (about ¼ teaspoon) prepared mustard. Roll the filets up, put in a jar, and cover with white or wine vinegar. Add to the vinegar 1 small onion, sliced, ½ teaspoon black peppercorns, ½ teaspoon mustard seed, and about ½ teaspoon of lemon peel. Let stand, covered, in the refrigerator for at least two weeks.

GEFILTE FISH

There are probably as many recipes for gefilte fish as there are Jewish grandmothers, and as with all such recipes, nothing is exact—you have to do it by taste and feel.

6 pounds fish (whitefish, pike, and carp)
Stock: Fish heads, bones, skin
4 onions sliced
3 quarts water
1 tablespoon salt
1 tablespoon black pepper
1 large onion, quartered
3 eggs
3 tablespoons matzoh meal or cracker meal,
   or 3 slices challah
¾ cup ice water
1 teaspoon salt
1 teaspoon white pepper
4 carrots, peeled and sliced

Filet the fish (or have it done for you); save heads, bones, and skin.

Make stock: In an 8-quart kettle, combine fish heads, bones, and skin with sliced onion, water, salt, and pepper; bring to a boil over high heat. (Add fish roe, too, if there is any.)

Grind fish with quartered onion. Beat in eggs, matzoh meal or cracker meal (or challah), ice water, salt, and pepper until well mixed. Then grind it all again (or put it in a large wooden bowl, and chop very fine). It should taste peppery. (You can do all this in a food processor, although that takes the fun out of it. Use the steel blade, and grind the fish first, probably in 2 or more batches. Then add the other ingredients, and continue processing until very smooth. The mixture comes out more like a fish mousse, and it is definitely not the way Grandma used to do it.)

Wet your hands, and shape a handful of fish mixture into a ball. Carefully drop ball into the boiling stock. Continue until all the fish is used. Add sliced carrot; cover pot; reduce heat; and simmer for 1 hour. Remove cover, and continue cooking for 30 minutes.

Let fish cool slightly; then remove from stock to a shallow serving bowl. Strain stock over it, and arrange carrots on top or around fish. Chill until sauce is jellied— 1 to 2 hours.
Serves 8 to 12.

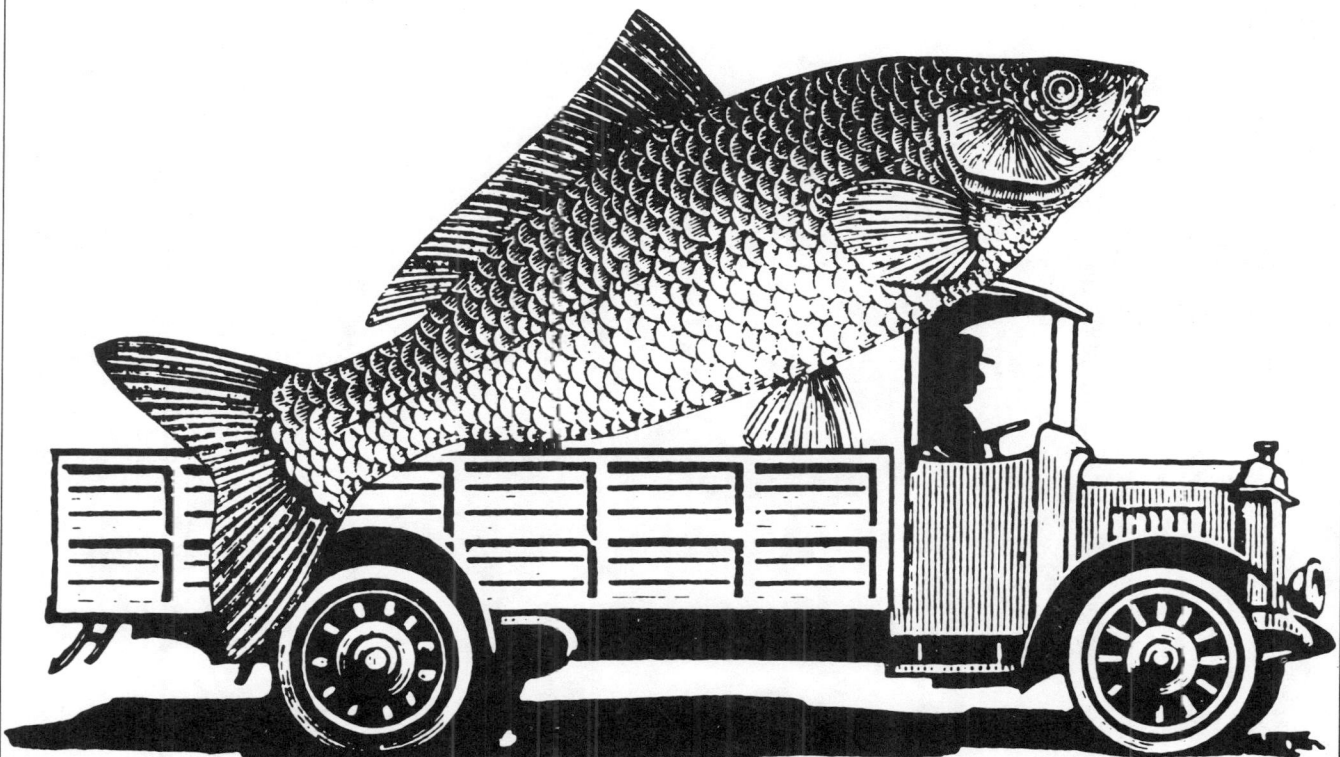

Deli

"When I was working in London, my wife used to ship me food from Zabar's—salamis, whitefish, things you couldn't get there. It was always successful, except once when there was a customs strike.

"I like to think Zabar's helped settle that strike. My wife sent me a whitefish, and forty-four days later, it was still on the dock, stinking up the entire place. They called me to please come and get it, and the strike was over almost immediately after."

Sol Kaplan

Zabar's meat department is an alluring world of more than 400 wursts and other goodies under one catalytic roof. There are old familiar foods, unusual ones you've always wanted to taste, and things you've never heard of. It's the ultimate in picnic chic, or a simple roast-beef, coleslaw, and pickle feast; an outrageous spread of pâtés and curious wursts; an unparalleled salad bar that makes any dieter feel privileged.

Look up! Stanley Zabar flaunts his salamis majestically from the ceiling, right over the deli counter. They're the crowning glory to an already ridiculously gorgeous assault on the senses.

At eye level, it's nothing short of mind boggling. More salamis and sausages, hams, roast beefs, pastrami, corned beef, bacon, and pâté share space with olives, pickles, and an incredible, ever-growing profusion of imaginative delicacies that Zabar's chefs prepare in the tiny kitchen in the back.

The man responsible for it all, under Stanley Zabar's watchful eye, is Harold Horowytz, a big bear of a man who looks as if he's tasted every one of the 423 items at his counter. He has. "The backbone of the counter is the kitchen and what comes out of it," Harold says. "We offer people an unreal variety that can't be found anywhere else."

CORNED BEEF

Zabar's corned beef is lean and trim, sweet and meaty—first-cut brisket of beef lovingly spiced and cooked—ready to be eaten as it is or to be made the center of attraction in an old-fashioned, yet instant, corned-beef-and-cabbage dinner.

Don't be misled by the name. Corned beef has nothing to do with corn. The Anglo-Saxons processed beef with a granular salt the size of corn kernels, and the name stuck. Corning is the pickling process the beef goes through before it's cooked. Each maker has his own time-tested, tried-and-true secret recipe, so the meat may be either dry-cured (rubbed with salt, sugar, and spices and layered and weighted down so it forms its own juice) or brined (soaked in a water, salt, sugar, and spice solution)—the same processes fish go through before they're smoked.

The spicing depends on the cut of meat and the flavor desired; cloves, peppercorns, and perhaps pickling spices are pretty standard and identifiable. Some chefs add more cloves and less salt and let the meat pickle for a shorter time. The result? A spicier corned beef. Many commercial corned-beef producers inject the brine into the meat; this cuts the curing time to as little as three hours.

After the beef has been corned, it still has to be cooked. It is washed to get rid of the salt; then it and

EASY CORNED BEEF AND CABBAGE

2 pounds corned beef, in one piece
1 medium cabbage, cut in wedges
Beef broth (about ½ cup)
4 medium potatoes, peeled and halved
  (optional)
Horseradish Sauce, below

Wrap corned beef in foil, and heat thoroughly in a low oven (325°F.). Takes about ½ hour.

Meanwhile, cook cabbage in ½ cup beef broth for about 10 minutes, or until tender. (If you like, add potato halves, increase cooking time to 20 minutes. The cabbage will be a little softer.)

Drain cabbage; place on serving platter with corned beef. Serve with Horseradish Sauce.
Serves 4 to 6.

all its whole spices are simmered in plain water for several hours. Carrots, onions, and more spices may be added, may not be. Now it's ready to eat, right out of the pot or glazed like a ham and baked. If you add boiled potatoes, carrots, onions, and cabbage, you'll have a New England boiled dinner in the time it takes to cook the vegetables. Fully cooked corned beef should be firm but tender, meaty, and not too salty or spicy. It has a grainy texture, but definitely not a stringy one.

"We sell about seven hundred pounds of it a week," boasts Harold.

It's corned beef, after all, that makes a Reuben sandwich a Reuben rather than a Max. Corned-beef

HORSERADISH SAUCE

3 tablespoons unsalted butter
2 tablespoons flour
1 cup hot milk
3 tablespoons white horseradish
2 tablespoons heavy cream
1 teaspoon dry mustard
1 tablespoon vinegar

Melt butter; stir in flour; continue stirring for 3 minutes. Gradually add milk, stirring until thick. Remove from heat, and add remaining ingredients. Reheat, but do not let boil. Serve hot.

hash is the quintessential American diner dinner. And simply sliced onto fresh rye bread or hard rolls, corned beef makes a sandwich that convinces you you've really been in a delicatessen.

PASTRAMI

Pastrami. The very thought of it, nice and spicy, piled high between pieces of fresh Jewish rye, slathered with mustard, pickle on the side, is enough to make even the most jaded appetite perk up. The first bite tells all: warm, pungent, and truly sensational. You can never get enough.

Pastrami. Its history is as mysterious and intriguing as the Transylvanian Alps where it was born 900 years ago. It wandered all over Eastern Europe and the Near East, like the lost tribes, for the next 500 years, searching for a permanent home. The Romanian Jews adopted it willingly, perfected it, cherished it, and brought it with them to the United States at the turn of this century. Their pastrami was pure beef (other cultures used meat from any animal that happened to be available—even camel), in observance of the Jewish dietary laws, and was filled with the wisdom of the ages.

The immigrants desperately tried to keep their recipes for pickling and smoking pastrami a secret. They couldn't. The Romanian method gradually became the one used throughout the pastrami-making world. Even so, they managed to keep some things to themselves. Try as anyone might, no two pastramis ever taste the same.

Zabar's uses first-cut brisket (lean and meaty) or

SWEET-AND-SOUR SUPPER

1 cup beef broth
½ cup dark brown sugar
1 bay leaf
6 whole cloves
½ teaspoon salt
Pinch cayenne pepper
1 large onion, thinly sliced
1 lemon, thinly sliced
½ cup raisins
1 pound cooked tongue, sliced ¼ inch thick

In a saucepan, combine all ingredients except tongue, and simmer for 10 minutes. Add tongue, and heat through.
Serves 4 to 6.

navel plate (fat and juicy), for pastrami. First, it is cured, like corned beef; then it is covered with a mixture of pepper, garlic, and spices and smoked over hardwood for several hours. After that, it is steamed. It isn't as firm as corned beef—more like pot roast—and it should be peppery, slightly fatty, and juicy.

Like corned beef, pastrami for sandwiches should be eaten hot, on rye, with pickles and coleslaw. Cream soda (any year is a good year) is the only correct beverage. Pastrami's spiciness makes a nice contrast to eggs, omelet or pancake style. And wrapped around water chestnuts, quickly broiled until crisp, it's the local version of *rumaki*, a South Sea Island hors d'oeuvre.

To New Yorkers, ex-New Yorkers, and would-be New Yorkers, pastrami and corned beef are the essence of delicatessen food. Zabar's sells nearly 400 pounds of pastrami a week. That makes an awful lot of sandwiches.

TONGUE

If pastrami is peppery and corned beef sweetly spicy, then tongue, the last in the triumvirate of corned meats, is meaty and rich, with that typical delicatessen taste and light, smoky flavor. It's made from beef or calves' tongues, and it is, by far, a most economical choice. There's no waste, no extra fat—it is all meat—and you'll easily get four to six servings per pound. It's soft, but still chewy enough to let you know it's around, and when sliced thin, it makes a great sandwich. Sliced about ¼ inch thick, it's perfect for quick, hot dishes, such as Sweet-and-

Sour Supper (see left column). It ain't bad with eggs, either.

In New York, where deli is king, corned beef, pastrami, and tongue are the forefathers of the royal family.

SAUSAGES

Sausages have been around forever, it seems. The Chinese had them first; the Babylonians ate them, too. Homer sang their praises in *The Odyssey*, and the ancient Romans feasted on sausage during the festivals of Floralia and Lupercalia. Both sausages, which were made of pork and pignolia nuts, and feasting were banned by Constantine, the first Christian emperor of Rome, who was rather shocked at the Bacchanalian goings on. But if Constantine was shocked, Petronius was so laid back that his satire on Roman life, *The Satyricon*, spoke of sausages as if they were lovers, to be fondled, relished, and adored.

By the Middle Ages, sausage-making had become a

CORNED BEEF AND POTATO SALAD

Garnish with lettuce and hard-cooked-egg quarters, and serve for lunch.

½ pound corned beef
2 large potatoes, boiled, peeled, and sliced
About ½ cup mayonnaise
1 large dill pickle, chopped; or equal
    amount chopped gherkins

DRESSING
1 tablespoon dry mustard
1 tablespoon dark-brown sugar (or more
    to taste)
3 tablespoons cider vinegar

Cut corned beef into julienne strips, about 3 inches long, ¼ inch wide. Put a layer of potato slices in a deep serving dish; spread with a thin layer of mayonnaise, and sprinkle with some of the chopped pickle. Cover with a layer of corned beef.

Make Dressing. Mix all ingredients (if you're using gherkins, which are sweet, use a little less sugar). Spoon a little over layers in dish.

Continue making layers until all the ingredients are used up; end with corned beef.
Serves 2 to 4.

true art, and sausages were named proudly after the cities in which they originated: Bologna, Lyon, Braunschweig, Genoa. And when the pilgrims landed on Plymouth Rock some years later, they found the Indians well into their own kind of sausage-making. The new settlers soon developed variations, using every part of the animal except, as they say, the squeal.

SAUSAGE BY ANY OTHER NAME

"Sausage" covers a whole variety of things and may mean something different to everyone. Salami is sausage; so are liverwurst, bologna, and mortadella. And frankfurters, bratwurst, and chorizos. But for easy identification, there are five basic types of sausage, and all fit into one or another of these categories.

FRESH SAUSAGE: Uncooked, uncured, and unsmoked. In other words, fresh sausage *must* be cooked before it's eaten. Breakfast sausages fall into this category, so do bratwurst and weisswurst, hot and sweet Italian sausages, and scrapple.

SMOKED SAUSAGE: Two types. One type is cooked, smoked, and ready to eat, such as frankfurters, bologna, kielbasa, and mortadella. The other is smoked but uncooked, such as mettwurst, and must be treated as fresh meat and cooked before eating.

COOKED SAUSAGE: Liverwurst is probably the most familiar example: bloodwurst is another. They're totally precooked.

SUMMER SAUSAGE: Also called semidry sausage. Originally made to last during the summer, before refrigeration was invented. Meats are cured, smoked, and dried and can be held safely for months without refrigerating. Cervelat, kosher salamis, and cooked salami are considered summer sausages.

DRY SAUSAGE: Chorizos, pepperoni, and most salamis are dry sausages, made of ground meat that is spiced and cured, sometimes smoked, and dried for up to six months. They are quite firm, since most of the moisture is extracted in the drying process.

WHEN WURST COMES TO WURST

"We have salamis that are all beef, all pork, or a combination of both; salamis that are smoked, dried, cooked, and cured in the San Francisco fog. We also have them coarse, fine, imported, spicy, bland, hard, soft, kosher and non-kosher," Harold Horowitz breathlessly recites. About 100 varieties, he conservatively estimates, from the very best wurst-makers in the world.

The spiciest is *Calabrese*, a coarse salami flavored with hot red peppers. It's nippy and devilish and straight from San Francisco. *Soppresata* is the coarsest, chunks of meat stuffed into a casing and studded with peppercorns. The finest are the Sicilian and Milano salamis, made here from authentic Italian recipes. Most Italian-style salamis are simply chopped, lean pork—sometimes with finely chopped beef added, whole black pepper, and other spices. They're dried for several weeks.

For Harold, Zabar's own *Love and Garlic* salami fits any situation. "It's something else," he says, and

it is. Garlicky, with just a hint of red wine, it's the kind of sausage to eat with someone who loves you dearly.

Genoa Piccolo is as hard as they come, with almost no give at all. Liverwurst is the extreme opposite—not a salami of course, but still a sausage—almost pâté-like and eminently spreadable.

What's the most exotic sausage at Zabar's? "I guess it's the *Coppa Veneziana*," Harold says. "It's an Italian salami with *coppa*—Italian-style ham— in the middle. You get a nice combination of tastes, the hard spiciness of the salami and the slightly salty softness of the ham. The best of both worlds."

Kosher salamis are all beef, only from "ritually clean" meat. Only the forequarters of the animal are used, and a Rabbi oversees the slaughter process to make certain everything is in accordance with the Jewish dietary laws.

The most expensive sausages are imported *German cervelat*—thick, peppery, cooked, and smoked, a sausage that does absolute wonders for rye bread—and *Zabar's Hungarian sausages*, a magic mixture of pork, lots of paprika, and years of Magyar culinary expertise.

HOW TO MAKE THE PERFECT CORNED-BEEF SANDWICH*

The best-tasting corned-beef sandwich, according to Zabar's, is made with fresh, hot corned beef, sliced just before you pile it on a thick slice of rye bread, the kind with crust so chewy that your jaws work overtime.

At least 5 to 6 ounces of the hot meat, sliced thin and across the grain at a slight angle (too thick, and it loses its special flavor; too cool, and it tends to dry out) are the bare minimum per sandwich. Distribute it evenly on the first slice of bread. The rye should be hand-cut, so each slice is about ½ inch thick. (If you try to put hot corned beef on thin, packaged rye, the bread will become soggy and fall apart.)

Spread the second bread slice with some good, spicy prepared delicatessen mustard and put it, mustard side down, on the corned beef. Cut the sandwich in half; add a good, juicy, sour pickle and a little coleslaw on the side, and plunge right in. This is a hefty sandwich for eaters, not diners, and should be washed down only with cold beer, celery tonic, or cream soda.
Pastrami is an acceptable substitute for corned beef.

THE REUBEN SANDWICH

The mystery of how this came to be called a Reuben may never be solved. Everyone has a different story. The filling, however, remains a classic all over the United States.

4 slices rye bread
2 tablespoons unsalted butter or margarine
About ¼ cup Russian dressing
½ pound corned beef, sliced
¼ pound Swiss-cheese, sliced
¼ pound sauerkraut, well drained

Preheat oven to 425°F.

Spread 2 slices of bread with butter or margarine, 2 with Russian dressing. Layer corned beef, Swiss cheese, and sauerkraut on the Russian dressing; top with other bread slices, butter side down. Wrap tightly in aluminum foil, and bake about 15 minutes, or until hot. (If you prefer, butter one side of all 4 bread slices. On unbuttered side of 2 slices, spread dressing and layer corned beef, cheese, and sauerkraut; top with other 2 bread slices, buttered side up. Sauté in a skillet, over medium heat, turning once, until bread is golden brown on both sides and cheese is melted.)
Makes 2 sandwiches.

Almost all of Zabar's wursts are domestic, by the way. The import of meats is heavily controlled by the government, and except for some smoked varieties from Germany, Denmark, and Romania, the others are made here, no matter by what regional name they're called.

If Harold had to choose one sausage as his favorite, it would be *kielbasa*, hands down. This Polish delight is no joke. It's dynamite with mustard or cooked into an infinite number of quick and interesting main dishes (see page 51). It has a spicy, smoky flavor, lingering and repeating, that tells you right away, and often several hours later, just what a hearty sausage you've put in your stomach.

FULL OF BOLOGNA

In the United States alone, more than one hundred kinds of sausage are made, and Zabar's has nearly all of them. World-wide, the figure is ten times that. The most popular, without rival in this country, are bologna and frankfurters.

A bologna sandwich on white bread might be the lunchbox choice of nearly everyone under 12—second only, maybe, to peanut butter and jelly. Why is that? Probably because bologna is so mild and sweet and inoffensive. It's ground beef and pork trimmings (kosher bologna, of course, is all beef), salted and allowed to stand for two days, then reground, lightly spiced with black pepper, sage, and maybe a touch of coriander and mace, ground once more, put in a casing, and dried overnight. It's smoked for an hour or two, then cooked in boiling water for half an hour or more, depending on its size. It comes out a rosy-pink color, soft and giving to the touch. It's easy to chew, mushes around nicely in the mouth, and tastes good but not overwhelming. It appears to have been invented solely to be put into sandwiches.

FRANKLY SPEAKING

Americans eat an astonishing eight billion frankfurters a year—more than all the Big Macs McDonald's has sold. Hundreds of pounds pass through Zabar's doors each week, all of them all-beef, kosher franks in assorted sizes.

Franks are much like bologna, only smaller, made

MAKING
YOUR OWN

Can you? Should you? Yes, and maybe. It's relatively easy to make fresh sausage—without a casing. But making cured, dried, or smoked sausage can be extremely time-consuming and expensive. Not to mention inconvenient if you have to buy a lot of equipment.

To make fresh sausage, the kind you shape into small patties and fry for breakfast, all you need are meat, seasonings, and a meat grinder or food processor. Lean pork, pork fat, salt, pepper, and sage are the basic ingredients, ground together quite fine by hand or machine. Shape patties and fry them until no more pink shows. Eat immediately (they don't keep). By varying the herbs and spices, using anything from garlic to nutmeg, adding wine, mixing the pork with beef or veal, you'll vary the flavor. Proportions are really a matter of taste; but a good start for fresh, country-style sausage might be 2 parts lean ground meat to 1 part fat, to which you can begin by adding (to 1½ pounds of pork and fat) about 2 teaspoons salt, ½ teaspoon pepper, ½ to ¾ teaspoon sage or a mixture of sage, thyme, marjoram, and savory.

A word of warning, and an important one. Start with a small amount, because you *should not* and *must not* taste the raw-pork mixture to check the seasonings. The trial-and-error method will never be a culinary disaster, although you may just not love the result.

DEEP-FRIED
MORTADELLA

This is also good made with ½ pound of mozzarella instead of the sausage, or with ¼ pound of each.

½ pound mortadella, cut into 1-inch cubes
About ¼ cup flour
1 egg, slightly beaten
½ cup bread crumbs
Oil for deep-frying

Dip the mortadella in flour, then in egg, then in bread crumbs. Set aside while you heat the oil; then deep-fry until golden brown. Drain on paper towels before serving.
Serves 4.

of beef and pork (except kosher ones, which are only beef), and a little more seasoned with garlic and spices. They can be eaten cold, like bologna (they're fully cooked), but they taste better hot. The easiest way to heat them is to drop them into boiling water and let them simmer for about five minutes. Some people prefer to broil them until the skin cracks, or split them lengthwise, spread them with mustard and a slice of Gruyère, and broil them until the cheese melts. That's still quick and easy.

Frankfurters got their name from the city of their birth, Frankfurt-am-Main, Germany. They may have made their first appearance in this country in St. Louis in 1876, when a German peddler who had been handing out gloves with his sausages so his clientele wouldn't soil their hands, decided to wrap his wares in rolls. And then again, they might not have.

At first, people called franks "dachshund sausages" —they do look rather like the little dogs. Then a newspaper cartoonist coined the phrase "hot dog" to describe the four-legged frankfurters that ran around his comic strip acting like people.

Franks came to be known as "Coney Island Red Hots" when a butcher from Coney Island—the first to make an all-beef frank—smothered them with a mouth-shattering combination of ketchup, mustard, onion, tabasco sauce, and pepper. You can hardly find them in Coney Island now.

As for the ballpark frank, although Babe Ruth didn't invent it, or even come up with the idea to make it a ballpark favorite, rumor has it that he often ate a dozen franks during the seventh-inning stretch. He might not have been so enthusiastic had he known that hot-dog vendors were selling their wares outside the stadium smothered in "rags and paint"—mustard and sauerkraut.

SAUSAGES AND SALAMIS—A TO Z

ABRUZZI: Dry Italian sausage, made from fresh pork and spices, cured and air-dried. Spicy and nice; for antipasto plates, hors d'oeuvres, or just munching.

BEEF JERKY: Completely cooked, dried and smoked beef, salty and chewy. It keeps practically forever; good for camping trips or emergency supplies.

BERLINER SAUSAGE: Coarsely ground pork and chopped beef; mildly cured. It has almost no seasonings, is smoked and cooked and quite bland.

BLOCKWURST: German-style, very similar to cervelat (below).

BLUTWURST: German delicacy, made with diced and cooked fat pork, beef, gelatin, and beef blood. Highly seasoned, very salty, but totally cooked. Good and surprising in chef's salad.

BOCKWURST: Mildly seasoned; veal, pork, milk, chives, eggs, and parsley. Similar to frankfurters, but white, and must be cooked. Can be boiled, fried, stewed, eaten hot or cooked and cooled.

BOLOGNA: Cured beef and pork, finely ground, lightly seasoned. Cooked, usually smoked. Perfect for sandwiches.

Ham Bologna (Schinkenwurst): Made from large chunks of cooked pork, smoked and cooked. From same cut as ham.

Hungarian Bologna: Heavily seasoned with paprika.

Kosher Bologna: All beef, packed in sheep's casing.

Lebanon Bologna: Thick and wide, encased in cheesecloth. Smoked, strong sweet flavor. Pennsylvania Dutch specialty, refinement of original Italian bologna to local tastes. Comes in three varieties at Zabar's: long, long and extra sweet, and midget size.

Smoked Bologna: Traditional beef-and-pork mixture, with a nice smoky flavor.

BRATWURST: Pork scraps, sometimes pork and veal, seasoned with sage and lemon juice. Must be cooked; then is eaten like franks. Especially good with lots of fried onions. (Zabar's also sells bratwurst precooked, smoked, and "Nuremberg-style.")

BREAKFAST SAUSAGE AND LINKS: Uncured and uncooked pork, with salt, pepper, sage, and sometimes other seasonings. Must be cooked—fried, usually. Comes in small links or in large, salami shape, to slice.

BUNDERFLEISCH: Swiss Alps air-dried beef, salty and spicy. Served and used like prosciutto.

SALAMI AND EGGS

A great quick supper, or a nice change from the usual bacon-and-eggs breakfast.

1 tablespoon unsalted butter or margarine
8 slices kosher salami
2 eggs, lightly beaten

Melt butter or margarine in a skillet, and sauté salami on both sides. Pour on eggs, and cook until set.
Serves 1.

CAPOCOLLO: Pork shoulder or butt, seasoned with red peppers, cured and air-dried. Spicy and hot.

CERVELAT: Thick and spicy pork sausage, dried and cooked. Usually eaten cold, particularly in sandwiches. Zabar's has several varieties:
Cervelatwurst: All beef, or beef and pork, tangy and spicy.
Farmer's Cervelat: Coarsely chopped pork and beef, no garlic, cured and dried.
Goettinger Cervelat: Dry and hard, very spicy.
Guteborg Cervelat: Dry, coarsely chopped, salty and very heavily smoked.
Landjager Cervelat: The Swiss version, dry, pressed flat, and smoked. Reddish-brown in color, and thin.
Thuringer Cervelat: Medium-dry version, tangy, but mild.

CHORIZO: Dry pork sausage, highly spiced with hot pepper, coriander, paprika, cumin, oregano, cloves, and vinegar. Spanish version of pepperoni; good as hors d'oeuvres, cooked with eggs, or added to beans, rice, chicken, or chili for special Latin touch.

COTEGHINO: Italian-style dried and smoked pork sausage, always big, with a special affinity for beans, particularly lentils. Traditional part of Italian *bollito misto* (mixed boil), a potful of everything from chicken to vegetables, beef, tongue, and spices.

CSABAI: Hungarian sausage, spicy rather than hot, with lots of paprika.

FRANKFURTERS: Finely ground and mildly seasoned, all beef or beef-and-pork mixture; always smoked. Don't need cooking, but much better hot. Zabar's sell only all-beef kosher franks.

FRIZZIES: Highly spiced, cured lean pork and beef, coarsely chopped. Dry sausage, like salami.

GELBWURST: Looks like liverwurst, but actually bland, spongy, pork-and-veal sausage.

GOTHAR: Dry, lean pork, finely chopped and cured. German-style sausage, ready to eat; not terribly distinctive.

GRIDDLES: Just another name for frankfurters.

HEADCHEESE: Cured hog's-head meat, sometimes including the tongue. It can be very spicy. Zabar's Hungarian version is made with blood and a ton of paprika. Meat and spices, combined with gelatin, are pressed into a mold and refrigerated until set. It's sliced like meat loaf. Not exactly a sausage, and not even appetizing to many, it's very tasty and appeals to Zabar's European customers.

ITALIAN SAUSAGES, HOT AND SWEET: Pork scraps and butt, with lots of seasonings. Fatty and fresh; must be cooked. Good with pasta, braised in red wine, browned and combined with zucchini, tomatoes, green peppers, onions, and artichokes.

KALBSROULADE: Liverwurst made from calves' liver; not smoked.

KIELBASA: Coarsely ground lean pork and fat, sometimes with beef blood, flavored with garlic, pimiento, and cloves; smoked and cooked. Polish or Hungarian in origin, depending on whom you talk to, and at Zabar's it comes Polish-style, long, or in loops, and kosher-style, made of all beef and very heavy on the garlic (sometimes called *knublewurst*). Very adaptable, can be eaten hot or cold, cooked or as is.

KNACKWURST (also *Knockwurst* or *Knoblauch*): Kosher, all-beef, ground, then dried and smoked. Similar to frankfurters, but with lots of garlic and cumin. Ready to eat, spicy, and tastes much better hot; boiled; split down the middle, filled with mashed potatoes, sprinkled with grated cheese, and broiled; or sautéed with onions, green pepper, zucchini, and tarragon.

LACHSCHINKEN: Lightly smoked pork loin, no seasonings. Dry. Eat it with a squeeze of lemon and a grind of black pepper.

LIVERWURST: Pork liver and meat trimmings, ground with onions and spices, cooked and/or smoked. Smooth, creamy texture; mild, livery taste. Comes in several varieties:
Braunschweiger: Smoked.
Fresh: Pork-and-beef-liver mixture, cooked but not smoked.
Long: Just indicates the length.
Smoked Goose: Made from goose livers.

LIEBERCASER: Liver loaf, German-style meat loaf, not terribly spicy.

LINGUICA: Portuguese-style sausage, spicy, but not very heavy.

LUNCHEON SAUSAGE: You can eat any sausage for lunch, but this one, made of big chunks of pork pressed with beef, olives, and pimientos, is particularly pretty and colorful.

LYON SAUSAGE: Dry sausage made of lean and fat pork, spices, and garlic. Cured and air-dried for four to five months. Best eaten cold as hors d'oeuvres; but it can be sliced, put on an English muffin, topped with slivers of sharp, aged Cheddar, and broiled. Good as part of a mixed-cold-cuts platter with Westphalian ham, cervelat, scallions, radishes, and black olives.

METTWURST: Sixty to 70 percent cured beef mixed with cured pork, pepper, and coriander. Mild, but tasty; must be cooked.

MORTADELLA: This is actually bologna, and according to some, the finest sausage in Italy. Smooth, delicious, subtle flavor, from finely chopped cured pork and beef, larded with back fat. It's smoked at high temperatures and air-dried, and may be as much as 18 inches in diameter. Zabar's has four versions: imported and domestic; with and without pistachio nuts.

PEPPERONI: In long strings for slicing, or sticks; a dry sausage made of beef and pork trimmings with lots and lots of red and black pepper and garlic. It's dried for a long time, and very chewy when it's cut into chunks. It's a super pizza topping, good in stews, baked beans, or with chili.

SALAMI: Basically, mixed meats with varying degrees of garlic and other spices. May be cured and smoked, cured and dried, or cooked. Zabar's has many kinds:

Allesandri: Italian-style, hard, dry, and spicy.
Alpino: Made from an old Alpine recipe; hard and spicy.
Arles: French-style, lots of garlic and red pepper.
Beef Log: Dry, smoked beef salami.
Cacciatore: Italian-style, in midget sizes.
Calabrese: Coarse salami with hot peppers.
Cooked Salami: Chopped beef and pork with garlic, black pepper, and other seasonings. Soft-textured and mild.
Coppa: Regular or sweet-style Italian salami, with bits of ham (*coppa*) in it.
Danish Salami: Smoked, small little sticks, like cervelat.
Filsette: Mild, Italian Genoa-style salami.
Genoa Piccolo: May be imported or domestic. Pork, beef, plus hearts, garlic, and pepper. Dried up to five months, which makes it hard and chewy.
German: Not very highly spiced, but heavily smoked.
Hard (Burgermeister): Pork and beef, seasoned with pepper and sage, and dried for two months. Most of the fat drips out, so this can be hard as a log before it's smoked.
Hungarian: Heavy on the smoke and garlic; either everyone you're with eats it, or you'll stand alone.

HAM CAKES AND RED-EYE GRAVY

*2 cups cooked ham (baked or boiled),
    ground or chopped fine*
½ cup bread crumbs
2 eggs
1 tablespoon grated onion
*Salt and freshly ground black pepper, to
    taste*
1 teaspoon prepared mustard
¼ cup flour (about)
5 tablespoons salad oil or bacon drippings

Mix ham, bread crumbs, eggs, onion, salt, pepper, and mustard together; shape into 6 flat patties. Lightly coat with flour.

Heat oil or bacon drippings in a heavy skillet; sauté ham cakes until golden brown on both sides, about 5 minutes.

RED-EYE GRAVY: Remove ham cakes from skillet and drain off all but 2 tablespoons of oil or drippings. Add to this 1 cup boiling water, and scrape up any particles that have clung to the bottom. Add 1 to 2 tablespoons of strong coffee and bring to a boil. Serve over ham cakes.
Serves 6.

Italian: In general, Italian salami is chopped pork and beef, mixed with red wine or grape juice, garlic, and spices.

Kosher: All beef, with garlic and seasonings, cured and smoked. It comes with Zabar's label in four sizes (two-pound, three-pound, long, and midget) and from Smulka Bernstein in the same four sizes, plus chicken salami (not made of chicken, just extra wide), cocktail salami, and salami on a string. Also comes in three stages—soft, medium, and hard.

Milano: Finely ground mixed meats.

Settecento Genoa: Another type of hard Genoa salami.

Sicilian: Finely ground pork trimmings with white and black pepper. Smoked and dried, spicy and flavorful.

Tiroler: Cooked sausage, like salami.

Toscana Soppressata: Coarsely ground pork, almost chunky, studded with peppercorns. No garlic, but pungent in smell and taste.

TV Sticks: Salami in two-inch logs, just right for munching while watching television.

SAUSSICHEN: Uncooked pork on a skewer; must be cooked.

SPECIALS: Super-jumbo fat kosher frankfurters. Particularly good with baked beans.

SULZE: Similar to headcheese, made with calves' feet that have been cooked for five to six hours, diced, mixed with hard-cooked eggs and sometimes other meats, and allowed to stand in its own broth until broth has jelled. Sliced like meat loaf, and served as an appetizer.

THURINGER EBONY: A type of spring salami made of beef, pork, white pepper, marjoram, and other seasonings, but no garlic. It's smoked long and slowly until the outside is black, hence the name.

THURINGER JUMBO: Summer sausage made of beef and pork, with hearts added, and lots of seasonings. Also smoked for a long time, so it has a heavy smoked flavor.

TOURISTWURST: Cervelat-style in rings or horseshoes; a big tourist attraction in windows of German butcher shops.

USINGER'S: Delicious sausages and old-fashioned liverwurst, both with or without garlic.

WEISSWURST: White veal sausage, seasoned with white pepper, among other spices; must be cooked.

WUNDERWUURST: A type of liverwurst with pistachio nuts.

ZABAR'S OWN: Salamis: *Love and Garlic* and *Wine and Garlic*; cured, dried, spicy, and hard; reeking with garlic and deliciously tasty.

HAMMING IT UP

In the Middle Ages, the Gauls salted their pork, smoked it for several days, rubbed it with oil, vinegar, and spices, and hung it to dry. In effect, they made ham. This meat became so gastronomically important that from then until the mid-nineteenth century, the cathedral of Notre Dame in Paris opened its square to a pre-Easter "ham fair" every year. Each town and region of France entered its best ham in an effort to win recognition. So prestigious were these fairs that they soon became international in scope and flavor; Westphalian ham from Germany, Prague ham, Parma hams from Italy, Jamon Serrano from Spain, Irish hams smoked over peat fires competed.

The early Massachusetts settlers were probably the first ham-smokers; but Smithfield, Virginia, soon became the place for the finest hams in the colonies. The Virginians fed their pigs a special diet of acorns, beechnuts, hickory nuts, peanuts, and corn, then salt-cured and smoked the fat ham cuts over low, long fires for several weeks. Finally, the meat was hung to cure further for a year or more. The result was hams of exceptional and incomparable flavor.

There were imitators, to be sure. Kentucky hams were similarly processed. Virginia hams other than Smithfields differed mostly in the length of curing and the wood used for smoking. But although they were close, Smithfield ham was still the prize. All the "country hams" had one basic thing in common, a heavy coating of mold, a natural result of the long curing process, which had to be soaked and scrubbed off before the hams could be used. They still do.

Zabar's is a ham fair all by itself.

There are about half a dozen kinds of baked ham, most of which started out smoked or boiled elsewhere and are boned, baked, glazed, or otherwise enhanced in Zabar's kitchen with whatever Stanley and Harold think will bring out the best in them. As Escoffier said: Fresh pork is not deserving of consideration, but ham is to be savored and honored.

Besides Zabar's own (see page 60), 40-odd other varieties—boiled, baked, smoked, dry-cured, air-cured —from all over the world are on the deli shelves. Each is subtly and wonderfully different, and the delicate nuances that distinguish them are lovingly and knowingly pointed out by Harold and his staff.

Take *prosciutto*. No real cook can live without it. It is a Parma ham, from pigs fed on chestnuts and whey. What makes it so special is the way it's cured: hung in caves where freely circulating air turns it almost translucently pink. At the moment, all prosciutto available at Zabar's is made domestically; there has been a government ban on meat products from Italy, Spain, and Portugal because of an outbreak of hoof-and-mouth disease in those countries. Harold thinks the disease is under control and the ban should be lifted any day.

In the meantime, Zabar's does have some of the very best domestic and Canadian (not considered im-

KIELBASA AND KRAUT

1 quart sauerkraut, drained
10 ounces beer, or 5 ounces white wine
 and 5 ounces water
1 onion, sliced
½ teaspoon salt
Freshly ground black pepper, to taste
1 loop kielbasa (about 1 pound)

Put all ingredients except kielbasa in a 2-quart pot; cover, and simmer about ½ hour.

Cut kielbasa into 1½-inch pieces. Brown in large hot skillet. Pour off fat; add kraut mixture; cover, and heat for 10 minutes.

Serves 4.

ported) prosciutto from Cittierio, Daniele (both sweet and Parma-style), Hormel, and Volpe. Wrapped around sweet, fresh melon, especially cantaloupe, or ripe, juicy figs. Prosciutto makes an incredibly delicious hors d'oeuvre or appetizer. Its salty, tangy taste and thin, almost dry texture are perfectly set off by cold, succulent fruit (it goes well with pineapple, too). Between thin slices of veal or chicken breast and Gruyère—Cordon Bleu—it's sublime, the perfect marriage of taste and texture. Draped over fresh asparagus, covered with slices of Fontina cheese, and baked until the cheese melts, it's not just pretty, it's sensational. And in a cream sauce for fresh pasta, with garden-fresh peas, prosciutto adds color, tex-

THE HAM YOU CURE MAY BE YOUR OWN

Given the patience and the right conditions, you can make your own version of prosciutto, as dry-curing is pretty easy. First, you must cure a fresh, boned ham by rubbing salt and sugar well into the meat. After making sure that every bit of ham is covered with the seasonings, put it into a large plastic bag, leaving a little space open at the top, and tuck it away in a cool, dry place for several days.

Then the salt and sugar must be scraped off, the ham dried and rubbed with garlic, sprinkled with some of your best cognac and crushed peppercorns, and wrapped securely in linen or canvas. Tie it all up with string, and hang it in a cool, dark place (a cave would be perfect) for at least six months.

ture, and an extravangantly savory zing.

Westphalian ham tastes very much like prosciutto and looks like smoked salmon, translucent and grainy. So does German-style *farmer's ham*. Both arrive at their respective flavors through heavy smoking. *Bayonne* (after the French, not the New Jersey city) and *Toulouse hams*, like prosciutto, are dry-cured and eaten "raw." The long curing and drying make them safe to eat with no further cooking. They are firm and chewy, just salty enough to be interesting, and slip cunningly between thin slices of buttered black bread or onto an hors-d'oeuvre tray.

If you want to be technical, *pancetta* is bacon, not ham (it's from the same cut of pork), and looks like a sausage. It isn't smoked, but air-cured after having been thoroughly coated with salt and spices. Then it's rolled up like a salami and sliced. It has a mild, fatty, pleasant taste, slightly salty, slightly spicy, and is used liberally in Northern Italian cooking, especially with veal. It's the secret ingredient that makes Spaghetti Carbonara so special. This is pasta served with a sauce of Parmesan and Romano cheeses, raw eggs, and pancetta sautéed with a little chopped garlic and white wine. (If you can't get pancetta, the next best thing, though not nearly the same, is bacon that has been blanched in boiling water two to three minutes, to get rid of the smoky flavor.)

Smoked *Black Forest ham* is a heady mouthful, rich and very smoky in taste. It's one of Harold's personal favorites, sliced about an inch thick, topped with a slice of pineapple, sprinkled with curry, and baked, covered, for about 45 minutes. He also recommends cutting it into chunks and serving it with a mustard dip.

Plain old *boiled ham* is neither plain nor old at Zabar's. It can be imported from Poland or Yugoslavia, although it arrives here canned. Any way you slice it, you'll have super sandwiches. Grind it, and mix it with mustard, salt, pepper, eggs, and bread crumbs, and fry it into extraordinarily good ham cakes.

Kügel ham from Germany is one of the few imported hams that is universally available. It's made in plants so spotlessly clean that it passes everyone's inspections, even the most stringent. It's very heavily smoked, "a hearty, peasanty ham," Harold calls it. "It's okay on sandwiches, but much better if you just cut it into cubes, stick a toothpick in them, and pass them around with cocktails." And better still, baked with stewed tomatoes and sprinkled with Parmesan cheese.

Mellow, moist, and tender *country ham* is naturally aged, cured, hickory-smoked, and fully cooked. It has a real country flavor, juicy and distinctive, is firm and chewy to the bite. Pleasantly salty and smoky, it shines best when it's fried and served Southern-style with grits and red-eye gravy (made from ham drippings, water, and coffee).

From Scandinavia comes lightly smoked, salty *Danish ham*, cured over hardwood, like bacon. *Turino* is an Italian-inspired pepper ham, studded inside and out with whole peppercorns and, not surprisingly, spicy and peppery. It's a little like pastrami and makes a good, flavorful sandwich.

Zabar's takes great pride in its highly seasoned, sharply biting *Smithfield hams*, and well it should. Whether you want a whole ham—bone in or out—still in its burlap wrapper, or one that's been pressed into a block for easy slicing, it will be right from the finest farms in Smithfield, Virginia. The hams have been dry-salted, spiced, aged, and smoked over hickory logs, then cleaned and totally cooked in the very best Southern tradition—slowly and basted with wine. Smithfields are amazingly versatile; the ham makes fine sandwiches and hors d'oeuvres, without doubt, and heated through, it becomes a main course for a

KIELBASA CASSEROLE

½ cup salad oil
1 cup chopped sweet red pepper
2 medium onions, chopped
2 large, ripe tomatoes, coarsely chopped
2 teaspoons sugar
¼ tablespoon salt
2 tablespoons hot paprika
½ pound kielbasa, cut into 1-inch cubes

Heat oil in a large skillet. Sauté pepper and onion in oil until onion is wilted. Add tomato, sugar, salt, and paprika; cover, and simmer about 15 minutes. Add kielbasa, and heat through.
Serves 2.

A THOROUGHLY ZABAR'S ANTIPASTO

Literally, "antipasto" means food served just before the pasta, and in Italy, it's an appetite-arousing but not stupefying plate of hard sausages and ham, fish, such as anchovies or tuna, cheese, vegetables, and olives. It can be a meal all by itself, too.

Start with some hard and spicy sausages or salami: Genoa salami is classic, but pepperoni, calabrese, or even kielbasa will do. You need only one—about two slices per person.

Then something milder: mortadella (the classic antipasto sausage), capocollo, Milano salami. Again, choose only one; 2 slices per.

Cheese: Provolone is always there, but try caciocavallo, fontina, bel paese, or smoked mozzarella. This is one time when you should precut the cheese, to make it more manageable.

A nice touch would be prosciutto or pancetta wrapped around slivers of cantaloupe or figs. Or if fruit is out of season, sesame bread sticks are nice.

Vegetables: Fresh ones might include celery or fennel, tomato wedges, green or red peppers. Pickled vegetables could be marinated mushrooms and artichoke hearts, pickled hot peppers or pepperoncini, pickled onions and beets. Or just use Zabar's antipasto salad. Pimiento and oil-cured black and green olives are a must.

If you want to do a little cooking, you might add a couple of homemade salads that are easy and nice: shredded carrot dressed with salt and pepper, oil and vinegar; a tuna salad of Italian-style tuna mixed with white beans (Great Northern or kidney, soaked overnight, cooked, and drained), sliced Bermuda onion, oil and vinegar; baby shrimp in a vinaigrette sauce; cold roast-beef salad.

Arrange everything on a large platter; add a few anchovies for taste and texture, and serve with a basket of Italian bread and a bottle of wine. *Buon appetito!*

company dinner that can't be beat. Smithfields are the closest to authentic Chinese hams and can be used in a tremendous variety of Oriental dishes.

Somewhere between ham and sausage are two of Zabar's more unusual offerings: capocollo, an Italian-style delicacy, and German *Lachschinken*. They are similar; both are made from cured pork and are not technically ham (which usually comes only from the hind leg, the most delicate part) or sausage, even though they're put into casings.

But there the similarity ends. Capocollo is highly spiced with hot red peppers and paprika, then air-dried, smoked, and pressed, not ground or chopped, into its casing. Lachschinken, on the other hand, has very little seasonings, is finely ground, and smoked until it reaches the color that gives it its name, which means salmon ham.

These are a little bit ham, a little bit sausage, unusual enough to be conversation pieces, delicious enough to make stupendous sandwiches, and distinctive enough to add special flavor to casseroles or any dish calling for smoked ham.

There's some ham in all of us, it's been said. Why not make it one of these?

BRINGING HOME THE BACON

There's more to bacon than simply unwrapping a package from the supermarket and tossing the bacon on a griddle. Good bacon is a true gourmet treat—for breakfast, with eggs, pancakes, waffles (bacon is the most popular breakfast meat in the country); for lunch, in sandwiches; for dinner, in traditional dishes like liver, bacon, and onions or classics like Quiche Lorraine. Zabar's offers you several singularly different choices, and not one of them is precut or wrapped in plastic.

Black Forest bacon is heavily smoked. Fry it up quickly to serve with scrambled eggs; its strong, unusually smoky flavor and its chewy texture contrast beautifully with the soft, bland egg mixture. Eggless? Sauté sliced apples in the bacon fat; sprinkle with sugar, and serve with strips of bacon. Good contrast here, and a nice and easy brunch or lunch dish.

A little bit of New England comes to you via Zabar's *maple-cured bacon*. It's long and lean, not too salty, with a distinct maple flavor that comes not just from the maple cure, but also from long, slow smoking over maple wood and corncobs. They've been making it that way in the South for over a century. Start cooking in a cold pan, says Harold, so it won't curl (that goes for all bacon). Try it with old-fashioned baked beans, an excitingly different way to serve them.

Canadian bacon is really pork loin with a very thin layer of fat and a large eye of meat. It looks like a slice of pork, round and smoky, and it's much more than breakfast food. "Buy a whole one and barbecue it," suggests Harold, "or glaze it like ham." (Whole ones usually weigh between three and nine pounds.) It's fully cooked, so it really needs only heating through, and it takes nicely to sautéeing, broiling, or baking.

All natural, *nonpreservative bacon* has a short shelf life before it turns an unappetizing gray, and it should be used within a week after being purchased. It has no nitrites or nitrates, so it will satisfy a longing for bacon and still be a "health food." Use it as you would any other bacon; it fries nice and crisp, with the traditional, wonderful bacon smell and flavor.

If you like a strikingly smoky flavor—and aroma—in your bacon, the Pennsylvania Dutch *double-smoked* is for you. It's lean and tender, almost sweet, but not quite, and just the thing with pancakes and lots of maple syrup, or wrapped around pineapple chunks or chicken livers and broiled.

Large-eyed *Irish bacon* is similar to the type that comes from Ireland, but it's made right here. Lean and meaty, with a medium-smoky taste, it's sold at Zabar's in rashers (slices) or gammons (whole sides). It's the star attraction in a stick-to-your-ribs Irish breakfast starting with porridge (oatmeal, actually), poached eggs, and Irish soda bread with sweet butter and marmalade.

Dry-cured, *hickory-smoked bacon* is sweet and lean, cured by rubbing each slab with honey and a sugar-and-spice mixture. It's smoked slowly, for several hours, over hickory wood, so its flavor is rich, concen-

---

SPAGHETTI CARBONARA

3 tablespoons olive oil
4 cloves garlic, minced (optional)
½ pound pancetta or bacon, cut into thin strips
¼ cup white wine
1 pound spaghetti, cooked and drained
3 eggs or 2 egg yolks
¾ cup grated Parmesan mixed with 4 tablespoons grated Romano
Freshly ground black pepper, to taste
1 truffle, thinly sliced (optional)

Over medium heat, sauté the garlic in the olive oil until golden; remove garlic with slotted spoon and discard. Add pancetta, and cook until crisp. (If using bacon, use only 1 tablespoon oil to cook garlic; sauté bacon until crisp.) Remove pancetta or bacon, and add wine to drippings in pan; let boil for 2 minutes and set aside.

In a small bowl, lightly beat eggs or yolks with cheese and pepper. Pour over cooked and drained spaghetti and toss to coat.

Put cooked pancetta or bacon back in the pan with the wine and heat for 1 minute. Pour over spaghetti. Top with sliced truffles if using.
Serves 4.

trated, and pronounced. It makes liver and onions a special treat, and in toasted sandwiches, with chicken slices, grated Swiss or Roquefort, and tomato, it's superb.

Although *Romanian bacon* is canned, it is sold by the piece at Zabar's. Sugar-cured, meaty and chewy, it takes the humdrum out of boring BLTs (sandwiches made with bacon, lettuce, and tomato) and makes a great topping for green beans. Fry it; sauté chopped onion in the bacon fat; add a little vinegar and sugar and some of the water you've cooked the beans in; crumble the bacon into the sauce, and pour it all over the the waiting beans. Simple, but delicious.

A PÂTÉ FOR EVERY OCCASION

Along with caviar and smoked salmon, pâté is one of the most asked for gourmet delicacies at Zabar's—even though, according to some cynics, it's nothing more than a high-class meat loaf!

Its beginnings can be traced back to the ancient tomb paintings of Egypt and old Greek and Roman chronicles. But the first *real* recipes came from France.

Everything and anything was made into pâté, not just livers, but all the edible parts of ducks, geese, swans, pheasants, peacocks, and larks. These were combined with fruits and vegetables and molded into fantastic shapes.

Pâtés were often prepared with a mortar and pestle so big they were attached to the ceiling with ropes on pulleys. At first, they were steamed; as ovens came into use, they were baked. *Pâté en croûte* (pâté in a pastry crust) was invented for Louis XV, an apathetic eater at best. His chefs drove themselves into a frenzy trying to come up with dishes to interest the king's palate. *Pâté en croûte* did it.

In the countryside, however, pâté was not royal fare, but robust peasant food. Meat was coarsely chopped, seasoned with a not always subtle hand, and the *pâté de campagne* was covered with melted lard to help preserve it for months. Pâtés still keep well—weeks in the refrigerator, months in the unopened can. They can be spreadable or sliceable, and all are delightfully different.

Pâté is always intriguing. Thin, chilled slices, simply arranged on a plate with black olives, cherry tomatoes, and a sprig of parsely or watercress, a bit of toast and butter are the perfect prelude to a dinner. Impressive, too! With plain crackers or good French bread and cornichons (small sour pickles), a mound of soft, creamy pâté is the ultimate hors d'oeuvre. For a deliciously light lunch a slice of pâté, steamed broccoli or asparagus, and a green salad are easy and splendid. Take pâté on a picnic, with crusty bread, pickles, tomatoes, hard-cooked eggs, raw vegetables, cheese and fruit for dessert, and a light or rosé wine. Elegant, simple, and extremely good. Even broiled hamburgers become peerless when you mix a little pâté, some chopped onion, and crumbled bacon into the basic meat mixture.

Zabar's has a dozen pâtés to offer, including: *maison*, of chicken livers, shallots, onions, thyme, bay leaves, and cognac, a smooth, creamy loaf, firm enough to be sliced; *campagne*, of mixed livers, dark and heartily flavored with thyme, pepper, and garlic, and laced with brandy and port; and *canard*, of duck livers, spices, and pistachio nuts. The campagne and canard are deliciously chunky and country-style as Harold fondly calls them—chewy and textured, tasting unmistakably of liver and spices. Wine is the perfect complement, a sweetish white for the smooth, pasty chicken livers; medium to light reds with the campagne and canard.

There are even *pâtés for the vegetarian*—all en croûte—broccoli, spinach, and artichoke and mushroom. They have a slightly semisweet flavor and vegetable crunchiness, all surrounded by a delightfully flaky crust. With a glass of white wine, they are an exceptional lunch.

For the semivegetarian, a combination of artichokes and chicken livers en croûte is a fine treat, with rich but not overpowering flavor. "The vegetable pâtés are unusual," says Harold, "mostly for people who don't like the taste of liver."

Imported pâtés are usually ground twice, so they are particularly pasty and fine-textured. Zabar's has five variations, all from France, ranging from simple *pâté*, made of 30 percent goose liver and 70 percent pork liver, to the more complicated *Suprême de Perigord*, a goose-and-pork-liver pâté with truffles in the center. In between are *pâté de foie*, with just a little bit of truffle, and *pâté maison*, heavily redolent of cognac. All should be thoroughly chilled, sliced very thin, and ringed with freshly made toast.

And, of course, there is *foie gras*, that very special Strasbourg or Perigord delicacy made from geese fattened specifically for that purpose—literally stuffed —and not allowed any exercise. Zabar's has it flown in fresh or *mi cuite* (slightly cooked) from France whenever it's available. It's rich and smooth, almost buttery in taste, with a faint flavor of fine brandy. Foie gras demands an equally rich, sweet wine to best set it off—a very good sauterne, for example.

NOTHIN' SAYS LOVIN' . . .

Many things make Zabar's a one-of-a-kind experience, but what truly sets it apart from any other store in the world is its kitchen and what comes out of it. That tiny little area is a magical monster, whose wizardry produces tons of exotic goodies each week. Three distinctly different cooking methods are used. Convection roasting allows heat to be evenly circulated around the meats and poultry; Slo-roasting is a low heat process that seals in the natural juices; Texas Barbecue is a low heat, natural smoke process (see page 62).

Harold and Stanley have an ace in the kitchen, a slight, handsome Russian named Boris. He used to run a kielbasa factory; now he runs Zabar's hot kitchen, with solid expertise and efficiency backed up by his unlimited imagination. He loves good food, and he loves the availability of fresh food products he finds here. Boris is one of the few cooks who admit they not only like to eat, but do, and often. He and Harold work together, and the sheer amount of food they cook is astounding: 300 ducks; 20 crates of whole chickens, plus another six of extra-large chicken breasts (more than most butchers retail in a week); 10 to 15 boxes of first-grade, Southern-grown, peanut-fed pork; a couple of thousand pounds of beef. And that's per week!

The best part is that almost everything that comes out of Zabar's kitchen never has to see yours. With a few exceptions, it's all ready to put on the table.

If you think duck, for instance, is something you should eat only in a restaurant, because it's so hard to prepare, wait until you see what Zabar's has to offer. *Smoked duck* has an exotically different taste, rich and succulent, sweet and dark, stuffed to bursting with fruit and vegetables. *French-style duck*—virtually fat-free—is crisp and tantalizing, stuffed with apple, onion, celery, and carrot, and probably the only duck anywhere, rich in breast meat, that's been designed specifically to be eaten cold. *Glazed duck* is another instant meal. Lightly coated with a sweet, syrupy glaze, it's juicy and flavorful, with just a hint of tartness. Add a salad and some wine, and preparing dinner will literally take five minutes.

Of course, you can warm the duck. Just cover it with aluminum foil and heat it at 350°F. for half an hour.

Thanksgiving means turkey, and that's the only time a lot of people ever think of that bird. Zabar's smoked turkey can change your mind. Its turkeys (toms, the meatier, male bird, rather than the drier, more common hens) come from just one farm in Colorado, which raises them especially for Zabar's and smokes them to succulent tenderness over hickory fires. The skin is crisp and brown; the meat mouthwateringly juicy. The smoky flavor is more pro-

ROAST-BEEF SALAD

If you've ever wondered what to do with leftover roast beef when you're tired of hash and sandwiches, this is it.

2 tablespoons wine vinegar
6 tablespoons olive oil
½ teaspoon salt
1 clove garlic, crushed
1 teaspoon dry mustard
2 teaspoons paprika
Freshly ground black pepper, to taste
½ pound roast beef, cut in julienne strips
GARNISH:
4 slices French bread
6 ripe black olives
8 cherry tomatoes
1 large pickle, sliced

Mix vinegar and oil in a jar. Mash salt into garlic clove. Add to oil and vinegar; shake well. Add mustard, paprika, and pepper, and pour over roast beef. Let marinate uncovered several hours.

When ready to serve, spoon salad onto French bread, and top with olives, tomatoes, and pickle slices.
Serves 4.

nounced when the turkey is served cold or at room temperature, as an appetizer or in a sandwich. If you want to tone down the smoky taste, put the turkey (they come whole, or by the breast alone) in a 350°F. oven for one and a half to two hours.

If smoked turkey is not your thing, fresh killed, slo-roasted birds are available, whole or parts. And boned and rolled *turkey thigh*, glazed to perfection with honey, soy sauce, and spices, can make you an accomplished Chinese chef in an instant. You can use it in any recipe calling for Chinese roast pork.

Tomes have been written about chicken, and Zabar's could easily fill one of its own. *Whole chickens* and *chicken breasts*—roasted, stuffed, glazed, smoked, fried in a Romano cheese batter, and barbecued—are always available, made with Zabar's special touch. But two in particular stand out: *Chicken Ballentine*, large, whole, boneless chicken breasts stuffed with a light and luscious combination of rice mushrooms, herbs, and spices, basted with sweet butter and baked to a delicate tenderness; and *Butterfly Lemon-and-Garlic Chicken*, one of Harold and Boris' many-day-marinating wonders. It's made from an old family recipe straight from the kitchen of Boris' Georgian grandmother. The pungent aroma of garlic and fresh lemon surrounds every delectable bite.

Other Chinese specialties are not ignored at Zabar's, and both the *spareribs* and the *roast pork* are made

from peanut-fed hogs. Meaty and tasty to begin with, these are glazed until they are crisp and slightly sticky on the outside, moist and juicy inside. You'll swear they came from a fine Chinese restaurant.

Zabar's turns a simple *pork roast* into an elegant feast by wrapping tenderloin in buttery phyllo pastry (Greek pastry leaves so thin they must be used in several layers, slathered with butter between each two) and roasting it with loving care. The crust is crisp, thin, and sweet; the pork pink, juicy, and well-cooked. It makes a dramatically different main course —a colossal pain if you were to try it yourself; no work at all this way.

Rare, red *roast beef*, lightly seasoned with salt, pepper, and a hint of garlic, is on the counter daily. It's one of the best-selling sandwich meats. But for something really different, try the *roast brisket of beef*, marinated for five days in a special Zabar's recipe. It's tender, juicy, and most unusual (brisket is more often used in pot-roasting, in braising, or for corned beef); roasting it was inspired.

If it's *corned beef* you're after, Virgina-style is glazed with brown sugar, mustard, cloves, and orange juice, just like Virginia ham, and ready to be sliced and served. Another version is roasted with tomatoes, peppers, and onions, an inviting and tasty blend of textures and flavors. Just one for dinner? Individual *meat loaves* are one-person size, made of a combination of ground beef and veal, seasonings, and a hard-cooked egg in the center. They can be eaten hot or cold, plain or fancied up with a favorite sauce.

Veal in all its glory is a special favorite with Zabar's customers. *Boneless veal roast* is stuffed with imported fontina cheese and ham, rolled, tied, and roasted into a fabulous blending of tastes—the sweetness of the veal, the tang of a good, nutty fontina, and the salty, pleasant flavor of the ham. It's easy to slice and elegant to serve. *Rack of milk-fed baby veal* (from calves no older than 12 weeks) is delicately seasoned and roasted. (The rack, by the way, is the first eight ribs, the tenderest, meatiest, sweetest part.) This is delicious served at room temperature, and for special occasions —or if you just want to be good to yourself—rub it lightly with warmed brandy, and ignite. When the flame has burned out, put the veal in a 325°F. oven just until it's heated through (about ½ hour).

Zabar's kitchen is a ham lover's heaven. Begin with the *fresh-roasted ham*, and work your way up, slowly and thoroughly, to the smoked and glazed varieties. You won't be disappointed. The fresh ham is pink and beautiful, with a thick layer of fat surrounding it. It has not been smoked or cured, so what you taste is just sweet, tender ham. It's perfect for a company dinner, and leftovers make great sandwiches, hot or cold; easy suppers when it's reheated and topped with a fruit sauce; ham loaf or sandwich spread. And what respectable pea soup doesn't have a ham bone in it?

Smoked hams have a distinctive taste that depends on the woods they were smoked over. *Hickory-smoked*

DELI

ham is sweet and smoky, with a touch of pepper; *applewood-smoked ham* is lighter and fruitier. The *glazed smoked hams* are almost candy-coated with molasses or honey, pear-shaped and lightly spicy. Serve them warm or cold, with mashed sweet potatoes, Brussels sprouts, or for a nice change, icy-cold fruit salad. Or try the *boneless, boiled Virginia ham,* baked and coated with pineapple slices, for a mild and mellow flavor with a tart, fruity kick.

THE EYES OF TEXAS

The deli department is easily the most edible area in Zabar's; instant gratification carried to its ultimate extreme. No place for dieters, this, or picky eaters. For in addition to all the delights from the kitchen, there's the *Texas Barbecue,* smoky, spicy, down-home-style, and exclusively Zabar's.

It was an inspiration that came to Stanley Zabar at a food show in Texas, where he saw the Texas Barbecue Oven, a slow-cooker that smokes food over hickory, oak, mesquite, or apple wood and does a remarkable job of keeping everything juicy and full of that scrumptious, natural smoked flavor. Stanley couldn't resist; he took a barbecue oven home and gave it to Harold. "Knock yourself out," Stanley told him. And Harold gave his imagination free reign—and his customers a whole new way of eating.

So far, Harold has successfully smoked succulent peanut-fed pork (tenderloin, roasts, and spare-ribs); rabbits; chickens; turkeys; ducks; veal; brisket; shell steak; standing rib roasts; and for the holidays, suckling pig, goose, or mini turkey. (You can, naturally, get the same succulent tender results without the smoked flavor with Zabar's slo-roasted meats and poultry.)

"Other places use liquid smoke as a flavoring," Harold confides. "Not us. We don't use any preservatives, additives, or artificial anything."

What's even more exciting about the Texas Barbecue foods is the smoky sauce that's sold with them—rich and spicy, heavy on the smoky flavor, and great on anything, even hamburgers.

The reaction to the Texas Barbecue has been tremendous—more than 2,500 pounds a week are sold—and New York's most insatiable food critic, Gael Greene, waxed poetic over its wonderfulness. Needless to say, it has been great for business. "And suddenly," she wrote, "the meat department is a hotbed of creativity. Texas barbecue has come to Broadway. ... The folks there have smoked almost everything but Harold [Horowitz]." (From *New York,* December 11, 1978.)

MY MOTHER'S
CHOPPED LIVER

Zabar's chopped liver is delicious, made totally from chicken livers. A lot of people think this version is even better.

½ *pound beef liver*
½ *pound chicken livers*
4 tablespoons rendered chicken fat with
grebenes or salad oil
2 hard-cooked eggs
2 large onions, chopped
Salt and freshly ground black pepper,
to taste

Broil chicken and beef livers until done, but not dry, about 5 minutes (turning once). Sauté onions in chicken fat or oil until golden. Put the livers, onions, hard-cooked eggs, through a meat grinder (or grate coarsely, or put in a food processor), and mix with chicken fat or oil left from sautéing the onions. Chill 3 to 4 hours until ready to serve.

To render chicken fat: Remove the fat and fatty pieces of skin from a chicken, wash, drain, and cut into small pieces. Cook in a heavy skillet, adding ¼ cup chopped onions per each cup of fat, until all the fat is melted and the onions are dark brown. The onions and pieces of skin are called *grebenes,* and for particularly delectable chopped liver, add them right along with everything else.

Serves 2 to 4 as an appetizer, with lettuce, tomato, Bermuda onion, and grated black radish (the traditional way to serve it). Chopped liver makes a great canape on crisp crackers, a terrific sandwich, a nice nosh.

On the Side

"It's the best food around when it comes to smoked fish, but I don't go in there, it's too crowded. My wife does it."
Joseph Heller

What goes best with deli? Pickles, for one thing, and coleslaw and potato salad, of course. Not to mention olives and sauerkraut. The usual. But a growing number of special salads that precisely and delectably set off the smoky-spicy deli meats in that department—uniquely and bewitchingly Zabar's own—are giving coleslaw and potato salad some heavy competition.

They're the province of the deli department, and made with unstinting care and attention in the "cold" kitchen, whose only purpose is to turn out glorious salads for the deli and appetizing departments.

As a side dish, *coleslaw* and *potato salad* are S.O.P. (standard operating procedure) anywhere and any time. They're to the deli department what cream cheese is to the bagel—irreplaceable. Zabar's chooses to have these standards made in the good, old-fashioned deli way, mild and creamy, not too heavy on

NOT ZABAR'S COLESLAW

Slaw, by the way, is from the Dutch word for salad, and this is a Dutch version of the old standard.

1 large head cabbage
½ cup water
1 tablespoon all-purpose flour
½ teaspoon salt
¼ cup sugar
1 teaspoon dry mustard
2 eggs
½ cup cider vinegar
¼ cup unsalted butter or margarine
Heavy cream
*1 teaspoon caraway or celery seeds
  (optional)*

Shred cabbage fine, and set aside. Combine water, flour, salt, sugar, and mustard; stir until smooth.

In top of a double boiler, beat together eggs and vinegar. Stir in mustard mixture, and cook until thickened. Stir in butter; remove from heat. Chill thoroughly.

Mix thoroughly with cabbage. If dressing is too thick, thin it with cream. For a special touch, add caraway or celery seeds. *Makes about 1 quart (4 cups).*

the mayonnaise. They're quite good, but they're only the tip of the salad iceberg.

The *antipasto* salad is made up of artichokes, cauliflower, peppers, baby corn, olives, onion, provolone, Genoa salami, prosciutto, and boiled ham. It's slightly spicy and vinegary, and very nice—almost a meal in itself, or for those lazy times when you don't want to bother creating an antipasto from scratch. Each and every component manages to retain its distinct flavor and taste, making each mouthful a wonderful new experience.

True to its Middle Eastern origin, the *eggplant salad* can be as blisteringly hot as the desert sands. What spices it up is a generous dose of hot peppers, onion, and garlic, and it does take a little getting used to. Maybe you should ease yourself into this one by starting with the milder version.

Vinegar and seasonings pickle most vegetables in a hurry, making them tender, tasty, and much more interesting than when they're let alone. The whizzes at Zabar's have chosen *artichoke hearts*, *asparagus spears*, and *hearts of palm* and marinated each separately for several days in a tangy vinegar-garlic dressing. Any one—or all—can be added to a plain green salad, served as part of an antipasto platter, or alternated on skewers with cherry tomatoes, green peppers, onions, and mushrooms, to be eaten cold or quickly grilled.

For something truly unusual, Harold Horowitz suggests *mushrooms marinated in Madeira wine*. They are superb, slightly on the sweet side, with just the right touch of garlic and spice. Sounds a little strange, but it works.

GERMAN-STYLE POTATO SALAD

This is traditionally served warm, but it's good cold, too.

6 slices bacon
2 tablespoons reserved drippings
2 tablespoons sugar
1 teaspoon all-purpose flour
Salt and freshly ground black pepper,
*   to taste*
¼ cup red-wine vinegar
½ cup water
1 large onion, finely chopped
2 pounds potatoes, cooked, peeled,
*   and sliced*
1 tablespoon chopped fresh dill (optional)

Sauté bacon until crisp. Drain, and crumble.

In bacon drippings, mix sugar, flour, salt, and pepper until smooth. Stir in vinegar and water, and bring to boil.

Add onion, and mix well. Add potato slices, stirring gently to make sure they're coated with dressing.

Transfer to a bowl to serve. Top with crumbled bacon and dill, if desired.
Serves 8.

FOUR-BEAN SALAD

Anyone can make three-bean salad, but
four-bean is a nice twist. Be sure not to
overcook the beans; they should be crunchy
and firm.

1 cup cooked, halved fresh green beans
1 cup cooked, halved fresh wax beans
1 cup canned drained red kidney beans
1 cup canned drained garbanzos (chickpeas)
½ cup finely chopped celery
1 medium Bermuda onion, sliced into
  thin rings
DRESSING:
¼ cup salad oil
2 to 3 tablespoons cider vinegar
Salt and freshly ground black pepper,
  to taste
1 teaspoon chopped fresh dill
¼ cup sugar

In a serving bowl, combine all beans
with celery and onion rings. Mix all dressing
ingredients, and pour over beans. Chill
well before serving.
Serves 8–10.

A low-calorie *California garden salad* is chock-full
of fresh raw vegetables—cauliflower, green beans, carrots, and more—in a vinegary sauce. It makes dieting
much easier, and not at all depriving. *Three-bean salad*
is made the classic way at Zabar's, with green beans,
red kidney beans, and chickpeas in a sweet-and-sour
dressing loaded with Bermuda onion. The *spiced fruit
salad*—chunks of pineapple, pear, apple, and whatever else is in season—is redolent with cloves and
cinnamon and goes nicely with sausage and ham, as
well as on its own. Topped with a little whipped cream
or spooned on vanilla ice cream or pound cake, it's
lovely for dessert. If you heat the salad and garnish it
with fried sausage links or patties, an unusual, light
dinner is a breeze.

The *dolmades*, Greek-style grape leaves stuffed with
rice and spices, are tiny enough to be part of a
large platter of appetizers; or they can be tooth-picked
and served as hors d'oeuvres or presented as a first
course all by themselves. Try them with *dilled baby
corn*—unusual enough by themselves, those perfectly
formed, tiny ears of corn, about an inch long—marinated in a vinaigrette sauce. Dill makes them particularly pungent and flavorful without being hot or spicy.

The Pennsylvania Dutch have a tradition of serving seven sweets and seven sours with every dinner.
Pickled watermelon rind is always one of the sweets,
the perfect, crunchy contrast to ham, pork, beef,
chicken, or anything else. Try the *kumquats*, too.

Salads can be, and should be, provocative, stimulating, lively, even rapturous. Zabar's gives you the opportunity to serve them that way—without any of the
work.

PICKLES

Pickles have been around since time immemorial;
cucumbers (and other vegetables) have always been
preserved in a salt or vinegar brine with a variety of
spices and seasonings. It's even been rumored that
Cleopatra ate pickles to keep healthy and beautiful,
and in fact, they do have a lot of vitamins (A, B_1, B_2,
and C) and minerals (calcium, iron, copper, phos-
phorus). And what do you think Amerigo Vespucci
was doing before he set out to discover new worlds?
Selling pickles, according to historians.

Zabar's has pickles by the barrel, in various stages
of doneness. The mavens in the deli department decide
when they're ready and whether you get *sour* or *half-
sour pickles.*

The really sour, face-puckering pickles, about four
inches long, fat and juicy, take about six to eight weeks
to get that way. They start out fresh and green and
end up a darker, more olivy color. Half-sour pickles—

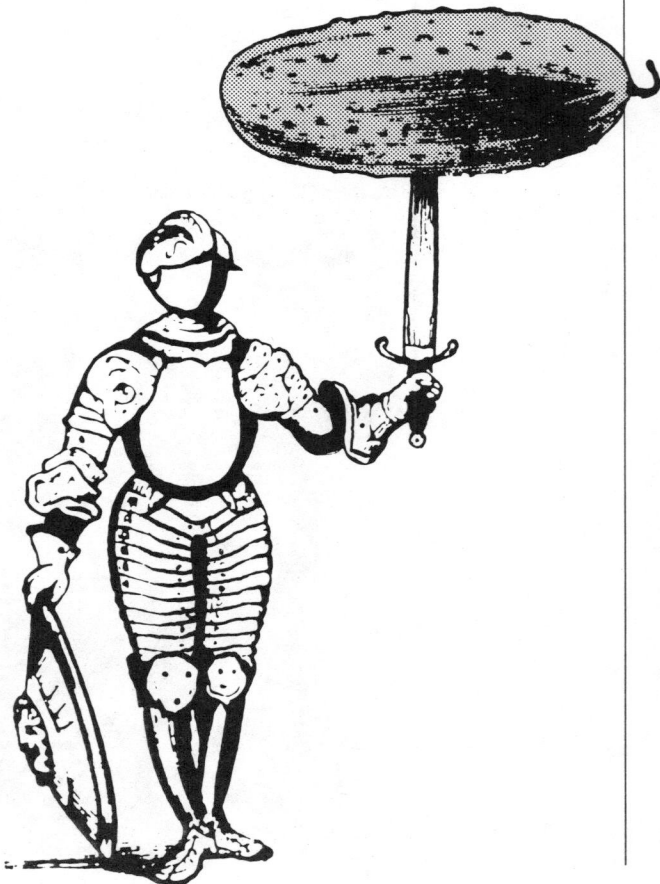

they're not sour pickles that have been cut in half—are taken out of the brine while they're still green. They taste like slightly pickled cucumbers.

There are several schools of thought about how to eat a sour pickle. Without question, the best way is to fish one out of the barrel, bite into it, and let the juice run sloppily down your chin. All the best flavor and fun come crunchingly through this way. Some people, however, prefer a neater approach, slicing pickles into little rounds, manageable spears, or bite-size chunks. *Chacun à son goût.*

The pickle can do other things besides lie on the side of a plate. Chopped and mixed with sour cream, they make baked potatoes come alive. In a stew or pot roast, they add an exciting mystery flavor, not immediately identifiable as the humble pickle. If you hollowed out a whole sour pickle, stuffed it with cream cheese, and sliced it into rounds, you'd have a totally different hors d'oeuvre for your next party. Diced, they're also a fabulous addition to potato salad.

Cornichons are those tart, crunchy little French vinegar pickles that so delightfully compliment rich and spicy foods, especially pâtés. Nibble them slowly rather than eating them whole, so the flavor lasts. *Gherkins*, conversely, should be eaten in one mouthful. They are sweet and tart at the same time, only about an inch to an inch and a half long. Try wrapping Genoa salami or smoked salmon around either corni-

---

HOMEMADE ANTIPASTO SALAD

½ small head cauliflower
½ cup artichoke hearts
1 large onion, sliced
½ cup baby corn
½ cup hot green pepper (peperoncini)
½ cup sliced carrot
½ cup chopped celery
½ cup green olives
½ cup ripe black olives
2 teaspoons drained capers
¼ cup red-wine vinegar
¾ cup olive oil
1 clove garlic, crushed
¼ teaspoon pepper

Break cauliflower into small pieces. In a large bowl, combine them with other vegetables, olives, and capers (be sure everything is well drained).

Shake vinegar, olive oil, garlic, and pepper in a jar; pour over vegetables. Let marinate in refrigerator 48 hours before serving.
Serves 8–10.

The word "grocer" goes back to England of the fourteenth century, when the Guild of Pepperers sold pepper from the Orient by the gross. They became known as wholesale grossers.

chons or gherkins; with cocktails, they are ideal finger food.

At the other end of the pickle family are *pickled tomatoes* and *pickled peppers*. The tomatoes, pickled while they're still small and green, are sour, firm, crunchy and a nice alternative to a pickle. Pickled peppers may be either hot or sweet and are usually small and red. The hot ones really are hot, and it isn't cricket not to warn people. *Peperoncini* are little green Italian devils, long and skinny, and they can be lethal. A little goes a long way; if you can't handle hot peppers whole, chop them and add them to French dressing, or mix them into hard-cooked eggs or cream cheese.

Exotic pickles in jars get a chance to show off on Zabar's endless shelves, too. Not just dills or mustard pickles, but *chow-chow*, which, according to Crosse & Blackwell, was created for Napoleon. Actually, it is mixed pickles in a mustard sauce. And *bread-and-butter pickles*, universally popular; how they got their name is a mystery. *Pickle chips* and *sweet mixed pickles*, perennial picnic favorites, are here, too. And *pickled vegetables*: everything from beets to zucchini, including carrots, cauliflower, green beans, onions—colorful, exciting, zingy in their tart, vinegary marinades.

You can eat these pickles right out of the jar if you're so inclined, or add them to salads or salad dressings to make them sing. Wrap bacon around a dill pickle or a chunk of pickled cauliflower, and broil until crisp. Spear a pickled onion and a square of smoked cheese together, or a chunk of smoked ham and a piece of pickled watermelon rind. Anything goes.

RELISHES

Do you relish relish? Good! So does Zabar's. That's why it has so many.

Chutneys, for example. A combination of fruits (usually tropical), herbs, spices, nuts, and seasonings, all pickled together. It may be sweet, it may be hot, it may be both at the same time; it may also taste sour or salty. The famous Major Grey's Chutney, named after a British army officer on duty in India, is actually made by several companies, all claiming to have the authentic original recipe. Name and recipe, however, do not necessarily have much to do with each other;

anyone can call his product "Major Grey's" as long as he turns out a sweetly hot, mango-based chutney. (Most Indian chutneys include mango because at one time this was the only fruit always available in India.)

Mangoes, papayas, peaches, apples, tomatoes—all can be chutneyed, seasoned liberally with ginger, garlic, vinegar, sugar, hot peppers, onion, according to the maker's recipe and how the chutney is going to end up. A really nice version is made from nectarines, chopped fine; it's sweet, almost like preserves. A chock-full-of-nuts chutney, on the other hand, is sweet and chunky; it's made with raisins, currants, mangoes, and walnuts.

Indians use chutney in the same unsparing way we use ketchup, mustard, and relish, to stimulate the appetite and enhance the flavor of food. It adds a sweet, fruit contrast to highly seasoned curries. But no need to stop there. Heated with a little sherry, a dash of Worcestershire sauce, and a jar of red-currant jelly, chutney turns into a piquant sauce for cold meat or fish. Spread chutney on toasted white bread; top with a slice of Swiss cheese, a slice of ham, and a slice of bread buttered on the outside; broil until the cheese melts—this gives the ham and Swiss a really fancy trimming. For canapés, try chutney mixed with cottage cheese on plain crackers; or top chutney on crackers with a slice of Cheddar, and broil. Served with thick slices of ripe avocado, chutney is a super appetizer.

Piccalilli is sweet-pickle relish by another name. The Shakers called their mess of chopped vegetables "Pickled Lily" for some reason, and there you have it. It's just one of the many *vegetable relishes* on Zabar's shelves, along with corn relish, golden-yellow and perky with bits of green and red pepper; old-fashioned hot-dog relish made with cabbage, sweet peppers, and sugar. There are relishes sweet enough for a child's hamburger or fiery enough to liven up any adult's dinner. Serve separately, as a side dish instead of salad; or add a spoonful or two to salad dressing, coleslaw, tuna salad, or chopped eggs; or mix with the yolks of hard-cooked eggs and stuff the whites for devilishly different deviled eggs.

SAUERKRAUT

Tart and zesty, crisp and crunchy, sauerkraut is nothing more than shredded cabbage that's been salted, packed tightly into stone crocks or barrels, weighted down, and allowed to ferment for several weeks. The salt draws out the natural juice in the cabbage and controls fermentation; this mellows the flavor but keeps the cabbage noisily crunchy.

It's a health food! Sauerkraut is so full of vitamin C that the British navy kept it on board all its ships as a cure for scurvy, and our Confederate army fed it to the troops.

Served cold, sauerkraut is a good change from the ordinary green salad. Combined with sour pickles, hot peppers, and sour (pickled) tomatoes, it's known to the delicatessen crowd as "sour stuff." When it is hot, its spicy taste is perfect with meats—especially pork and sausages—but the longer you heat it, the milder it becomes. As a vegetable, mix it with apples and a little sugar, and warm until the apples are tender; or try it with sautéed onions, tomatoes, and brown sugar, simmered for half an hour.

OLIVES

You must have olives to be a deli, and Zabar's has about 10 kinds: black *Greek olives*, shriveled and coated with olive oil; hot green *Sicilian olives*, flavored with hot peppers; mammoth, spicy green Sicilians; *Israeli green olives*; *Moroccan olives*, plain or with hot peppers and garlic; *French niçoise*, tiny green or black olives; and calamata. And there's an *olive salad* that will blow your mouth out: a combination of hot Moroccan and Sicilian olives, celery hearts, oregano, hot peppers, and garlic, hot enough to begin with, but with a delightful habit of becoming even more torrid the longer it stands. "Definitely not for the fainthearted," the deli staff warns.

You can make a less spicy version by using ripe olives, black and green, marinated in olive oil, vinegar,

SAUERKRAUT SALAD

½ pound sauerkraut, drained and chopped
1 green pepper, chopped
1 onion, chopped
2 tablespoons chopped parsley
2 carrots, shredded

DRESSING:
2 tablespoons wine vinegar
6 tablespoons olive oil
Salt and freshly ground black pepper, to taste
¼ teaspoon dry mustard

Combine sauerkraut and other vegetables in a bowl. Mix dressing ingredients, and pour over vegetables. Let chill before serving.
Serves 4.

CONDIMENT GLOSSARY

BUTTERS: Fruit purées boiled with sugar until very thick. They can be spreadable or allowed to set so they can be sliced.

CHUTNEYS: Fruits and/or vegetables cooked with vinegar, spices, and sugar until thick.

CONSERVES: Whole or sliced fruit preserved in syrup and eaten with a spoon. More syrupy than jam, sweeter and richer, too. Sometimes nuts and raisins are added.

JAMS: Sugar and fresh fruit, crushed or ground, boiled until thick, but not as firm as jelly.

JELLIES: Sugar and juice of fresh fruit, clear and firm, shimmery and shaky.

MARMALADES: Bits of cooked fruit in heavy syrup; translucent.

PICKLES: Vegetables that have been washed, salted, soaked in brine, rinsed, repacked with spice vinegar, and cooked.

PRESERVES: Whole or large pieces of cooked fruit in thick, almost jellylike syrup.

RELISHES: Chopped vegetables and spices, cooked in vinegar for shorter time than chutneys.

SPICED FRUIT SAUCES: Thinner and smoother than chutneys and relishes, like ketchup and plum sauce.

and garlic for half an hour. Not nearly as hot, but good nevertheless.

Americans consume more than 10 million gallons of olives a year, mostly as decoration for the martini glass. But olives can, and should, be used to bring ordinary, everyday foods out of the pits.

Zabar's shelves of fabulous canned goods offer even more olives—stuffed with onions, pimiento, or celery; ripe black ones; little yellow-green ones. Try a mixed selection on an hors d'oeuvre tray, and for special company, stuff pitted green olives with a tiny bit of pâté.

There's so much material to work with that, armed with a sense of adventure—even a cookbook, if you like—you can add sparkling new sensations to your cooking and entertaining.

CONDIMENTS

The entire right rear wall of Zabar's is filled with a profusion of condiments, seasonings, oils, vinegars, mustards, honeys, jams and jellies, herbs and spices from all over the world. You'll find the pungent cinnamon of Ceylon; the sharp mustards of England and the subtler ones of France; sweet and unusual preserves from as far away as Israel, as nearby as Pennsylvania—all the wonderful things to put on, in, or around food to make something even as ordinary as a piece of toast excitingly different.

PASS THE MUSTARD

Forty-two, count 'em, 42 kinds of mustard from every corner of the globe.

To the French, mustard is a subtly important cooking ingredient, long admired for its distinctive regional peculiarities. Americans are just beginning to get beyond the supermarket shelves and into a new universe of taste and flavor.

QUICK MUSTARD DIPPING SAUCE

Terrific as a dip for sausages; chilled, cooked shrimp; or raw vegetables. A nice variation, spicier and more piquant, substitutes ¾ cup tomato paste and 1 tablespoon vinegar for the water and cream. Add a pinch of sugar, a dash of salt, 1 tablespoon horseradish, and some chopped chives. Use 2 tablespoons dry mustard.

2 tablespoons dry mustard
Cold water
½ cup heavy cream, whipped
Paprika

Blend mustard and enough cold water to make mixture creamy. Fold gently into whipped cream, and sprinkle with paprika.
Makes 1 cup.

ZABAR'S MUSTARD MART

DIJON MUSTARDS

Fine-grained, piquant mustard, flavored with white wine, vinegar, and spices.

Dijon (Maille)

Dijon—extra strong (Moutarde de Meaux)

Dijon—grained mustard with Meursault Burgundy (Maître Jacques)

Dijon—extra strong (Maître Jacques) 2 sizes

Dijon—grained mustard with Burgundy (Maître Jacques) 2 sizes

Dijon—with tarragon, mild and sweet (Maître Jacques)

Dijon—extra strong, salt free (Maître Jacques)

Dijon—lemon flavored (Maître Jacques)

Dijon—with green pepper (Maître Jacques)

Dijon—with hot red pepper (Maître Jacques)

Dijon—with Herbes de Provence (Maître Jacques)

Dijon—extra hot (Pikarome)

Dijon—with white wine (Grey Poupon)

Dijon (Devos Lemmens)

Dijon mustard is perfect for anything—salad dressings, sandwich spreads, on steak, in sauces, a good all-around mustard with nice variations.

FLAVORED MUSTARDS

Mustard with green pepper (Maille)

Mustard with red pepper (Maille)

Mustard with tarragon (Maille)

Mustard with shallots (Maille)

Mustard with lemon (Maille)

Mustard with lemon (Amora)

Mustard with shallots (Amora)

Mustard with herbes de Provence (Amora)

Mustard with tarragon (Amora)

Mustard with green peppercorns (Amora)

Mustard with green peppercorns (Devos Lemmens)

Mustard Provencal (Zabar's) with champagne, thyme, savory, basil, fennel, lavender flowers, and other spices

These are especially nice in salad dressings and as special flavors for white sauces, stews, and special casseroles.

OLD-FASHIONED FRENCH MUSTARDS

Old-style mustard with white wine (Maille)

Moutarde Complète à l'Ancienne (Pluquet), made in the same farmhouse style since the 16th century

Old-fashioned mustard (Amora)

Coarse-grained Moutarde à l'Ancienne (Queens Gate)

On broiled or barbecued meats, fish and poultry, these old-fashioned mustards are rich and tasty. Their flavor, collectively, is strong and mustardy, but not overwhelming.

HOT MUSTARDS

Devil's Brew (Reese)

Hot Mustard (Hengstenberg)

Extra Hot Mustard (Hengstenberg)

Hot English Mustard (Colman's)

Hot, pungent, nice with cold meats and in sauces that need an extra flavorful zip.

THE 10 WURST MUSTARDS

Smokey Mustard (Reese)

Düsseldorf Mustard (Reese)

Bavarian-Style Mustard with Moselle Wine (Reese)

Sweet Mustard (Hengstenberg)

Mustard (Savora)

Dry Mustard (Colman's)

German-Style Mustard (Colman's)

Sharp and Creamy (Nancy)

German Mustard (Frenzel)

Inniemore Scotch Mustard, made on the Island of Mull in the Hebrides, coarse mustard seed, stone ground flour, oatmeal, sugar, spices, and malt whiskey.

Just made for wurst, from hot dogs to kielbasa. Sharp, creamy, aromatic, and delicious. Good with hamburgers, too.

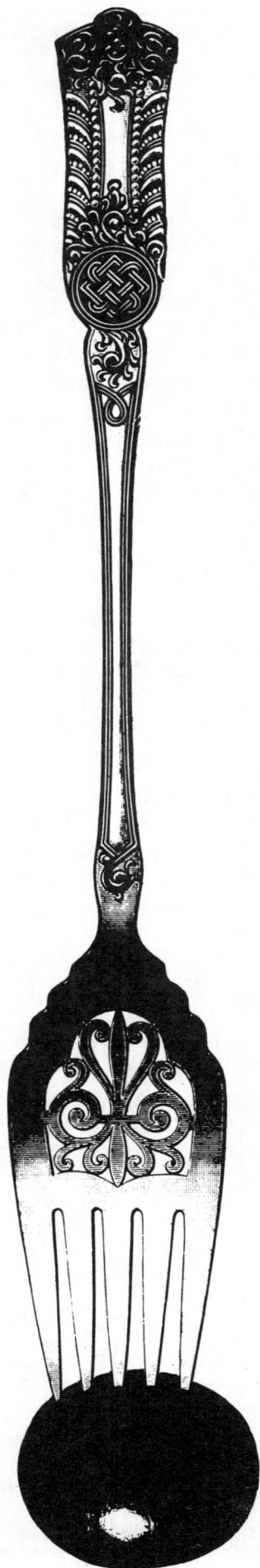

There are, at Zabar's, 16 Dijon mustards alone, because they're all exceptional. Dijon mustard is sharp and heady, flavored with spices and wine in the original Dijonnais manner. The old, familiar Grey Poupon, made with white wine, is in fine company with Dijons from Meaux that are extra-strong; from Maître Jacques, flavored with Meursault burgundy (in reusable canning jars), extra-strong or zippy with green peppers, hot red peppers, tarragon, lemon, *herbes de Provence*, whole-grain or smooth, and even salt-free. Pikarome has hot Dijon mustard; Maille and Devos Lemmens offer their own special Dijons.

These mustards come in different sizes, sometimes in interestingly shaped jars and crocks, but the real contrasts are in the subtleties of their individual flavors. Dijons are characteristically light and understated, with a definite punch; the range from mildly pungent, like Grey Poupon, to very strong—with hot red peppers, for instance. All the Dijons work wonderfully in salad dressings; on steak just before it's broiled or barbecued; in sauces, especially with white wine and butter; and particularly well in leftover-turkey sandwiches.

And that's just the Dijons. From *Meaux* also comes *Pommery mustard*, "Served at the tables of the Kings of France since 1632," according to its label. It's a smooth, full-flavored mustard with lots of little

POTATO SALAD CHORON

DRESSING:

1 cup mayonnaise
1 tablespoon olive oil
1 tablespoon cider vinegar
2 teaspoons Maille's Dijon mustard
½ teaspoon celery seed
Salt and freshly ground black pepper, to taste

SALAD:

4 cups sliced, boiled potatoes
2 hard-cooked eggs, chopped
1 cup celery, chopped
2 tablespoons chives, chopped (or scallions)
½ cup green pepper, chopped
¼ cup chopped pickles (sweet or mixed)
2 medium carrots, julienned
8 strips bacon, fried and crumbled

In a jar or bowl, mix dressing ingredients together. In large bowl, mix remaining ingredients, pour dressing over all and toss to mix. Cover and refrigerate several hours before serving.
Serves 8.

cracked mustard seeds shot through it. *Maille* has mustard with green pepper, tarragon, red pepper, shallots, and lemon, and even plain. From *Nancy* comes a sharp, creamy mustard that's particularly nice to cook with. *Reese* offers three kinds: smoky, Düsseldorf, and Bavarian-style, fabulous with wursts and dark breads. *Moutarde à l'Ancienne*, from *Pluquet*, made with champagne and white wine, is prepared according to traditional methods. "The grains are crushed gently with a grindstone, without heating, to allow them to recall the taste of the best mustards of yesteryear."

Hot, extra-hot, and sweet mustards are available from *Hengstenberg*, and with German sausage, such as bratwurst or bauernwurst, they are splendid, indeed. Another French exporter, *Amora*, has small jars (three and a half ounces) of old-fashioned mustard, as well as mustard with lemons, shallots, *herbes de Provence*, tarragon, or green peppercorns. Small enough jars to try a few. Mustard from *Savora*, mustard sauce from *Bocquet*, and hot English mustard and dry, powdered mustard from *Colman* complete the picture.

There's mustard for hot dogs or pastrami, for wursts of any description. Add a little to pot roast or stew; spread a dab of tarragon mustard on hamburgers before broiling. Try Pommery mustard, lemon juice, and peach preserves as a glaze for chicken, or extra-hot mustard mixed with brown sugar and cloves for ham. And that's not all. Stirred into melted cheese, mustard makes a terrific sauce for steamed vegetables. Dry mustard added to a bread-crumb or flour mixture makes a particularly tasty coating for fried foods.

Mustard actually comes from seeds, which are dried, powdered, and mixed with liquid. When the Romans added must (unfermented grape juice), they called the result mustard. Since then, everything from champagne to vinegar has been mixed with mustard powder to give it expressively different flavors.

Hot mustards are hot because they are blended with cold liquids and stirred incessantly. A chemical reaction between the pungent elements in the seed and the cold comes out virtually flaming—at least in your mouth. Milder mustards are mixed with hot, usually boiling liquids, so the reaction is inhibited.

You don't always have to use mustard from a jar. You can make your own. To about a quarter cup dry mustard, add three to four tablespoons liquid (water, wine, milk, flat beer, vinegar, champagne) and a bit of salt. Stir, and let stand for about 20 minutes, so the flavor develops fully. If it's too hot, tone it down with a little olive oil, sugar, or mild herbs. If it's not hot enough, add garlic, hot peppers, horseradish, curry powder, almost anything at all. If it's not bright and yellow enough, add a little turmeric; that's what commercial producers do for mustardy color. And for Chinese mustard, the kind that's on every table in every Chinese restaurant, mix dry mustard with cold water, and stir until your arm feels as if it's about to fall off. According to one Chinese gourmet, the more you stir, the hotter the mustard becomes.

And don't forget the mustard plaster. It'll cure anything from sinus trouble to arthritis, they say!

OIL AND VINEGAR

The right *olive oil* can make all the difference between a good salad and a great one. Zabar's carries eight olive oils, imported from France and Italy, each characteristic of the region it comes from and the type of cooking done there.

From the finest olive groves of France and Italy come the "extra-virgin" oils—the absolute top of the line—from the first pressing of the olives. They taste distinctly like green olives and smell like them, too, especially those from Sicily. You can see the difference in color and smell the distinctly olivy aroma when you compare those oils with even the very best "virgin" oils, which nevertheless are several times better than oils with no designation. The rating system depends in large part on the weather, the type of olive, the moment they were picked, the acidity in the soil— much like wine.

And you should treat olive oil like fine wine. Protect it from bright light and too warm air, so it won't turn rancid (no need to refrigerate it, though; a cool cupboard will do). And although it may be more economical to buy olive oil in gallon sizes, if you don't use a lot, stick to small quantities, so the oil will be fresh and fragrant when you need it.

Walnut and *hazelnut oils* from France have an entirely different taste, light and delicate. They are a salad-maker's dream come true, nutty and sweet, beautiful on fresh, crisp greens. Don't cook with these, though; high heat would break them down and alter the flavor.

For cooking (and salads, too), try one of the light, winsome oils made from *safflower, cottonseed, corn, apricot kernels*, or *grape seeds* (also low in polyunsaturated fats), and *peanuts* (and, of course, olive oil). *Chinese sesame oil* lends a special, nutty flavor to salad dressings and cooked foods. It has a pervasive taste, however, so use it in small doses. Try it with a light vinegar on sliced cucumbers; it's remarkable.

The finest oils must be perfectly matched by the finest vinegars to make a salad dressing that stands out but doesn't stomp out your salad. So which one you choose can make a tremendous difference. Vinegar is a natural product: The juice of fruits or grapes, left to stand, ferments, and ultimately, when the alcohol turns to acid, you have vinegar. *Apple-cider vinegar* is made just this way; so are most *malt vinegars*.

Distilled, or white, vinegars are made by distilling the alcohol from corn, barley, malt, and rye, much as liquor is made. The grain is mashed with water, which releases sugar, and yeast is added. The mixture ferments, and then it is boiled; the alcohol vaporizes and is condensed. Distilled vinegars are the most acidic— great for pickling.

75

Wine vinegars, which start with red or white wine that is allowed to ferment past the drinking stage, are the mildest. Cider and malt vinegars are in the middle. Generally, all bottled vinegars are marketed at 5 percent acidity. Wine vinegar at Zabar's may be made from red or white wine or from sherry or champagne. These vinegars are light and mild, slightly sweet, and good for just about anything. Zabar's has its own sherry wine vinegar imported from Jerez, Spain. It is bottled in sherry bottles at 7 percent acidity and is one of the best sherry vinegars available.

Vinegars flavored with lemon or herbs (basil, tarragon, mint, garlic, or oregano) are particularly exciting in salad dressings; the full flavor of the herbs is truly distinguishable, but certainly not overpowering. Try *barley-malt vinegar* on your next order of fish and chips. That's the way the British like it!

It's easy enough to make your own flavored vinegar —and fun, too. Start with good quality white vinegar. Choose any one of the ingredients listed below—or a combination. Add 3 tablespoons of fresh herbs to each pint of vinegar and steep (let stand) for about two weeks. You'll have fragrant, herby vinegars that are dynamite any way you use them. Fresh herbs, such as basil, tarragon, rosemary, chervil, mint, dill, summer savory, oregano thyme—just a few sprigs, lightly bruised to release the flavor (crush them between your palms) —can be quite lovely and delicate. Chili peppers, peeled whole cloves of garlic, or shallots are terrific used by themselves or combined with other flavors. Onions, horseradish, celery, and capers create special effects with unusual flavor. Dried herbs and spices work pretty well, too, but strain them out before using and only use 1½ tablespoons per pint. Leave the whole spices; they look beautiful. If you put up your vinegars in pretty jars or crocks, you can use them as Christmas presents and easily be the most appreciated gift-giver on the block.

SWEETS TO THE SWEET

Zabar's buyers work diligently to find the very best imported foods in the world—not just the tastiest, but also the most unusual, the hardest to get, and the most diverse.

Anyone who comes across a gourmet goody that's unique and delicious can recommend it to Saul or Stanley or Murray. If it is stupendously different and unmatched by anything else, it's more than likely to find a place on a shelf.

Honey is a good example of Zabar's "seek and ye shall find" philosophy. In the honey department, honeys—solid, liquid, or still in the comb—from 21 countries and innumerable blossoms stand ready to be counted. Thick and golden, sweet-smelling wild flower, orange blossom, and lotus; grassy alfalfa, clover, heather, linden, acacia, and tupelo; spicy thyme and pungent eucalyptus; light and syrupy buttercup honey. From New Zealand or Florida, mild like clover or strong like buckwheat, the darker the honey, the

stronger it will taste. It all depends, of course—taste, color, and flavor—on the flowers the nectar comes from.

To sweeten tea or cakes, to add an unusual zing to ham or chicken, good aged honey is like vintage wine. Once you get hooked on it, you're spoiled for life.

If honey crystallizes, put the jar into a pan of hot water; the honey will liquefy in minutes. And when you're measuring honey, coat the cup or spoon with oil; the honey will slide right out instead of being a sticky, drippy mess.

Almost everything under the sun, from apples to ugli fruit, has been jammed, jellied, preserved, conserved, or marmaladed somewhere in the world, and Zabar's has found most of them. The choices are truly stunning; there even are rare jams laced with Benedictine or Dry Sack; boozy marmalades made with good Scotch whisky or Cointreau. Toast will never be the same!

Zabar's has a host of *jellies, jams, preserves, conserves, marmalades.* You'll find just about all the fruits of the earth, alone or in tantalizing combinations: strawberries, wild blueberries, dark, sweet Bing cherries, Damson plums, kiwi fruit, small pitted cherries suspended in cherry jelly, currants, mirabelle plums (those yellow, sun-ripened Alsatian dainties) —whatever your taste buds might hanker for, and then some. Hard-to-get fig preserves will make Christmas fruitcake a singular creation; preserved orange slices in a bittersweet marmalade, from Israel, have a deliciously sun-drenched, tart flavor that makes any morning bright. Whole, peeled chestnuts in jamlike syrup are as French as the Eiffel Tower. Tiptree preserves, handmade, hand-packed, are delightfully English—for breakfast or high tea.

Fruit butters are not left out. Apple, rich with spices and cider and sweet, full, old-fashioned good-

EASY TRIFLE

12 slices pound cake, soaked in sherry
1 12-ounce jar raspberry preserves
1½ cups cooked tapioca pudding
1 32-ounce jar spiced peaches
1 cup heavy cream, whipped

For individual servings, place a slice of pound cake in a dish; spread with preserves. Top with pudding and a peach, and cover with whipped cream.

Or, in a punch bowl, arrange slightly overlapping cake slices spread with preserves. Add pudding and peaches. Top with whipped cream. It makes a beautiful finale for a dinner.
Serves 12.

ness; Lekvar, Hungarian-style prune butter, a purée of sweet, plump prunes that is the perfect filling for cakes and pastries.

This is the ultimate breakfast dream, a baker's Nirvana, a sweet-freak's happy hunting ground. And if you can think ahead to dessert, snappy *fruit syrups* (raspberry, strawberry, red currant, black currant, and cherry) go right from the bottle onto ice cream or cake or into a glass of club soda.

SPECIAL SPECIALTIES

Beyond Zabar's fish counter, beautifully packed into antique glass jars, are the dried fruits and nuts, abundant, tempting, colorful. Raisins, prunes, currants, apricots, papaya, pineapple, peaches, apples, dates, figs, carob, almonds to walnuts—everything you would want to use in baking or cooking, as snacks, desserts, or natural sweets. Canned pâtés of various natures are also there, and some canned fish.

But the real celebrities are the dried mushrooms and the truffles.

MUSHROOMS

Mushrooms have always been, and always will be, slightly mysterious and certainly intriguing. In foods,

on foods, stuffed, fried, raw, they are incredibly capricious and can change a simple dish into a gourmet creation. But there's more to mushooms than the fresh white ones and canned varieties found in every supermarket.

Dried mushrooms from all over the world are absolutely wonderful to cook with. They add a touch of the forest and exciting new wildness to everything they flavor. And they have several advantages over fresh ones: They keep for months and months in a cool, dry place; the water they're soaked in (and they must be soaked for 15 to 20 minutes in warm water) is an excellent base for stock or a replacement for liquids in cooking; they're almost always available.

Dried Polish mushrooms at Zabar's are strung in two-foot lengths. They're strongly flavored, so one or two in a dish is enough. If your kitchen doesn't get hot and humid, let them hang. They're as attractive as they are flavorful.

The woodsy, concentrated flavor of *dried Italian mushrooms* will add zest to any dish, Italian or not. Since, they, too are earthy and pungent, use them only for seasoning, never as a vegetable. Look for large, light-brown ones, and use them sparingly.

French dried mushrooms are seasonal. Chanterelles are a summer crop, a bit more delicately flavored than morels, the spring version. Cèpes are pretty much year-round; they're flavorful. All have that wild, woody taste and earthy smell, but they're not as heavy as the Polish and Italian varieties. Still, a small

78

FRENCH-FRIED ONION RINGS

BATTER:
¾ cup sifted flour
½ cup flat beer
Salt and freshly ground black pepper, to taste
1 teaspoon salad oil
1 egg, separated (optional)

3 large onions, sliced thinly and separated into rings
1 cup milk
1 cup water
Vegetable oil for deep frying

Mix batter ingredients together and let stand at room temperature 3 hours. If you are using the egg, add only the yolk at this time. Just before frying, beat egg white until stiff and fold into the batter mixture.

Soak the onion rings in the milk and water for ½ hour. Drain and dip into the batter. Deep fry, in 2 inches of oil, a few at a time, until golden—about 1 minute.
Serves 4 to 6.

---

amount is enough to add a lot of flavor.

Although whole dried mushrooms look best, it's cheaper to buy bits and pieces when they're available. And since they mostly go into stews and sauces, it doesn't really matter.

There are several varieties of Chinese dried mushrooms. Usually they're shredded or cut into small wedges, so only a few pieces are needed for each dish. Stir-fry them quickly; the more they cook, the stronger the flavor becomes.

TRUFFLES

They've been called black gold and the black diamonds of Perigord, and they are priced to fit. They are so costly because they are so rare and because no matter how hard scientists, agricultural specialists, and gourmets have tried, truffles simply cannot be cultivated. The soil, the climate, and the roots of the native oak trees of the Perigord countryside where they are found have never been duplicated precisely enough for truffles to be grown on demand.

And found is exactly the right word. In France, pigs root out the treasured black truffles; dogs do the same for the equally precious white Italian truffles—only during December and January. No man or woman has yet been born with a nose sensitive enough to sniff out a truffle. They are expensive, too, because they are harder and harder to find. In 1900, French pigs

dug up 130 tons of the delicacy; last year's yield was only 10 tons.

Truffles are so dear, so valuable, that the French sometimes lock them in their safes with their jewels and papers. And yet, they are round and wrinkled, rather unattractive, and have a strong, almost overpowering odor. And they do add an unalterable, unique flavor to whatever they're in or on.

You can get fresh truffles at Zabar's—in season, of course. They must be well washed, virtually scrubbed, and should be sliced extremely thin. Add them at the very end of cooking, to flavor omelets, stuffings, or pâté; or chop them fine, and sprinkle them on a finished casserole. Canned truffles are used exactly the same way.

HERBS AND SPICES

Whether it's a salad you want to dress or a leg of lamb waiting to be covered with a crusty, invigorating coating, herbs and spices are indispensable. In small quantities, so they're never overwhelming, they make ordinarily boring foods exciting and do for great food what precious gems do for a beautiful woman—enhance, entice, and electrify.

In any case, herbs and spices are generally lumped together as "seasonings," although spices are stronger and add their own flavor to foods; herbs, milder and more often used fresh, accent flavors already there rather than introducing their own.

HERBS

ANISE: Sweet-smelling and spicy, with a subtle smell and taste of licorice. Used mostly to make liqueurs, such as Anisette and Pernod, but it livens up cookies and breads like nothing else. King Edward IV used it as sachet. Steep one teaspoon of seed in one pint of good brandy for an interesting after-dinner drink.

BASIL: L'herbe royale, sweet, aromatic, yet pungent and peppery. It symbolizes hatred or love in many medieval texts and is also said to keep flies away. It's especially good on tomatoes, with fish or eggs, and in pesto green garlic sauce for fresh pasta.

BAY LEAF: The foundation of all French cooking. It's also the symbol of glory and success, a protection against evil, and the leaves were woven into wreaths to decorate the brows of poets and heroes. Pungent and flavorful in soups, stews, marinades, and a special treat when thrown onto hot coals for barbecuing fish.

CHERVIL: Sweet and delicate, it's one of the fine herbes and delicious in omelets, with asparagus and cauliflower. It symbolizes sincerity.

CHIVES: Strong and oniony; can be used instead of 79

HOT MUSTARD

81

onions in most dishes. Chives are a must for vichyssoise or mixed with sour cream for baked potatoes. Adds zest to plain mayonnaise, too.

DILL : Delicate, yet bitter ; use it with fish, cucumbers, pickles, cabbage, or squash.

FENNEL : One of the nine sacred herbs of the ancient Greeks. Less pungent and sweeter than its relative, dill. It's a symbol of flattery and heroism and goes nicely in fish and pork dishes.

FINES HERBES : A combination of tarragon, parsley, chives, and chervil, most often seen in omelets, but good in soups and sauces, too.

GARLIC : The essence of vulgarity, according to Horace, and either loved or hated, but never in between. The larger the head and the thicker the cloves, the sweeter it will be. Using dried garlic is a sin when fresh garlic is so available.

HORSERADISH : Strongly pungent, sinus-clearing root that's grated and mixed with lemon juice and vinegar

POTATO PANCAKES (LATKES)

This is another one of those very personal recipe preferences. Every one seems to have his or her favorite method for making latkes. But if you're tired of the same old French fries all the time, try these—especially with a little applesauce on the side.

1½ pounds potatoes (5 or 6)
2 eggs
2 tablespoons flour or matzoh meal
Salt and freshly ground black pepper, to
  taste
3 tablespoons grated onion
Oil for frying

Peel and grate potatoes coarsely (this can be done in a food processor). Put them in a linen dish towel or double layer of cheesecloth and squeeze to extract as much liquid as you can (there should be about 2 cups of grated potatoes when you're through). Put in a bowl and add eggs, flour, or matzoh meal, salt, pepper, and onion. Mix thoroughly.

Heat about ¼ inch of oil in a heavy skillet, and drop the potato mixture, about 3 tablespoons per pancake, into the hot oil. Fry until golden brown on both sides, turning once.
Serves 4 to 6.

MACARONI SALAD

4 cups cooked, drained, cold elbow macaroni
  (8 ounces uncooked)
1 cup mayonnaise
2 tablespoons cider vinegar
2 teaspoons prepared mustard
½ teaspoon celery seed
1 tablespoon grated onion (or more, to
  taste)
1 cup celery, chopped
½ cup parsley, minced
¼ cup pimiento, chopped
Salt and freshly ground black pepper, to
  taste

Mix mayonnaise with vinegar, mustard, celery seed, and onion ; pour over macaroni, and toss to coat. Add remaining ingredients and toss again. Chill thoroughly for 2-3 hours.
Serves 4 to 6.

to add an almost mustardy flavor to roast beef, tongue, and, of course, gefilte fish.

JUNIPER : Bittersweet, tasting slightly of pine. Berries are used in sauerkraut, game marinades, and to make gin. It's the symbol of protection, probably based on the legend that when Mary took the baby Jesus to Egypt, they found refuge behind a juniper bush.

MARJORAM : Aromatic, sweet, and spicy ; used in stuffings or rubbed into meats before roasting ; in soups and with vegetables. Used extensively in northern Italian cooking, though the name is Greek for "joy of the mountains." It symbolizes protection against epidemics.

MINT : The symbol of virtue ; the ancient Greeks used it to clean tables or sweeten bathwater. There are many varieties : spearmint, peppermint, applemint, and so on. It goes into candies, jellies, salad dressings, sauce for lamb, and tea. Peppermint tea aids digestion, spearmint tea makes a good skin lotion.

OREGANO : A variety of wild marjoram, the spiciest of them all, and the mainstay of southern Italian cooking. Use it anywhere, anytime.

PARSLEY : Known as the "herb of health," it is rich in vitamins, iodine, iron, and minerals. Most people simply use it as a garnish, but its tangy, sweet taste adds flavor and color to almost anything. Chewing it rids the breath of garlic and onion, and as a symbol of revelry and victory, it was used to crown champions.

POPPY SEED : Nutty, subtle flavor, not from the opium poppy, but a different plant altogether. Good in cakes and pastries or with noodles. It takes 900,000 poppy seeds to make a pound.

ROSEMARY : So fragrant it was once burned as incense; its strong taste is perfect with lamb, pork, and roast chicken. It was used as a charm against witches and as a symbol of remembrance, friendship, and fidelity— legend has it that it grew only in the gardens of the righteous.

SAGE : Warm, piquant, slightly bitter, camphorish taste; goes well with pork and veal because they are so mild; gives special zing to stuffings and sausages. It was a symbol of domestic virtue as well as a healing herb thought to whiten teeth, keep moths away from clothes, and serve as a remedy for snakebite, constipation, and epilepsy.

SAVORY : Called the bean herb because its strong, aromatic, spicy—almost peppery—flavor has a special affinity for beans, particularly peas and lentils.

SESAME : The nutty flavor is most apparent when the seeds are toasted or fried, and they add good flavor to cookies, candy, breads, and chicken. Sesame is high in polyunsaturated fat.

TARRAGON : Fragrant and sweet, with a slightly bitter, licoricy edge; it does magic things to chicken, fish, eggs, asparagus, and artichokes. It must be in a good Béarnaise sauce, and it makes a lovely vinegar. Symbolizes unselfish sharing and was thought to be a cure for insect bites and stings.

THYME : Very strong and sharp, sometimes overpowering, although some of its varieties, such as lemon, mint, and orange thymes, are warm and pleasant-tasting. Use it in bouquet garni, stuffings, sauces. It aids the digestion of fatty foods. It's the symbol of courage: Roman soldiers put it in their baths to absorb some.

SPICES

When spices were first introduced into England, they were so expensive and valuable (one pound of mace, for example, was worth three sheep), the guards at the London docks had their pockets sewn up so they couldn't steal.

ALLSPICE : This is not a mixture, but a plant unto itself that combines the flavors of cloves, cinnamon, and nutmeg (in France it's known as *quatre épices*). Use it in pickling, spice cake, pot roast, pâté, marinades, pea soup, and with yellow vegetables. It stands for compassion. (Available ground or whole.)

CAPERS : The unopened flower buds of a Mediterranean shrub, picked by hand and always packed in salt or vinegar to bring out their strong flavor. They are good in salads and dressings, sauces, antipastos, and with vegetables.

CARAWAY : Pleasantly sharp and spicy; you'll find it

good in sauerkraut, rye bread, potato salad, cheese, cakes, and cookies. It's a Dutch spice, always thought to prevent theft, evil, and infidelity and to cure hysteria.

CARDAMOM : A popular spice in first-century Rome, used to flavor coffee. The Scandinavians use it a lot; the Orientals chew the seeds after dinner to sweeten the breath. The dried ripe seeds are used whole or ground in curries, cakes, and cookies. (Available ground or whole.)

CAYENNE : Very small, very hot red peppers; used judiciously to flavor meat, egg, and cheese dishes. (Available ground, whole or flaked.)

CELERY SEED : From wild celery, called smallage, not the cultivated type. Strong-flavored, so should be used sparingly in soups, salad dressings, pickles, potato salad, and coleslaw.

CHILI : Made from Mexican peppers with cumin, garlic, and oregano; hot and spicy.

CINNAMON : Warm and aromatic, it's the oldest spice known. The bark of cinnamon trees was used to make perfume in Biblical times. When it is used in cookies, cakes, breads, stews, its delicious aroma is immediately identifiable. (Available ground or in pieces.)

CLOVES : It takes 4,000 to 7,000 dried cloves to make one pound of spice. These sun-dried flower buds of the clove tree, shaped like nails, got their name from French *clou*, or nail. Cloves symbolize dignity and add a touch of refined elegance to pastries, soups, and sauces. An onion stuck with cloves is the classic French seasoning for stocks and stews. (Available ground or whole.)

CORIANDER : A member of the parsley family, it was the first seasoning grown in this country. The whole seed is used in pickling; crushed, it's part of curry powder and can be mixed into cottage or cream cheese. It's the symbol of hidden worth.

CUMIN : To the Greeks, it symbolized greed, but today it's regarded as a good source of vitamin A, calcium, and iron. It's strong, spicy, and aromatic; used in chili powder and curry powder.

CURRY : Not one spice, but a blend of many, among them ginger, chili, coriander, cumin, cinnamon, fenugreek, turmeric, cardamom, pepper, and cloves.

FENUGREEK : Slightly bitter in taste, but something like celery in smell. It's used in curries, halvah, imitation maple-syrup flavoring.

GINGER : Hot, sweet, clean-flavored. The root may be used fresh, preserved in syrup, or crystalized, or it may be dried and ground. It's essential to Chinese cuisine and often used in baking.

HERBES DE PROVENCE : A combination of tarragon, basil,

thyme, and rosemary, all dried on their branches to make them more flavorful.

MACE: Similar to nutmeg, and actually a layer between the nutmeg shell and its husk. Mace and nutmeg can be used interchangeably.

MARYLAND CRAB SPICE: Peppercorns, bay leaves, and mystery. Extraordinary with shellfish.

MUSTARD SEED: It symbolizes indifference, yet was touted as a digestive stimulant. It's pungent, spicy, and versatile. Use it in pickles, salad dressings, sauce, dips, on sandwiches.

NUTMEG: Sweet, warm, and spicy, but not quite as pungent as mace. Best when freshly grated; adds zip to sweet foods; puts the nog in eggnog. (Available ground or whole.)

PAPRIKA: The soul of Hungarian cooking, it is ground pepper; and comes in three strengths: sweet, half-sweet, and hot—and the hot is very hot. Its bright-orange color is decorative on pale foods; its flavor blends beautifully with anything.

PEPPERCORNS: Dried berries of the pepper plant—the black are from ripe berries with the hull still on; the white from those with the hull removed. White is a little milder and particularly useful in white or pale dishes, in which specks of black pepper would be unsightly.

PEPPER, GROUND: Less pungent than whole peppercorns, but with the same spicy flavor.

PICKLING SPICES: A combination of dill, mustard seeds, coriander, and bay leaves.

SAFFRON: The most expensive spice, it's also the richest source of vitamin B_2. Spicy, aromatic, and very pungent; a very little goes a long way, especially in rice. It comes from the stigmas of the autumn crocus, picked by hand. It takes 75,000 blossoms to make one pound, and not surprisingly, saffron is the symbol of the necessity of guarding against excess.

SEA SALT: Salt from the evaporation of sea water, containing trace materials ordinary salt doesn't. It's also free-flowing and noncaking.

TURMERIC: The dried root of a tropical plant similar to ginger; has a mildly peppery taste. It's used in pickles and relishes, and adds that bright-yellow color to curry and mustard. It's also used as a vegetable dye.

VANILLA: The dried bean of an orchid, delicate, sweet, and spicy. It's unique for sweet foods. (Available in liquid extract form, or whole bean.)

Cheese

AND CRACKERS

"I used to go often, but the last ten times I couldn't get waited on, so I'm thinking of giving it up."

Saul Bellow

From simple country *chèvres* (goat's-milk cheeses) to winy, aged Cheddars, the cheese department at Zabar's sings out its offerings like a Lorelei on the Rhine. It's tempting, enticing, and hopelessly irresistible. Zabar's brings in 80% to 90% of their French cheeses themselves—about a container (2,000-3,000 pounds) a week—direct from their own private cheese broker in France.

Three, four, even as many as five hundred different cheeses can be found. For the "turophile" (writer and critic Clifton Fadiman's words for cheese lover) or the novice, Zabar's has cheese to please everyone.

Just about everyone, from Mother Goose to Shakespeare, has had something to say about cheese. One of the oldest stories bears a strange resemblance to a tale told about the discovery of yogurt. An Arab trader, one of those historical schleppers always on their way to or from someplace across the desert on camelback, was in fact schlepping across the desert on camelback. He had with him a portion of milk, probably sheep or goat, that he carried in a pouch made from the stomach lining of an animal. Between the desert heat, the not-so-gentle rocking of the camel, and the chemical presence of rennet—a natural curdling agent found in animals' stomach linings—the milk separated into solid curds and liquid whey. The trader, who was desperately hungry by this time, drank the liquid, which wasn't half-bad, and ate the curd, which was, as a matter of fact, quite delicious, not to mention filling. Cheese—or yogurt, depending on which legend you believe—had been serendipitously discovered!

Leaping ahead to the Middle Ages, somewhere around 1070, one finds Charlemagne studiously trying to pick the mold out of Roquefort. He was diplomatically advised that he was throwing away the best part and decided to eat it as it was. He loved it!

Shakespeare made much ado about cheese, little of it flattering. " 'Tis time I were choked by a bit of toasted cheese," he says in *The Merry Wives of Windsor*, and Macbeth complains, ". . . you lily-livered boy, you whey-face." Obviously, the Bard's experiences with cheese left a bad taste in his mouth.

Robert Louis Stevenson's were better. "Many the long night I've dreamed about cheese—toasted mostly," Ben Gunn laments in *Treasure Island*. And even Mother Goose couldn't resist: "Heigh-ho the dairy-O, the cheese stands alone." And who will ever forget poor Little Miss Muffet?

MAKING IT

According to an old gypsy recipe for making cheese, first you steal a cow. Actually, it could also be a goat or a sheep, as long as it gives milk. The finished product will depend very largely on the quality of the milk, which in turn can depend on what the animals were fed, the time of day they were milked, whether the milk is pasteurized, and so on.

If you were merely to leave fresh milk alone at this point, it would sour and thicken of its own natural accord, and drained and salted, would be the most basic type of cheese known to mankind.

But in commercial cheese production, the next step is to pasteurize the milk to knock out any harmful bacteria (not all cheese is made with pasteurized milk, especially not in Europe). Rennet is then added to start the curdling process.

When curd has formed, it's separated from the whey —the liquid portion sometimes used to make certain cheeses, such as Norwegian Gjetost, and some ricottas. Exactly what follows depends on what type of cheese it is to be. The curd may be cut, cooked, drained, molded, and pressed, or simply collected and set out to cure and ripen. At this stage, cheese has no flavor or shape. Ripening gives it both.

Salt may be added now to inhibit moisture and harmful bacteria, as well as to add flavor and texture. As the salt spreads, the cheese becomes more solid. It is here, too, that a cheese may be treated with the bacterial cultures that give it its special characteristics— interior or exterior molds, and so on.

"Fresh" cheeses, by the way, such as cream cheese, mozarella, and ricotta, among others, are not cured, ripened, or aged at all, but are ready to eat almost as soon as the curds and whey are separated.

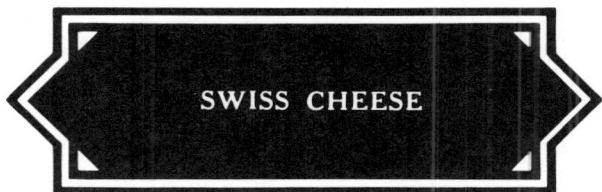

SWISS CHEESE

It's the third most popular cheese at Zabar's, and the only one you can have sliced to order. ("Almost everyone wants it for sandwiches," explains Harvey, "And it doesn't muck up the slicing machine.") Zabar's sells only imported varieties, mellow and milky, sweet and fine-textured, with a deliciously nutty flavor.

When you ask for, and get, Swiss cheese, it's actually *Emmentaler* from Switzerland, a cheese rigidly controlled by the Swiss government. The huge wheels, sometimes weighing up to 200 pounds, are officially stamped on the rind with the word "Switzerland" within concentric circles. If the cheese doesn't have that stamp, it doesn't come from Switzerland. It might be Swiss-type cheese from Norway, Denmark, Finland, Holland, Alsace-Lorraine, or Austria, made in a similar way and with a similar taste, but not the real McCoy.

Genuine Switzerland Swiss cheese is usually made from raw milk, and it is the ripening period that is critical to its success; it takes 7 to 10 months for the flavor to fully mature. The holes everyone associates with Swiss cheese are caused by gasses (carbon

CHEESE AND BABIES

In Switzerland, where cheese cellars are as common as wine cellars and just as proudly stocked, the birth of a child is celebrated with a large wheel of cheese, usually Emmentaler or Gruyère. It is marked with the baby's name, birth date, and other vital statistics. The cheese is eaten only on the most special occasions: graduations, promotions, new jobs, betrothal, marriage, births, and so on. The last of the cheese—many years later, it was hoped—would be eaten as a final tribute by the mourners at the individual's funeral.

An old British custom called for making a large wheel of cheese on the day the expected birth of a child was announced. Slices were cut from the cheese wheel daily—from the center out—until, just before the baby's birth, only a large ring of cheese was left. The newborn would be passed through the ring on his christening day.

dioxide, a product of ripening) that cannot escape from the ripening cheese and so explode into holes, or eyes.

A second cheese from Switzerland is *Gruyère*, from the same family as Emmentaler, but creamier, a bit saltier, and aged longer. This also carries the official Swiss-government stamp on its rind.

"People come from all over just for our Gruyère," Harvey boasts. "It's very well aged, so its flavor is perfect." According to Harvey, Gruyère is made by a slightly different process than Emmentaler, so only a few, small holes develop. The aging process is critical here, too. Five months to a year, and the longer it's aged, the better and deeper the flavor.

Emmentaler and Gruyère are often used interchangeably in cooking. Both melt easily and add tre-

mendous pizazz to whatever they're combined with.

Of course, Switzerland produces a great variety of other cheeses, some, such as *Appenzeller*, *Beaufort*, and *Saanen*, somewhat similar to Gruyère and Emmentaler; others that are totally different, such as *Sapsago*, *Tête de Moine*, and *Vacherin*.

But real Swiss cheese, the one with the holes, that goes so well with ham on a sandwich is Emmentaler. All the rest are simply Swiss-made cheeses, known by their individual names.

CHEDDAR & CO.

Cheddar, Harvey says, is a tricky cheese. Like Brie, it can be superb or barely edible. It depends on proper aging—as little as two months, as long as two years—and on its being regularly turned as it mellows, to assure even ripening and an interior texture just this side of crumbly. "The longer the better," claims Harvey. "But you have to be careful. Cheddars can be too strong, too carbon-dioxidy, or too rubbery if they're aged improperly."

Pretty much everything sold under the broad category "American cheese" is, or was, a member of the

CHEESE SOUP

This is quite filling, so small servings are in order.

1 large onion, chopped
3 tablespoons unsalted butter
⅓ cup all-purpose flour
¼ teaspoon salt
Freshly ground black pepper
4 cups milk, scalded
2 cups shredded sharp Cheddar cheese
2 tablespoons tomato sauce
1 tablespoon Worcestershire
Dash Tabasco

In a large saucepan, sauté onion in butter until golden. Sprinkle with flour, salt, and pepper to taste; stir, and cook for about 3 minutes.

Add hot milk slowly, stirring all the while. Add cheese, and stir while it melts. Simmer, covered, about 15 minutes.

Add tomato sauce, Worcestershire, and Tabasco; simmer 10 minutes longer. Serve immediately.
Serves 7 or 8.

THE BIG CHEESE

A gigantic Cheddar cheese, weighing half a ton and truly fit for royalty, was made and given to Queen Victoria as a wedding present. It was nearly as big as the one made in Massachusetts to honor Thomas Jefferson; that cheese required the milk of 800 cows and weighed 1,235 pounds. But these were small potatoes compared with the 17-ton Cheddar exhibited at the 1964 World's Fair in New York.

From Ontario, where it was made cooperatively by 15 Wisconsin and Canadian cheese factories, it was sent to New York by special horse-pulled wagon and train. It was delivered to Flushing Meadow with great fanfare and flourish, and the floor of the exhibition hall promptly collapsed under its weight.

The story doesn't end there. The cheese remained in the hall for six months, under a glass-domed roof, until Thomas Lipton, the tea importer, bought it and had it shipped to England. It had not been kept under ideal conditions, and that showed. But surprisingly, after a few weeks in the English air, it had totally recovered—except for a foot-deep layer, which was easily cut off. The cheese was sold to a London restaurant, who triumphantly served it in his establishment and kindly sent a large chunk of it home to its makers in Canada.

The adventurous journey, from Canada to New York to England and back again, took about two years, and the great Cheddar, it was reported, had only improved with age.

Cheddar family. However it gets to the table in crocks, cylinders, bricks, wheels, chunks, barrel or sausage shapes, or cocktail cubes; white or yellow; flavored with pimiento or wine or anything else, it's still Cheddar. Nearly half the cheese eaten in the United States is Cheddar in some form, and while it's not quite as American as so-called American cheese, it's certainly as American as the apple pie it so often accompanies.

Real, honest-to-goodness aged Cheddar, however, is a treat. At its very best, it is rich, tangy, with a sharp, nutty taste. Hundreds of tons of Cheddar are produced in this country yearly, and the quality varies tremendously. Zabar's chooses only the very best and treats Cheddars with the same reverence oenophiles give to vintage wines.

American Cheddar-makers follow the traditional English methods and recipes, except, usually, using pasteurized rather than raw milk. The British age their Cheddars in the caves of Cheddar Gorge in the

West Country; Americans have settled on Wisconsin, New York, Vermont, and Oregon.

"There isn't very much real English Cheddar available in the States, although we have it when it is," Harvey says. "There's much more Canadian Cheddar around."

The Canadian cheese, like the English, is made from unpasteurized milk. But what sets it apart even further from American Cheddar is the color: It is almost always white; American Cheddars are, for the most part, orange-yellow. The color comes from annato, a vegetable dye first used in mining camps during the Gold Rush to color McIntosh cheese. The miners called this cheese "edible gold," and farmer McIntosh's dairies in Washington and Oregon were famous for their golden Cheddars. One of them, Tillamook, in Oregon, still produces a fine Cheddar, distinct and special, it is claimed, because of the excellent quality of the mountain grass.

No matter where it comes from, though, Cheddar is deliciously versatile. You can, of course, add it to macaroni or steamed vegetables; use it in soups, soufflés, or breads and rolls; or serve it plain with crisp Golden Delicious apples, peaches, or oranges, crusty French bread or crackers, and beer, cider, or a light red wine. (The English drink elderberry or dry, vintage apple wine with their Cheddar.)

VARIATIONS ON A THEME

There are a whole bunch of Cheddarlike cheeses at Zabar's, smoked, spiced, aged, mild, spreadable, and endless combinations of these qualities. But a few stand out as distant cousins to Cheddar.

Longhorn Colby is very moist and soft, aged, at most, for three or four weeks. It's mild and mellow, with a pleasant, tangy taste—a little like sour cream —but technically it's a stirred- or granular-curd cheese (the curds are stirred or kneaded, like dough) rather than a true Cheddar (whose curds are cut and stacked). In New England, Colby is called "Crowley," after the family of cheese-makers who invented it.

Another relative of sorts is *Monterey Jack*, which is more like Colby than Cheddar, but still considered to be in the Cheddar family. It's mild and slightly sweet and has a soft, almost rubbery consistency. It's a nice melting cheese for topping casseroles.

Monterey Jack was one of the first dairy products to come out of California. The original recipe came from a Spanish monk, although it was a Scottish dairy farmer, David Jacks, who actually put the cheese on the market.

Washed-curd cheese is yet another variation. This is quick-cured and has a high moisture content, because the curds are actually washed or soaked before they're pressed. It tastes very much like Cheddar, but doesn't keep nearly as well or have the distinct flavor characteristics of a well-aged cheese.

Zabar's sells them all: the *Cheddars* from England;

CHEESY ITALIAN BREAD

1 loaf Italian bread
1 cup grated Jarlsberg
¼ cup minced onion
¼ cup minced shallot
3 tablespoons unsalted butter, softened
1 teaspoon oregano
1 clove garlic, minced
1 tablespoon milk

Preheat oven to 350°F.

Slice top off bread, and remove soft, doughy interior, so loaf looks like a canoe. Mix remaining ingredients until smooth, and spoon into hollowed-out bread. Put top slice back on; wrap in aluminum foil, and bake about 20 minutes, or until cheese is melted. To serve, slice in 1-inch-thick slices.

Makes 20 slices.

Black Diamond "Extra Old" and *Maple Gem* from Canada; *Seward Family Cheddar* from Vermont; *Longhorn* from Wisconsin; New York State *Cheddar;* even a *raw milk Cheddar,* and New England *goat's-milk Cheddar,* unusually tasty and particularly pungent. And Cheddar logs, Cheddars coated with pistachio nuts, mixed with dried fruit and pecans or wine, thinned with cream to a spreading consistency. "Anyway you like it, we've got it," Harvey Pearlman says with pride. And he isn't kidding.

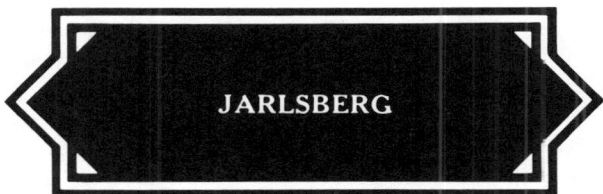

JARLSBERG

Next to Cheddar, the best-selling cheese at Zabar's (a hefty 1,000 to 1,200 pounds a week) is Norwegian Jarlsberg.

"Most people ask for it instead of Swiss," Harvey says. "It's very popular with our customers." It's softer and milder than Swiss, aged only three to six months; but it has holes.

It's a real old-timer, going back to the first Vikings in Norway who found cheese-makers producing big wheels of a firm cheese which was called Jarlsberg after the biggest estate in the area. At one time, Jarlsberg was Norway's most popular cheese—the answer to hard-to-get Emmentaler and Gruyère. But as new types and tastes in cheese became more and more available, Jarlsberg took a nosedive.

In the past few years, however, its mild and nutty flavor has enjoyed a resurgence of popularity in Norway—at least partially due to the cheese's importance here—and no *landgang,* the Scandinavian version of the six-foot hero sandwich, is complete without its Jarlsberg.

Norway produces more than 60 varieties of cheese, and Jarlsberg is easily number one. It's very close to that here, too. It's good eating all the time, as a snack or in a sandwich, with fruit and bread, or in cooking.

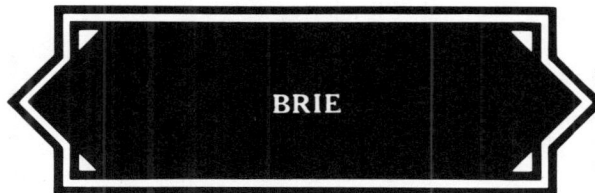

BRIE

Zabar's sells over a thousand pounds of Brie a week. That's a lot of cheese! It's all imported from France, and all of it must meet the absolute standards set by Saul Zabar and Harvey Pearlman.

"Brie is very tricky, very touch-and-go," Harvey says with grave authority. He's more than merely in charge of cheese; he's second in command to Murray Klein, and he trained with Zabar's best cheese expert, Irving Horowitz, who spent twenty-five years in the cheese department before he retired.

"We have gone without Brie when it hasn't met our standards," Harvey continues. "The best time for Brie used to be the fall, but now it's made weekly, or even every few days, so it's very changeable. We have special refrigerators for the Brie to ripen in for one or two weeks, and it's rotated and checked daily. It's as carefully treated as a new baby."

The French, according to Harvey, often eat Brie that is overripe, brown, and slightly ammoniated. (Brie and Camembert release ammonia during ripen-

THE CHEESE THAT FAILED

Everything at Zabar's is perfect—almost. Sometimes even *Zabar's* makes mistakes, and they are usually whoppers.

When it looked as if the price of Jarlsberg cheese would go up astronomically, Zabar's bought 5,000 pounds of it and stored it against the future. And forgot about it. By the time it was discovered, it was too ripe to sell in the store.

Sometimes Zabar's isn't that lucky. A 450-pound shipment of Brie, which tasted fine to Saul Zabar at the importer's, didn't taste so fine at the store. The importer wouldn't take it back, and it wound up in the garbage.

SURPRISE BISCUITS

⅓ *pound Brie or Camembert, crust
  removed, and softened*
4 tablespoons sweet butter, softened
1 egg
Dash salt
Freshly ground black pepper, to taste
1 cup all-purpose flour
¼ *teaspoon cayenne pepper*

Preheat oven to 350°F. Lightly grease cookie sheet.

In a bowl, beat softened cheese, butter, egg, salt, and pepper until smooth. Add flour, a little at a time, beating after each addition. Add cayenne. If dough is too soft, use a little more flour. Roll into a ball, and chill for at least 1 hour.

On floured board, roll out dough about ¼ inch thick. Cut in 2-inch rounds. Place on cookie sheet and bake 15 to 20 minutes, until browned.

Makes 11 or 12 biscuits.

ing as the amino acids react to the enzymes. If the odor is pronounced, the cheese is too ripe.) Neither he nor his customers stand for that. Brie is either perfect, or it's not there. When it's on the counter, it's uniformly ripe, with no hard, chalky line in the middle; slightly bulging, but not runny. If by some chance it's not quite ready, Harvey or one of his assistants might advise holding it a day or two before using.

Brie de Meaux is the best of the French Bries, from the region known as Ile-de-France (not to be confused with the brand name "Ile de France"), a lush, fertile area east of Paris. It's Brie made of cow's milk from the evening milking that has been allowed to ripen (stand overnight to start the enzymes forming) mixed with fresh milk of the following morning. To reach its most nearly perfect stage—an even, creamy interior that almost oozes like paste when it's cut, covered by a white rind lightly flecked with brown— it must ripen for at least three to four weeks at a constant temperature of 52° to 54°F. Its flavor can range from mild and delicate to pungent and almost nutty. The cheese has a very short life span, especially when it's fully ripe. It must be served at room temperature (take it out of the refrigerator at least 2 hours before).

While Brie de Meaux is the supreme Brie, that's not to say Brie from other areas are not good. They're just different.

"We don't always have Brie de Meaux," Harvey says. "It depends on what's available. But we always have the richest and creamiest Bries."

BLUE CHEESE

"Blue cheese" is any cheese that has developed, during the ripening process, a bluish-green vein of interior mold. This can happen naturally, because of conditions in the ripening area, or the mold may be injected by the cheese-maker. There are many varieties of blue, and almost half of them are attempts to imitate Roquefort. At the moment, Zabar's has eight varieties, from Italy, France, Great Britain, and Denmark.

Most of the French *bleus* are Roquefort copies, made with cow's milk rather than sheep's. The cheeses are named for the areas where they are made: *Bleu des Causses* and *Bleu d'Auvergne* come from the Massif Central, a mountainous region with superb pastureland; *Bleu de Haut Jura* is from the Jura Mountains on the Swiss border; *Bleu de Corse* is a Roquefort made in Corsica. They vary somewhat in intensity, and their pastes range from white to yellow, hard to buttery, mild to rather strong; but all share a creamy pungency and rich, tangy taste—said to be good for the digestion.

"If you want to taste something a little different," offers Harvey, "try *Saga*, from Denmark. It's like a Brie with a vein of blue running through it. It's a modern hybrid that combines the best of two great cheese types." He also recommends *Blue Castello*, a Danish mixture of blue cheese and triple crème, rich, tangy, slightly sweet, and very piquant.

BONAPARTE AND THE CHEESE

In the small French town of Camembert, Marie Harel, the wife of a local farmer, was the village expert in producing a type of cheese very well-known in the area. Napoleon visited the town in the 1790s and was served some of Madame Harel's cheese. He was so excited by its flavor that he kissed not only Madame, but the waiter who had served the cheese. Napoleon decreed, then and there, that a statue be erected in honor of the cheese (from then on to be called Camembert) and its maker. The statue stood proudly in the town square until German bombs knocked it down during World War II.

GOUDA, GOUDA FOR YOU

As the story goes, an illustrious and imaginative commander of a naval fleet from Montevideo, Uruguay, one Commodore Coe, was a military strategist of extraordinary resourcefulness. In 1847, he repulsed his attackers, the navy from Buenos Aires, with an unusually effective weapon.

Having run out of ordinary cannonballs, Commodore Coe bombarded the Argentinians with what he had handy—red-wax-coated Gouda cheeses! Or so the story goes.

Danish blue cheese, *Danablu*, is sharp, strong, and often quite salty. It easily accounts for the majority of blue cheese imported into this country, and it's more popular in England than British blue-veined *Stilton*, a rich, sweet, almost spicy cheese.

Of the blue-veined cheeses, *Gorgonzola* is perhaps one of the oldest. It has a tradition 1,000 years old, when it was aged in caves for a year or more, to give it a very strong and pungent flavor. Today's factory-made Gorgonzolas are milder, though still quite tangy and flavorful, slightly gamy, and on the spicy side. Its mold is greenish, rather than blue.

"It makes a terrific salad dressing," Harvey says. "Strong, chunky, and tasty. You only need a little bit of cheese, oil, vinegar, salt, and pepper. Let it stay in the refrigerator for a couple of hours."

The same can be said for any of the blues that are more crumbly than pasty. But the real treat is to serve them at the end of a meal, with crusty French bread or plain crackers, sweet butter, fresh fruit—especially pears or peaches—and good, hearty red wine. The British recommend a vintage port with Stilton; the French like full-bodied "great" Bordeaux or burgundies or Côtes du Rhone with their *bleus*. And according to the Italians, nothing is better with Gorgonzola than a good, robust Chianti or barolo.

GOUDA AND EDAM

Making Gouda on farms near the small town of Gouda is still, as it has been since the thirteenth century, women's work. The men are in charge of taking the cheese to market and playing the age-old haggling-over-prices game. It's well worth the odd division of labor, however.

95

"We're very proud of our aged, farmhouse Goudas," Harvey boasts. "They have a deep, delicious flavor that most people don't associate with ordinary Gouda."

Factory-made Gouda is produced all over Holland. It is bland, almost sweet, with a mild tang. It may be spiced with cumin, but it's always a good, reliable cheese—no surprises; you always get just what you expect.

Edam is similar to Gouda in taste and texture, buttery and mellow, smooth and yellowish. It's made with a little less fat and is a bit softer, but both are almost rubbery in consistency. Edam is a sphere, like a grapefruit and is coated in red wax. Gouda is less spherical, and its wrapping may be red or yellow.

Both keep extremely well, especially Edam. A polar expedition in 1956 found an Edam that had been left at the South Pole in 1912. It was in perfect condition.

MÜNSTER VERSUS MUENSTER

Münster is not the same thing as *muenster*. The first is Alsatian, the second American, and the difference is great.

American muenster is rather bland, sometimes even tasteless. It's made mostly in Wisconsin and the Midwest, from pasteurized milk, and has a short aging period—a week to a month. It's very mild, with almost no smell, and has a sweet taste and somewhat chewy texture. It's light, uncomplicated, inoffensive, and goes with everything—fruit, vegetables, bread, crackers. It melts well, too, and makes a nice topping for casseroles.

True münster, on the other hand, is a strong, rich cheese, first made, it is said, in the seventh century in the Vosges Mountains by a band of nomadic Irish monks. It's a very tasty cheese, with an earthy flavor and aroma, both of which strengthen with age. Ripe münster with German beer and crusty bread makes an ideal snack.

Münster is considered one of the finest of the cheeses that originated in monasteries. They were made by the monks for their own use and often were named after saints. Similar in texture, smooth and relatively soft, they may be quite mild or tangy, or very strong and flavorful, with a long-lasting, somewhat mushroomy aroma.

Port du Salut is a mild version, still made by Trappist monks at the Abbaye de Notre-Dame de Port du Salut. The monks also supervise a factory operation near the monastery where *Port-Salut* is made. This is a different cheese altogether, closer in type to *Saint Paulin*, tangy and intense. Port-Salut is actually a brand name rather than a type of cheese.

Pont l'Évêque, *Saint Nectaire*, and *Tomme de Sa-*

BOYS WILL BE BOYS

A bunch of handsome young French shepherds, more interested in chasing shepherdesses than in tending their flocks, tucked away their lunches in a cave. Things being what they were, they forgot about the food until several days later, when they found their lunch packets full of blue-green mold. Being hungry and fearless, they ate the cheese—and thought it much improved. They ran home to tell the local cheese-makers of their discovery, and Roquefort has been aged in caves ever since.

Only the sheep's-milk cheese that has been aged that way—in nooks and crannies of caves in limestone cliffs near the village of Roquefort-sur-Soulzon—can truly be called Roquefort. The natural circulation of air and moisture through these caves encourages the mold to develop and grow, and though the milk may come from anywhere, to be officially called Roquefort, the cheese must be ripened here. By edict of Charles VI, only the cheese-makers of Roquefort-sur-Soulzon have the exclusive and legal right to produce this cheese. Genuine Roquefort always has an identifying red symbol with a sheep on its wrapping.

voie are similar cheeses, are mild and creamy, quite smooth in texture. Switzerland produces *Tête de Moine*, which means monk's head and is so-called because at one time the cheese was shaped like that. Another theory, however, credits the name to the practice of paying one's church taxes with cheese rather than cash.

All are perfect cheeses to serve with bread and wine at the end of a meal. Dry to fruity red wines, depending on the age and ripeness of the cheese, are the general rule.

AMERICAN CHEESES

The United States produces more cheese than does any other country—more Swiss than Switzerland, more mozzarella than Italy, more Cheddar than England. It adds up to an astounding 3.3 billion pounds of cheese a year. Almost half of it is made in Wisconsin, followed by New York, Vermont, and California.

Despite all that, only five cheeses are truly American in origin: *Brick*, a purely American invention, is shaped like a brick and originally was pressed under the weight of bricks. It's a semisoft cheese, easy to slice, with a mellow, sweetish taste. It's good with black bread, fresh peaches, and beer. *Cream cheese* (see page 105) and *Monterey Jack* (see page 92) are numbers two and three. Fourth is *Liederkranz*, created by a New York cheese-maker at the end of the nineteenth century to satisfy his German customers' yearnings for a mild, but pungent cheese like the one they loved at home. (Today, Liederkranz is packaged and processed only by Borden, and it's a registered trade name.)

Almost every other cheese from America, even good, old-fashioned "American cheese," had its origin someplace else. What you get when you ask for American cheese is basically Cheddar or a Cheddar type, usually processed and pressed into loaves. Its yellow color comes from annato. White American cheese has no coloring added.

When the Dutch, English, French, and Scandinavians came to this country, they brought along their cheese-making skills and began almost immediately to duplicate the cheeses made in their countries for centuries. It was strictly a farmhouse industry until the first cheese factories came into being in the nineteenth century.

Cheese production in the United States today is a huge industry, with strict quality, processing, packaging, and manufacturing controls. And extremely strict import laws (cheese must be aged for at least 60 days or made from pasteurized milk), designed more to protect American cheese-makers than to protect health.

However, American versions don't seem to taste the same, and imports keep increasing. There are some cheeses, such as Roquefort and Pecorino, that have no

STUFFED MUSHROOMS

This can also be made with goat cheese, such as Montrachet.

¼ cup unsalted butter, softened
½ cup blue cheese
1 to 2 tablespoons cream
12 large mushroom caps

Mix butter, cheese, and cream until smooth. Stuff into mushroom caps. Really pile up cheese mixture; it not only looks great, but tastes great.
Serves 12.

FRIED GOAT CHEESE

An interesting hors d'oeuvre.

1 pound goat cheese e.g., Chevrotin or Lezay)
1 egg, slightly beaten
About ½ cup bread crumbs
Oil for deep-frying

Cut cheese into 1-inch cubes. Dip in egg, then in crumbs. Heat 2 inches of oil in a deep skillet. Deep-fry cheese cubes until golden brown.
Serves 8.

American equivalents, and some that are just not enough in demand to be produced here.

Zabar's is always on the lookout for new American-made cheeses in an effort to help the American cheese-makers, but most of what is sold—and what customers ask for—is imported from all the great cheese-making centers of the world.

CHÈVRES AND SHEEP'S-MILK CHEESES

On an average day, Zabar's might have 25 kinds of *chèvres*, the generic name for French cheeses made of goat's milk.

All *chèvres* are similar in some basic ways, although they can be mild or strong, depending on how long they're aged. They are usually small, the paste is soft-textured, and they have a definite goaty smell—rather like a barnyard, earthy and somewhat musty—more pronounced in some cheeses than in others. They may be cured for as little as a week or as long as three or four months, in anything from mud to chestnut leaves.

They do vary greatly in appearance. *Chèvres* arrive here shaped like cylinders, pyramids, horseshoes, flowers, logs, balls, cones, almost anything you can think of. Harvey Pearlman is convinced that the shape is often as much, if not more, of a selling point than the flavor. He may be right.

Banon is also round and flat; it's sprinkled with summer savory and wrapped in fragrant chestnut leaves. Not only does it make a pretty package, but its strong, almost nutty flavor, enhanced in the ripening with wine or brandy, grows even stronger as it ages. In Provence, where Banon is made, it is fermented by a secret method in stone jugs for at least five weeks before it is ready to eat.

From Touraine, "the garden of France," comes *Cabichou*, a goat cheese with a short ripening time. It's usually pyramid- or cone-shaped, redolent and intensely pungent, and one of the goatiest in taste and smell of them all.

Chevrotin, says Harvey, is sometimes a combination of cow's and goat's milk. It's aged like no other cheese: left for several weeks in cages atop high poles, so cool air can circulate around it. The cages are surrounded by shade trees, so the sun won't quicken the fermentation. The French like Chevrotin best when it's still fresh, accompanied by salt and garlic or sweetened with sugar and double crème.

Like the fine white wine of the same name, *Montrachet* comes from Burgundy. A light, mild-tasting *chèvre*, it is available in logs and cylinders, plain or covered with cinders, in cups, or wrapped in chestnut leaves, rosemary, *herbes de Provence*.

"It's one of our best sellers because it doesn't have a real strong taste," Harvey says.

Other goat cheeses at Zabar's may be covered with salt, charcoal, or ashes (scraped off before eating), which are a little bit for show, but mostly to preserve the cheese, or flavored with herbs, spices, olive oil, wine, or brandy. Zabar's selection is so varied that you could try a different goat cheese every day for nearly a month without repetition.

The best-known sheep's-milk cheese is *Roquefort*, but Greek *feta* is almost as popular. It's made today almost exactly as it has been for centuries, the very same method, according to Greek myth, set down by Polyphemus, the one-eyed shepherd in Homer's *Odyssey*.

On farms, the milk is hung in leather sacks until it forms curds. In factories, it's hung in cloth or put in molds. In both cases, the cheese is salted or brined and left to ripen in a mixture of the brine and whey. It's sold still packed in liquid, and to keep the salty, slightly sourish taste fresh, that's the way it should be stored. (If there isn't any brine, make your own by adding two tablespoons of salt to two cups of water, and cover the cheese with it. It will last several months or longer.)

Almost all the cheese eaten in Greece is feta in some form. Running a close second is *Kasseri*, a kneaded cheese molded into large wheels before it's set out to ripen. It's firmer and more elastic than feta.

The other sheep's-milk cheeses on Zabar's shelves are from Israel, Hungary, and Czechoslovakia. Often they are a little salty or a little strong, but they're always interesting, especially with dark bread and a light red wine or beer.

SAGANAKI

Made with with sheep's-milk cheese, this is a classic Greek appetizer, and the classic drink to accompany it is Retsina. A hearty red wine will do nicely, too.

⅓ pound Kasseri cheese
2 tablespoons unsalted butter
1 tablespoon lemon juice

Preheat broiler, if necessary.
Slice cheese about ¼ inch thick. Melt butter in a shallow, ovenproof pan. Add cheese in slightly overlapping layers. Broil, about 3 inches from heat until golden brown and crusty. Sprinkle with lemon juice, and serve immediately with crusty Italian bread.
Serves 4.

THE MOON IS MADE OF GREEN CHEESE AND OTHER ODDITIES

"This is our strangest cheese. It's green!" The unanimous decision of Zabar's cheese department is that *Sapsago* is truly the only one of its kind.

"It's a hard cheese, flavored with herbs and a particular kind of clover that has no other reason for being than as an ingredient in this cheese," Harvey declares. Its taste can be so spicy and sharp that only a little makes a piece of bread a whole meal. But its main use is as a grating cheese, to flavor omelets and stews.

Not nearly as exotic, but quite unusual, is *Raclette* (also known as Bagnes), a mild, nutty cheese, similar in taste to Gruyère. It's used mainly to make the melted-cheese dish of the same name. Traditionally, a large chunk of cheese is cut and placed near a fire to melt. The melted part is scraped onto plates or slices of bread and served with baked potatoes, onions, and sweet pickles. This is virtually the national dish of Switzerland, tremendously popular at ski resorts.

Gjetost from Norway is another cheese that stands alone. It's made from goat's-milk whey with sugar and cream added, which may account for its taste—somewhere between chocolate and butterscotch, with a leaning toward peanut butter. It's very nutritious, in any case, according to the Norwegians, and was the cheese the Vikings ate to give them strength.

CHEESE FROM ITALY

The Italians love cheese, and the art of cheese-making is an ancient one in Italy. *Parmesan*, for instance, is literally as old as the hills of Rome. Its recipe came from an ancient Etruscan one, its name from the province of Parma, where it has always been made. In the *Decameron*, Boccaccio describes his own fantasy-land as having "a mountain made of nothing but grated Parmesan cheese, and on top of it, people making nothing but macaroni and noodles."

Parmigiano Reggiano, made on the south side of the River Po, is strictly controlled by Italian authorities. Only the cheese from five provinces in that specific area can be called Parmigiano Reggiano. It can be made only from April 1 to November 11. It is cured up to three years (at least two before it can be sold), sometimes coated with a mixture of dirt and oil. The crust becomes so hard that to test it, it must be hit with a special hammer and listened to rather than cut and tested. It's pale yellow, slightly salty, but mellow and tangy. *Grana Padano* is an almost identical cheese, made on the north side of the River Po. It's not as strictly policed, so it's not quite as reliable as Parmigiano.

"If you need Parmesan just for cooking," the cheese staff recommends, "buy domestic. It's about a third the price of the imported." Some chefs disagree vehemently, claiming you certainly can tell the difference. It's all a matter of taste. Imported Parmesan is easy to identify at the cheese counter, however. The rind is etched with the words "Parmigiano Reggiano" in little dots, and part of the rind is always on every piece.

The Italians call all cheese made from sheep's milk *pecorino*. These cheeses are grainy and hard, with a sharp, biting taste. They are aged for almost a year and usually are used for grating. *Pecorino Romano* is the oldest and best-known version, still made from a recipe recorded in the first century A.D. Most good Italian cooks combine Pecorino and Parmigiano in cooking—Pecorino is sharper and more powdery when grated, and it gives the milder Parmigiano a nice boost.

MAMA MIA'S MOZZARELLA IN CARROZZA

4 slices Mozzarella
8 slices fresh Italian Bread, about ½ inch thick
2 eggs, lightly beaten
4 tablespoons olive oil
4 tablespoons butter

ANCHOVY SAUCES:
4 tablespoons olive oil
4 tablespoons unsalted butter
10 cloves garlic, coarsely chopped
2 2-ounce cans anchovies

Put each slice of mozzarella between 2 slices of bread. Dip in egg, and set aside.

In a large skillet, heat about ¼ inch olive oil. Melt butter in oil. Sauté sandwiches in this mixture until they are golden brown on both sides, and cheese begins to ooze out.

Meanwhile, make Anchovy Sauce: In saucepan, heat oil and butter. Add garlic and anchovies; cook until anchovies are dissolved and garlic is lightly golden.

Serve sandwiches hot, with hot Anchovy Sauce.

Serves 4.

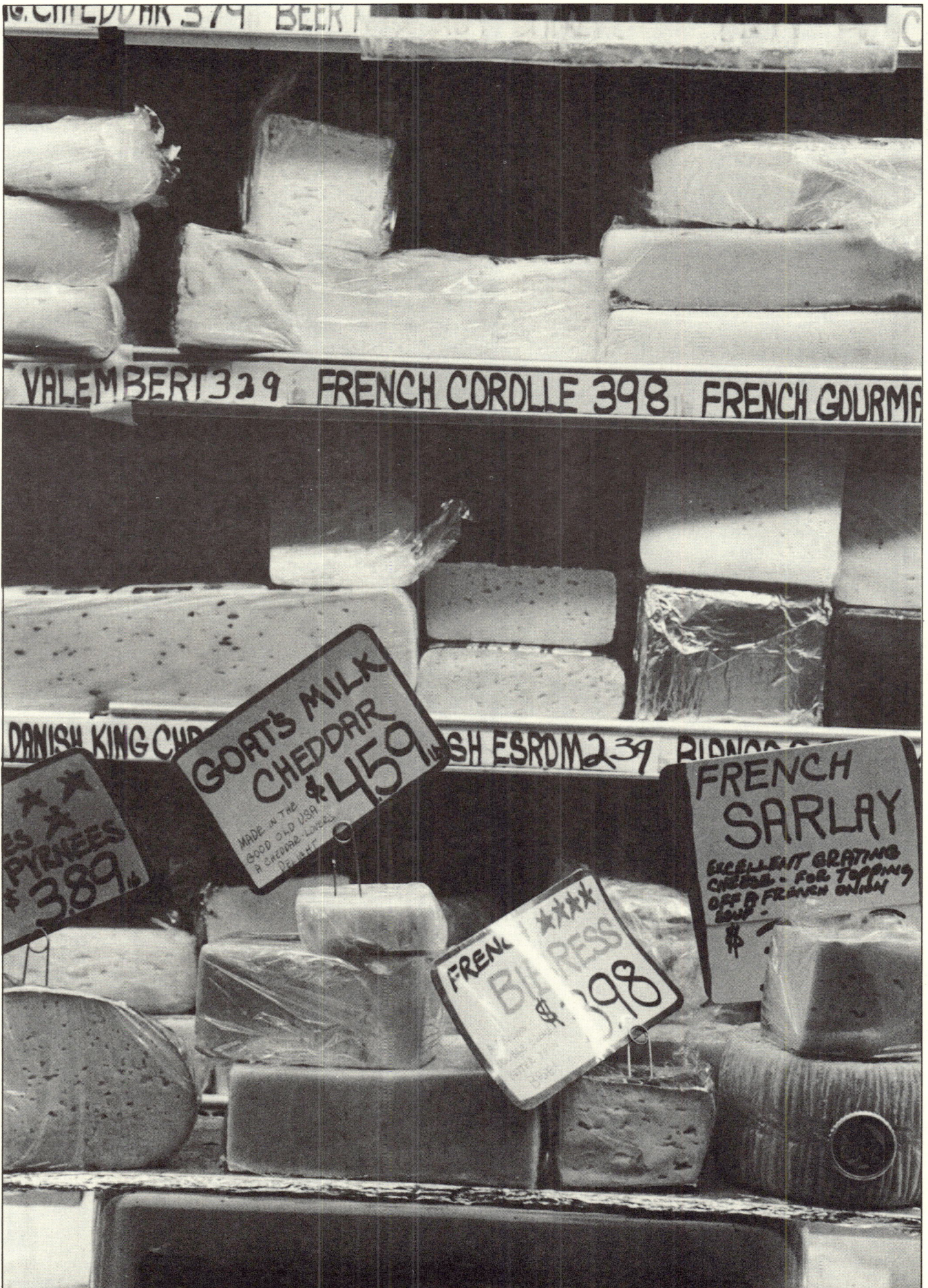

©Burt Glinn/Magnum

BLINTZES

Nothing but Jewish crêpes, filled with cheese, but oh, so good.

Serve them hot, with cold, fresh sour cream.

BATTER:
2 eggs
1 cup water
¼ teaspoon salt
1 cup sifted all-purpose flour
Unsalted butter or margarine

FILLING:
½ pound farmer's cheese
1 egg yolk
3 tablespoons sugar
½ teaspoon vanilla extract

Make Batter: Beat eggs and water together. Add salt and flour, and mix well. It will be thin, but don't worry.

Grease well with butter the bottom of a 7-inch skillet; heat until it sizzles. Pour about 2 tablespoons batter into pan, and swirl so bottom is covered evenly. Cook about 1 to 2 minutes, and slide blintz onto plate. Repeat until all batter is used—you should have 12 blintzes.

Make fillings: Mix all ingredients. Put about 2 tablespoons in middle of uncooked side of blintz; roll up, and tuck in ends. Repeat until all blintzes are filled.

Sauté in butter in skillet until golden brown on all sides.
Makes 12 blintzes.

Ricotta is technically not a cheese at all, since it isn't made from curds, but from whey left from making some other cheese—in Italy, usually provolone (in this country, ricotta is made from whole or skim milk and is made from curds). It's a fresh cheese, white, smooth and creamy, bland and soft. At Zabar's, it's sold two ways: freshly scooped to your liking from a large bucket or slightly dried and firm, for slicing or grating. It is not, Italian cooks emphasize, interchangeable with cottage cheese.

The type of cheese known in Italy as *formaggio di pasta filata*—cheese with an elastic curd that's kneaded or drawn—is usually shaped or sculpted as the last step before it's ripened. *Provolone* is the best example. You'll recognize it immediately, as it's the large, round cheese hanging from the rafters. No respectable cheese seller, especially not Zabar's, is ever without his gently swinging provolones, smoked or plain. The cheese can be sweet to sharp, depending on how long it was aged, and is always present on any authentic antipasto platter. It's particularly good with sausages or with fresh pears at the end of a meal.

Caciocavallo, another *pasta filata*, literally means horse cheese or cheese on a horse, probably because early Roman cheese-makers shaped their creations like a horse's head or sometimes braided them and hung them in pairs over a pole, "on horseback." Caciocavallo may even, at one time, have been made of mare's milk, but no longer. It's slightly salty, but with age it has a more pronounced, spicy, almost smoky taste, whether or not it's been smoked. Usually, it's shaped like a gourd and hangs beside the provolone.

What's a pizza without *mozzarella*? Not much. But mozzarella in this country has little or no resemblance to the real Italian version, sometimes still made with buffalo's milk, as it used to be. American mozzarella tends to be rubbery and tasteless, not fit for much else except pizza, veal parmesan, and other dishes on which it's melted. In Italy, however, fresh mozzarella is eaten while it's still dripping from its holding bath, creamy and sweet, accompanied by ripe, juicy tomatoes, anchovies, and a little salt and pepper.

Zabar's has a smoked mozzarella and a mozzarella laced with pancetta or prosciutto. These are particularly nice additions to omelets, and they melt beautifully. Their fresh whole-milk mozzarella is a delicious treat.

Italy, naturally, has many other cheeses, including *bel paese* and *fontina*. The first is a semisoft cheese, creamy, mild, and sweet; nice for dessert with fruit

JUDY'S CHEESECAKE

2½ pounds cream cheese, softened
1 ¾ cups sugar
3 tablespoons flour
5 eggs plus 2 yolks
1 teaspoon vanilla
¼ cup heavy cream

Preheat oven to 450°F.

Combine softened cream cheese with sugar and flour; beat until smooth and creamy. Add eggs and yolks, one at a time, until all used up; add vanilla and cream. Beat until smooth.

Pour into a greased 9-inch springform pan and bake at 450°F for 10 minutes. Lower heat to 250°F and continue baking for 1 hour longer. Remove from oven and let cool. Refrigerate for several hours before serving. (Warm cheesecake is terrible.)
Serves 10 to 12.

and light white wine. Imported bel paese always has a map of Italy on its wrapping; the American version has a map of North America.

Fontina is considered by some to be one of the world's greatest cheeses. It has a slightly nutty, sweet flavor, delicate and gentle, and a smooth, resilient texture; it's soft and giving, but sliceable. It is such an important cheese in Italy that its name is protected by law and reserved for cheese made from the raw milk of the Valle d'Aosta, in the Piedmont mountains.

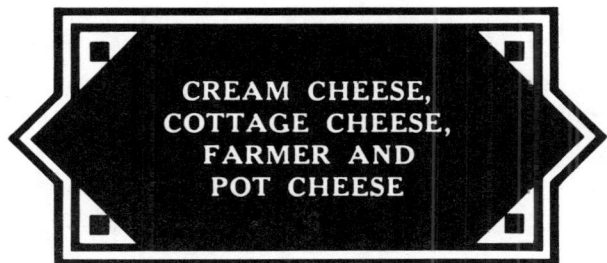

CREAM CHEESE, COTTAGE CHEESE, FARMER AND POT CHEESE

Almost universally, fresh, uncured cheeses are described as tasting like something else: milk, cream, freshly cut grass, a summer's morning. Also, they are rarely eaten alone, but usually are mixed with or garnished by vegetables, fruits, herbs, spices, even other cheeses.

Cream cheese is made of milk and cream. It's soft and spreadable and has a slightly sour, tangy taste. It's best known for being something you put on a bagel; however, it is also the basic ingredient in stupendously flaky pastry, essential to good cheesecake, and a boon companion to scrambled eggs. *Neufchâtel*, American-style, is nothing more than cream cheese with less fat. (French Neufchâtel is ripened for three to four weeks and has a fresher, cleaner taste than the domestic product.)

Petite Suisse is French cream cheese, less salty and not quite as sour as the American version. It got its name because a Swiss peasant working on a French farm suggested adding cream, as was done at his home, to fresh cheese being made.

Of all the fresh cheeses, *cottage cheese* is definitely the most popular. It's soft, creamy, slightly acidy; cream was added to the curds for smoothness. (To be called "creamed cottage cheese," it must have at least four percent butterfat.) It comes in two versions: large curd (also called "country" or "California" style) and small curd ("old-fashioned" style); there's no difference in taste. It's low in calories (120 per half-cup for regular; 80 for low-fat), low in cholesterol, high in protein and calcium. New Yorkers alone eat six pounds of it per person a year. Most

PETIT CHEVRE
DE LEZAY

A CREAMY GOAT CHEESE
WITH THE TEXTURE OF
A BRIE.

229

FRENCH COULOMMIER lb 350

often they eat it mixed with raw vegetables and sour cream, with noodles, in blintzes, or on berries.

Pot cheese is similar, but has larger curds than even large-curd cottage cheese, and skim milk, rather than cream, was added to it. It also has less salt and is a little drier than cottage cheese.

Farmer's cheese is made from whole milk and pressed into bricks or loaves. Because it's so compact, it's very filling and you tend to eat less.

At Zabar's, farmer's cheese is very special. It's studded with strawberries or blueberries or raisins and nuts and baked until it's crusty on top. It's like cheesecake without the cake.

THE FRENCH CRÈMES

"French double and triple crèmes are very, very rich, with sixty to seventy-five percent butterfat," Harvey Pearlman says. "The best ones, like *Brillat Savarin, Segala, L'Explorateur, Caprice de Dieux,* and *Fontainebleau,* taste like pure butter."

Crèmes are sinfully luxurious, soft, almost whipped, and utterly delicious. Double crèmes contain at least 60 percent butterfat and are ripened for 2 weeks or more; triple crèmes have 75 percent butterfat, and are ripened for at least 3 weeks. They may be plain or flavored with herbs, spices, garlic, crushed peppercorns, scallions, nuts, raisins, or wine. They are best known by their brand names, such as *Boursin* and *Boursault.* Because they are so rich and laden with heavy cream, they should be served instead of dessert, with plain crackers and good, hot coffee or perhaps a slightly sweet wine. For a totally self-indulgent luncheon treat, try Segala or L'Explorateur on thinly sliced black bread, with fresh strawberries or a sweet, ripe pear on the side.

ZABAR'S OWN

Zabar's may have the largest cheese department anywhere in the country, and some of the finest offerings are made right in its own kitchen.

"Our *Hungarian Liptauer,*" Harvey Pearlman discloses, "is made from our best cream cheese, a lot of paprika, anchovies, and a few secrets. It's very spicy and very spreadable." It's also the perfect illustration of the fact that cheese spreads can be far more exciting and wonderful than Cheddar mixed with pistachio nuts.

The *bacon-horseradish combination* is another

RICOTTA PANCAKES

These are nice for breakfast or as dessert. They are also good with jam or jelly instead of the confectioners' sugar.

½ pound ricotta cheese
2 tablespoons all-purpose flour
2 eggs
Dash salt
2 tablespoons granulated sugar
Butter
Confectioners' sugar

Mix cheese with flour, eggs, salt, and granulated sugar. If mixture is too thin to shape into pancakes, add a bit more flour. Shape into flat, oval cakes.

Heat griddle or heavy skillet. Add some butter, and cook pancakes until golden brown on both sides. Add more butter as necessary.

Serve sprinkled with confectioners' sugar.
Serves 2 to 4.

cheese spread that is tantalizing and tangy. Its distinctive aroma pervades the cheese department, because of the pungent horseradish that's mixed with cream cheese and the best bacon the deli has to offer. It's second in popularity only to Zabar's *scallion cream cheese*—which may have other rivals to contend with: *lox and cream cheese, cream-cheese-and-caviar spread à la Boursin* (Zabar's swirls a good-quality pasteurized caviar through plain cream cheese), *and double-creme Roquefort.*

Cottage cheese with herbs and garlic is another homemade delight. *Spiced cream cheese* has a loyal band of followers. Both are superb as a dip or a schmear. *Fromage Blanc* has a tangy, almost sour taste.

One other Zabar's specialty—butter flown in from Isigny-sur-Mer, on the Normandy coast. Its high butterfat content makes it the purest, freshest-tasting, buttery butter you could ever hope to taste.

THINK THIN

"Don't think cheese is unhealthy or even always fattening," says Harvey Pearlman. "We have a big selection of low-cholesterol and low-salt and low-fat cheeses. They're very big with our health-conscious customers, even when they're not dieting."

BOBBIE'S PASTA WITH FOUR CHEESES

This is very rich, as well as scrumptious and very fattening. Serve it with a green salad, hot bread, and a full-bodied red wine.

1 pound spaghetti
½ pound sweet butter
Freshly ground black pepper, to taste
¼ pound fontina, diced
¼ pound Gorgonzola or Roquefort, crumbled
¼ pound provolone or bel paese, diced
½ cup grated Parmesan mixed with 4 tablespoons grated Romano, if desired
1 cup heavy cream (optional)

In a large kettle, cook spaghetti in plenty of boiling water until *al dente*. Drain, and set aside.

In a large, heavy saucepan, melt butter; add pepper, fontina, Gorgonzola or Roquefort, and provolone or bel paese. Heat, stirring, until melted. Add Parmesan and Romano, stirring until well blended. Add cream, and heat thoroughly, but do not let boil.

Transfer spaghetti to serving bowl, and pour cream mixture over.
Serves 4.

MRS. BREAKSTONE'S RUGGELACH

CREAM CHEESE PASTRY:
¼ pound unsalted butter
¼ pound cream cheese, softened
1 cup sifted flour

FILLING:
½ cup (¼ pound) walnuts, finely chopped
1 cup sugar
1 teaspoon cinnamon
½ cup raisins

Preheat oven to 350°F.

Cream butter, cream cheese, and flour together. Form into a ball and freeze for at least 1 hour. When ready to use, cut the ball into quarters, and roll out one quarter at a time, keeping the rest in the freezer.

Roll the dough into a rectangle and cut into small triangles. Mix the filling ingredients together and put about ½ to 1 teaspoon of filling in the center of each triangle. Start at wide edge and roll tightly until the small point is at the top; bend into crescent shape.

Place on ungreased cookie sheet and bake about 20 minutes, until golden brown.
Makes about 2 dozen, depending on how big they are.

Swiss Chris and *Swiss Lorraine* are part-skim-milk cheeses with no added salt. *Cholesterol- and salt-free Goudas* and *low-sodium Cheddar* are also perfect for those on salt-restricted diets.

For calorie counters, *Saint Otho* from Switzerland has the lowest fat content of any natural cheese; *Appenzeller Rasskase* is also relatively dietetic. There's a *low-cholesterol cheese* (Chol-Free) made with nonfat milk, vegetable oil, lactic-acid culture, and rennet, and even a *yogurt cheese* that tastes great and is low in fat and cholesterol.

Harvey has an unusual test for his doubting customers: He offers them three cheeses—salt-free, low-salt, and regular—and asks them to identify which is which. Most of them can't.

AND CRACKERS

Crackers can do a lot of things. They can hold caviar, pâté, or chopped liver. Be dipped into delectable mixtures and popped into the mouth. Temptingly encircle a bowl of steaming chili. They can be sweet or not, crunchy or soft, simple or complex, round, square, triangular, big or small. But best of all, crackers go with cheese as if they were truly made for each other.

Zabar's has crackers for any occasion—and any cheese—an absolutely huge assortment of the very best packaged goods from all over: France, Germany, Scandinavia, England, Italy, Canada, and the United States. From Pepperidge Farm to Carr's, there are *crackers for cheese, digestives, flatbreads, crispbreads,* thinly sliced *black breads* crunchy with grain and heavy with the aroma of molasses, even *animal crackers* for the young at heart. The variety could drive even the inveterate muncher crackers.

Plain and simple crackers are particularly good with crèmes, Brie, Camembert, and all the spreadable cheeses. Toasts, such as *Melba,* of course, square or round; Grielles from France and Jos. Pobel's British crackers are perfect. *Water biscuits* are suitable for almost any kind of cheese. Choose from Carr's, in tins or boxes; Bent's; Jacob's; Belin; Oulevey; Verkade; and Pelletier, the best of the plain crackers. The big difference among them is shape and thickness. A cracker, after all, is only flour, baking soda, water, and salt. Some may be thicker and crisper than others, rounder or squarer, but it is really a matter of individual preference. What you don't want, and won't get with any of these, is a flavor to compete with the cheese. Crackers are merely texture—and the best way of getting cheese into your mouth.

With hard cheese, you might like a little more zing, and Zabar's has such things, too. From Scandinavia there's an assortment of flatbreads and crispbreads, really crackers, flavored with rye or caraway. *Bremner Wafers*, in packages or tins, come in several flavors, and Carr's offers an assortment of crackers for cheese and *wheat-meal biscuits*, sweet and wheaty, almost like a cookie. Jacob's also has assorted crackers, plus some made with heavy, sweet cream instead of water. For an unusual twist, you might try Oriental-style *rice crackers* or *sesame crackers*. They're light, nutty, and nice with a mild, unassuming cheese such as Swedish Ambrosia.

Bread sticks sprinkled with sesame seeds are good to wrap slices of Swiss cheese around; and Weston's Stoned Wheat Thins are crunchy, grainy crackers that go extremely well with a firm slicing cheese such as Jarlsberg.

If you are serving several kinds of cheese, it's important to have several kinds of cracker, choosing the types you believe go best with the varieties of cheese on the board.

I HAD A LITTLE LIST

There are 1,200 cheeses in the world with specific names—and countless others known only to the makers and their friends. France alone has over 400. Zabar's has almost as many. The following is only a partial list.

BLUE CHEESES

BLUE CASTELLO: (Denmark) Creamy blue of the triple-crème type.

DANABLU: (Denmark) Semisoft, strong, sometimes salty; Danish answer to Roquefort.

GORGONZOLA: (Italy) Strong, crumbly, yet still soft and creamy.

LADY BIRD BLUE: (Denmark) Creamy double-cream blue.

NORMANA: (Norway) Norwegian Roquefort.

PIPO CRÈME: (France) Delicate double-cream blue.

SAGA: (Denmark) A combination of *bleu* and *Brie*.

STILTON: (England) Very strong and intense, moist, soft, crumbly.

GRATING CHEESES

ASIAGO: (Italy) Sharp and salty; must be aged at least a year to be gratable; can be substituted for parmigiano.

LOCATELLI ROMANO: (Italy) Hard and tangy.

PARMESAN: (Argentina; domestic) Good grating cheese.

PARMIGIANO REGGIANO: (Italy) Hard and sharp.

PECORINO ROMANO: (Italy) Made from sheep's milk; tangy.

SAPSAGO: (Switzerland) Tangy, spicy, green, and very hard. For grating and flavoring only.

MILD CHEESES

AMBROSIA: (Sweden) Rich, fat; with a mild, smooth taste, buttery paste.

BEAUMONT: (France) Creamy, mild; nice with berries.

BEL PAESE: (Italy) Semisoft; sweet, mild taste.

CHIBERTA: (France) Semisoft, mild and simple; smells earthy, but has a clean taste.

DANBO: (Denmark) Semihard, mild and buttery; good as lunch rather than dessert cheese.

EDAM: (Holland) Firm, light, bland.

ESROM: (Denmark) Similar to Port-Salut, sweeter and milder, with small holes. Gets more pungent with age.

FONTINA: (Denmark, Sweden) Other versions of the Italian original, but really no resemblance whatsoever.

FONTINA: (Italy) Buttery, resilient, semisoft cheese, sweet and delicate.

GOUDA: (Holland) Firm, clean-tasting, bland, and reliable.

GOUDA, AGED: (Holland) A farmhouse rather than a factory cheese; firm, sharp, well-defined, and slightly salty.

HARVARTI: (Denmark) Soft, creamy, slightly acid, but generally clean, mild taste. Can be sharp when aged.

MARIBO: (Denmark) Fresh-tasting, with caraway seeds, sometimes called "King Christian IX."

MIMOLETTE: (France) Bland and buttery, similar to Edam and Gouda.

MORBIER: (France) Semisoft cheese, made in two halves joined together with a streak of ash (which doesn't affect the taste). Mild and buttery; good for snacks.

MUENSTER: (U.S.) Semisoft natural cheese that ranges from bland to tasteless. (Plain, caraway, seeds, sweet.)

MÜNSTER: (France) Soft, tangy, delicately rich; usually strong by sale time.

PONT L'ÉVÊQUE: (France) Varies from mild to strong.

PORT DU SALUT: (France) Mild and creamy, with nice tang.

REBLOCHON: (France) Semisoft, creamy, slightly nutty flavor.

ST. ALBRAY: (France) Semisoft, sweet, anytime cheese, "the greatest thing to come out of France in a long time," according to Harvey.

ST. MARCELLIN: (France) Mild and creamy, wrapped in chestnut leaves. At one time was part goat's milk; now all cow's.

ST. NECTAIRE: (France) Smooth and bland, with a nutty taste.

ST. PAULIN: (France) Semisoft, tangy, can be slightly sourish.

SAMSOE: (Denmark) Buttery and mild, slightly sweet and nutty.

TALEGGIO: (Italy) Semisoft, creamy, and slightly tart; especially nice for dessert.

TILSIT: (Denmark, Germany) Mild, with slight sharpness; good with dark bread and dark beer.

TOMME DE SAVOIE: (France) Mild and nutty.

VALEMBERT: (France) Mild and smooth, tastes faintly like Brie but firmer.

CHEDDARS AND CHEDDAR TYPES

CAERPHILLY: (Wales) Mild, but distinct buttermilk taste, slightly acidy and salty.

CANTAL: (France) Looks and smells like Cheddar, but has a nutty, slightly sweet flavor. The oldest French cheese.

CHEDAR. (Scotland) Tangy flavor.

CHEDDAR: (Canada) Firm, usually well-aged and nicely sharp.

CHEDDAR: (England) Tangy and sharp, nice, mellow taste. Aged, with a good, sharp flavor.

CHEDDAR: (U.S.) Bland to rich, depending on aging; taste can vary dramatically.

CHESHIRE: (England) Firm, mild and mellow, more crumbly than Cheddar.

COLBY: (U.S.) Cheddarlike, but softer, moister, more-open texture.

DOUBLE GLOUCESTER: (England) Very firm, mellow and fresh-tasting.

DUNLOP: (Scotland) Very mild Cheddar.

GOAT'S-MILK CHEDDAR: (U.S.) Very pungent and sharp.

MONTEREY JACK: (U.S.) Mild, sweet, semisoft.

RAW MILK CHEDDAR: (U.S.) Mild and crumbly.

SALT-FREE CHEDDAR: (U.S.) Mild, nice flavor.

VERMONT CHEDDAR: (U.S.) Firm, with a slightly sharp flavor.

WENSLEYDALE: (England) Semisoft, mild and tangy Cheddar type.

SWISS-TYPE CHEESES

APPENZELLER: (Switzerland) Firm, mild to sharp and strong.

BEAUFORT: (France) Faintly salty, few small eyes, very rich taste.

EMMENTALER: (Switzerland) Firm, nutty taste, the real Swiss cheese.

GRUYÈRE: (Switzerland) Varies from mild to sharp—totally different taste than Emmentaler.

JARLSBERG: (Norway) Firm, from mild to nutty taste.

RACLETTE: (Switzerland) Similar to Gruyère; melting cheese.

"SWISS" CHEESE: (Austria, Denmark, Finland, Holland, etc.) Imitations of Emmentaler; can be very good.

WESTBERG: (Holland) Copy of Norwegian Jarlsberg, but much milder and softer.

FRESH CHEESES

COTTAGE CHEESE: (U.S.) Plain, or with herbs or garlic.

CREAM CHEESE: (U.S.) Soft; sourish tang; plain, or with herbs and garlic, caviar, scallions, or chives; natural, no gum.

FARMER'S CHEESE: (U.S.) Firm, fresh cheese, pressed into loaves. Also available baked with fruits, nuts, and scallions.

MOZZARELLA: (Italy; U.S.) Soft, mild, fresh; great melter.

PETITE SUISSE: (France) French version of cream cheese; sweeter, slightly aged.

RICOTTA: (U.S.) Smooth, creamy, fresh, bland cheese, used for lasagna, cheesecake, etc.

BRIE AND CAMEMBERT TYPES

BEL BRESSAN: (France) Soft, rich, very much like Brie.

BRIE DE COULOMMIERS: (France) Soft, mild-tasting white mould cheese; high butterfat.

BRIE DE MEAUX: (France) "The jewel of the Ile-de-France."

CAMEMBERT: (France) Soft-ripened, spreadable; can be mild or tangy.

CHAOURCE: (France) Mild, soft-ripened, almost nutty flavor; can be pungent and/or salty.

DOUBLE AND TRIPLE CRÈMES

BOURSAULT: (France) Triple crème, very rich, slightly tangy.

BOURSIN: (France) Triple crème, sometimes flavored with herbs and garlic or peppercorns.

CREMA DANIA: (Denmark) Double, almost triple crème.

FONTAINEBLEAU: (France) Triple crème, rich and delicious.

L'EXPLORATEUR: (France) Triple crème; fresh, exquisite cheese.

ST. ANDRÉ: (France) Triple crème, fresh and mild.

SHEEP'S-MILK CHEESES

BRINDZA: (U.S.) Strong, salty, similar to Feta.

FETA: (Greece) Crumbly, moist, salty-sourish.

KASHKAVAL: (Czechoslovakia) Spicy taste, firm texture.

KASSERI: (Greece) Strong taste, salty; good for melting.

PECORINO ROMANO: (Italy) Sharp and tangy; perfect grating cheese.

ROQUEFORT: (France) The king of the sheep's-milk cheeses; strong, sharp flavor, blue-veined.

SARDO: (Argentina) Hard cheese. For grating.

GOAT'S-MILK CHEESES

BOUCHERON: (France) Log-shaped; fairly mild; fresh.

CABICHOU: (France) Cylinder-shaped; sharp-tasting; peppery and smelly.

COROLLE: (France) Soft and creamy, soft-ripened cheese.

LEZAY: (France) Brand name for mild goat cheese; comes in pyramids, logs, plain or covered with cinders.

MONTRACHET: (France) Soft, spreadable, quite mild; comes in cups. Available also in olive oil with pepper, rosemary, or *herbes de provence*.

OLIVE GOAT CHEESE: (France) Studded with pimiento-filled green olives.

PEPPER GOAT CHEESE: (France) Covered in crushed peppercorns.

SALT-FREE AND FAT-FREE CHEESES

CHOLESTEROL-FREE: (U.S.) Made with nonfat dry milk.

LORRAINE SWISS: (U.S.) Part skim-milk cheese, low in salt and butterfat (20%; compared to 40% for regular cheese).

MAGRELAIT: (France) Mild, low-fat cheese.

MONVELAY ALLEGE: (France) Mild, semisoft cheese.

ST. OTHO: (Switzerland) Very-low-fat content.

SALT-FREE CHEDDAR: (U.S.) Still tasty, but no added salt.

SALT-FREE GOUDA: (Holland) For sodium-restricted diets.

SWISS CHRIS: (Switzerland) Low-fat content, about 25%.

PROCESSED CHEESES

GOURMANDISE: (France) Semisoft; flavored with walnuts or kirsch.

LA GRAPPE: (France) Covered with grape seeds.

MARGOTIN: (France) Semisoft; covered with crushed peppercorns or garlic.

RAMBOL: (France) Coated with walnuts or crushed peppercorns.

REYBIER: (France) Coated with walnuts or pistachio nuts.

RONDELE: (France) Spiced with garlic and herbs.

SPICY CHEESES

BROTHER BASIL: (Germany) Natural smoked cheese; quite heavy smoke flavor.

LEYDEN: (Holland) Harsh, always spiced with cumin and caraway.

LIVAROT: (France) Strong, soft cheese.

MAROILLES: (France) Strong, tangy, and smelly.

NOKKELOST: (Norway) Firm; spiced with caraway and cumin.

POMPADOR: (Holland) A Gouda with herbs.

SAPSAGO: (Switzerland) Hard green cheese, spicy, good for grating.

MISCELLANEOUS CHEESES

FROPAIN DE MAGES: (France) Semisoft; shaped like braided bread. Mild taste, similar to Port du Salut.

GAPERON: (France) Soft-ripened; moldy rind; made with buttermilk; flavored with garlic.

GJETOST: (Norway) Hard whey cheese, sweet-tasting.

"Maybe it's a little crowded. You take your life in your hands. Nobody leaves their line. They call you over. 'Hey, Mel Brooks, come here and bring a pencil and paper. I want your autograph.' Jews never get off their lines, so I always wind up at the end of someone else's line.

"Zabar's is a good place if you're not a celebrity; otherwise, you can't stay on your line.

"But seriously, I love their crazy black bread with the raisins and the Jamaica Blue Mountain coffee. All their stuff is fabulous, and it's the only place in the world that has it."

Mel Brooks

Coffee. It's a Zabar's special, and coffee fanatics come from all over just for it. Shiny brown beans, fresh-roasted, whole, or ground any way you like them. Surrounding them, brewers and equipment to satisfy every need and every desire.

The kids who sell it try to be experts. They'll sell you not only the coffee and the pot, but the cup as well, if you like, and add a detailed lecture on how to brew the coffee.

Of all Zabar's customers, the coffee buyers are the most single-minded, barreling straight to the back of the store, zeroing in on the coffee department, never pausing to look right or left. And if they can't get there in person, they'll have coffee mailed to them. That's devotion.

SAUL ZABAR, COFFEE MAVEN

So many millions of pounds of assorted coffee are shipped to the United States every year that choosing among them has become quite an art. The man who does it for Zabar's is Saul Zabar, and to put it mildly, he is zealous. Just about the only people he doesn't drive crazy with his quest for perfection are his customers.

Saul has been handling bean coffee since he was a kid working behind the counter in one of his father's supermarkets. When Zabar père plied his trade on Broadway in the 1940s, his green coffee was bought from suppliers, sent out to be roasted, and, it was hoped, returned to the store without mishap. Sometimes already roasted coffee was bought from brokers. The control was totally out of Zabar's hands, in any case.

THE GREEN BEAN

Actually, Saul's involvement with coffee starts well before it gets to his roaster. Coffee is grown on plantations or small holdings or estates, as big as two million trees or as small as 500. The beans are harvested, processed, bagged, and shipped in their green state to importers. Most bean coffee retailers buy roasted coffee without ever seeing or sampling the beans. Saul doesn't. He obtains small green samples to roast, cup, and taste. Then he makes a commitment for a specific lot of usually 125-250 bags, weighing 132-150 pounds each.

When a shipment is accepted, the bags of coffee are stored. At any given moment, Zabar's could have as much as 75,000 to 100,000 pounds of green coffee in the warehouse. Green coffee will retain its character and quality unroasted from four months to a year, depending on the coffee.

Because Zabar's maintains a healthy reserve, it was able to hold its coffee prices down during the recent

MAIL ON WEDNESDAYS!

Saul Zabar roasts only as much coffee as he needs for a week, to sell at the store and to fill mail-order requests.

All the coffee that is shipped is sent out on Wednesday, less than 24 hours after being roasted. The reason is this: Ship on Wednesday, the coffee usually reaches its destination by Friday, in time for a weekend of good coffee drinking.

Unequivocally, the coffee at Zabar's ranges from merely excellent to absolutely stupendous. Which is why nearly 1,000 people each month pay an extra 50 cents a pound, for minimum five-pound lots, to have coffee shipped to them all over the United States.

coffee shortage of 1976–78. While frost and storms were driving up the wholesale costs, and coffee sellers all over the country were hoisting their prices to match, Zabar's, according to Murray Klein, was not only selling its coffee for less than the competition in New York, but encouraging customers to switch to tea and support the nationwide coffee boycott.

SAMPLING, CUPPING, AND TASTING

With a lance-like trier in hand, Saul attacks a random sampling of beans from his stock. He pokes his trier into the top, middle, and bottom of several bags, to make sure that they are uniform. He then roasts beans in quarter-pound batches in a sample roaster in production.

He watches constantly; all his roasting is done by eye in six-hundred batch roasters. One fine day, with a precious shipment of Jamaica Blue Mountain in the roaster, a few seconds too many went by between color checks, and the beans were too dark for regular roast. Saul had to continue roasting until the priceless beans darkened to the Italian stage. Zabar's customers were treated to very special cups of espresso from that batch.

Once the right color is reached, the coffee is cooled.

It is ground and measured by weight into waiting glass cups, and boiling water is poured over it. Saul prefers to taste the coffee at moderate temperatures, when maximum flavor appears. "But good coffee will have an interesting taste at every temperature," he says, "from hot to cold."

The cups are placed on a revolving table. First, Saul checks the aroma.

Then comes the actual tasting. Saul sucks the coffee from a spoon, mixing it with as much air as possible, so that it will spray over his tongue and immediately spits it out. Then on to the next cup, and the next, until all 10 or 12 samples have been tasted. Each cupful is tasted again, to see what the coffee is like when it has cooled even further. The purpose of this whole process, known as cupping, is to evaluate a given coffee on three levels: acidity, body, and roast level.

Acidity is a positive and much-prized quality, and when missing, makes a coffee dull. Fine Kenyan and Tanzanian coffees are renowned for their acidity.

Body is just what it sounds like: the weight or heaviness of the brew.

Only after Saul has completed his sampling and approved the roast and beans, is the coffee shipped to Zabar's. Saul does all the roasting personally. The big roasters hold 600 pounds of beans. Zabar's sells about 5,000 pounds of coffee a week. To get that much, Saul actually has to roast about 7,000 pounds because 16 to 24 percent is lost through shrinkage. He does at least 12 to 14 roasts a week.

Saul usually works with two roasting machines at a time. It takes 12 to 15 minutes to roast a full load, so with filling and emptying time, he can do three roasts an hour. Working with two machines also means that he can make blends of some coffees, one batch a little light, one a little darker, to get exactly the mix he wants.

From the roaster, the coffee is sent into cooling cars, where air is circulated to cool the beans. It's then sent down a chute into waiting bags, and after sampling and approval, is sealed, and loaded onto a truck pointed toward Broadway and 80th Street.

A BRIEF HISTORY OF COFFEE

The coffee tree still grows wild in Ethiopia, as it has for thousands of years. The fantastic and fabulous legends about its discovery are as varied as coffee itself.

By far, the most oft-repeated tale is about an Ethiopian goatherd who munched some red berries growing on a hillside after he noticed how frolicsome they made his goats. He felt pretty good himself. He gave some berries to the head of a nearby monastery, who boiled them into a potent brew and gave it to his monks, to

FROM QAHWAH TO COFFEE

The Arabs of the sixth century called it *qahwah*, that which gives strength. The same word was used for wine, a drink forbidden by Muhammad to his followers, and *qahwah* (coffee) became known as "the Arab's wine."

Over the years, the corruption of *qahwah* became *café* in French and Spanish, *caffè* in Italian, *kafeo* in Greek, *kahve* in Turkish, *khavi* and *koffie* in Finnish and Dutch, respectively. In English, the word went through some rather strange changes before settling down to *coffee* around 1700. In 1598, the English called it *chaoua*, then *cahoa* and *cahue* over the next 50 years, ending with first *coffey* and finally *coffee*.

help keep them awake during long religious services. News of the drink traveled fast and far, and in a short time, monks all over the country were sipping the bitter potion—and praying more and longer because of it.

Word of the powers of the legendary drink spread throughout the Arab world like a fever. Dervishes drank a coffee brew during their exercises, to keep them whirling, and as they visited new religious centers, they offered the drink to their converts. Between the eleventh and sixteenth centuries, the introduction of coffee seemed to follow right on the heels of Islam.

The coffee the Arabs carried with them was always roasted. No green beans were permitted to leave the Arab world; no foreigners were ever allowed close enough to the coffee trees to pocket a few beans to take home.

But you can keep a secret only for so long. Some pilgrims managed to smuggle a few precious coffee beans to India and plant them there early in the seventeenth century, and eventually the Dutch, who already had been trading for roasted coffee with the Italians—who got it from the Turks—were able to plant coffee in their own hothouses in 1690. They carried seedlings to their colonies in Ceylon and Java in 1696, and within ten years, the first Javanese coffee crop had been harvested. The Dutch were generous with their coffee. They sent seedlings as gifts to their friends all over Europe, but only Louis XIV, who didn't even like coffee, managed to keep the plants alive.

As coffee spread, so did coffeehouses, rife, during the sixteenth, seventeenth, and eighteenth centuries, with radical and antireligious thought.

As early as 1511, Muslim coffeehouses were closed, burned, suppressed, and coffee was generally forbidden as against the laws of Islam. Alleged violators were beaten, tortured, or drowned.

Catholics called coffee the "invention of Satan" and tried to have the Pope ban it. Unfortunately, the Pope liked it, and he thought the cafés in Venice's Piazza San Marco were a splendid idea.

In 1689, the Café Procope, the first in an endless stream of French cafés, opened. It was a second home for the likes of Diderot, Beaumarchais, and Voltaire, who is said to have drunk 40 cups of coffee mixed with chocolate every day. During the French Revolution, one could find Marat, Robespierre, and Danton deep in conversation over coffee, and, in fact, the very speech that caused the citizens of Paris to storm the Bastille was made just outside the Café Foy.

Ironically, the British, now a nation of tea drinkers, probably drank more coffee in the late seventeenth and early eighteenth centuries than anyone else in the world. British coffeehouses were known as "penny universities," where for a penny, and two cents more for coffee and a newspaper, a man could sit and listen to distinguished conversation for hours.

Even in America, where coffeehouses were usually just inns or taverns that also sold coffee, political ideas were debated and exchanged, radical ideas were fomented, and men such as John Adams and Paul Revere set up the "headquarters of the American Revolution" over steaming mugs of coffee.

THE BREW THAT IS TRUE

PERCOLATED COFFEE

There's only one thing coffee aficionados seem to agree on: The worst possible way to make coffee is in

THERE'S AN AWFUL LOT OF COFFEE IN BRAZIL

There might not have been any coffee in Brazil had the Dutch and the French not had a boundary dispute over their common border in Guiana. Both were producing coffee, and a full-scale border war would have been a disaster. A Brazilian army colonel was chosen to arbitrate. Not only was he successful in settling the difference between the two rivals, but he charmed the wife of the French governor so completely that when he left, she gave him a huge bouquet of flowers, in the middle of which were hidden some coffee seedlings. He took his prize home to Brazil, and the rest is coffee history.

an *electric percolator*. What, you say? It's fast, easy, and instantly fills the room with the scintillating aroma of freshly made coffee.

Unfortunately, according to the experts, it doesn't make a *good* cup of coffee, and you'll not find a single electric percolator at Zabar's. Electric percolators keep sending boiling water over already saturated grinds for too long, so the result is overextracted coffee.

The same experts (Zabar's included) have kinder words for the *stove-top percolator*. It's more controllable, and with careful, conscientious, and unhurried attention, you can make good coffee in it.

If you must perk, do it right. Get the correct grind of coffee to begin with—regular or percolator. For each six ounces of water (the standard, recommended cup size for coffee, no matter how big the mug you drink from) use one standard coffee measure (two level tablespoons) of coffee.

Measure the water into the pot; bring it to the boil, and remove it from the heat. Put the coffee in the basket; put the basket in the pot; cover, and return to low heat, so it perks gently but steadily for six to eight minutes. No longer! Violent or extensive perking would make bitter, muddy coffee, not a stronger brew. Use a timer if you have to, or watch the clock.

THE DRIP METHOD

The standard, old-fashioned *drip coffeepot*—a bottom with a spout and a handle, a middle basket to hold the grinds, and a top to hold the water while it drips—is probably the easiest and most nearly foolproof way to make good coffee. Just be sure to measure the water correctly (six ounces per cup); use the correct grind (fine or drip); measure one coffee measure (two level tablespoons) per cup; have the water just at the boil when you pour it into the top. It will take four to six minutes for the water to drip through, so you might keep the pot on a hot plate or over very low heat while the coffee brews, to keep it hot.

FILTER-CONE COFFEE

The Melitta, Chemex, and Tricolator are the best-known *filter-cone coffeepots* (a variation on the drip pot), and all work the same way. This is the method Zabar's recommends; it makes the perfect cup of coffee.

The Chemex is an all-in-one glass pot, cone and bottom fused together, with a wooden band around the middle for easy handling. The Melitta and Tricolator have glass bottoms and plastic or ceramic cones to hold the paper filter. Use the standard measures of coffee (fine for Melitta and Tricolators, regular for Chemex) and water. Boiling water is poured over the grounds in the filter—a little at a time for Chemex, as much as the cones will hold for the others.

Don't pour all the water over the grounds at once—unless you want a foaming, bubbling, unevenly wetted mess. Pour half, with a circular motion; give it a quick zigzag stir with a spoon, to make sure all the grinds

IRISH COFFEE: Strong coffee, sugar, Irish whiskey, and whipped cream.

MEXICAN COFFEE: Strong coffee, chocolate syrup, whipped cream flavored with sugar, cinnamon, and nutmeg.

BRAZILIAN COFFEE: Dark-roasted coffee, made by putting 2 tablespoons of fine-ground coffee into a cloth strainer, holding it over the cup, and pouring 4 ounces of boiling water through it. Strong and rich, it's usually drunk sweetened, and called *cafezinho* in Brazil, *tinto* in Colombia, and *demitasse* elsewhere in Latin America.

BELGIAN COFFEE: Hot coffee poured over ½ cup of whipped cream, mixed with vanilla and a stiffly beaten egg white.

VIENNESE COFFEE: Hot coffee topped with *Schlagobers*, whipped cream made from the top of the milk when it is skimmed.

TURKISH COFFEE: Also Greek or Middle Eastern Coffee, made with very finely ground dark-roasted coffee, sugar and water, boiled till it foams, and served in tiny little cups.

DANISH COFFEE: Made with eggs, lemon peel, sugar, brandy or cognac, and extra-strength coffee.

CAFÉ BRÛLOT: A French treat, made by putting cognac, cinnamon sticks, cloves, sugar, chocolate syrup, orange and lemon peel into a chafing dish, igniting the cognac, and then adding double-strength black coffee. The whole thing is then strained into small cups.

SPANISH COFFEE: Extra-strong coffee with sugar, Cointreau, and grated orange peel.

HAWAIIAN COFFEE: An iced drink made with coffee, pineapple juice, sugar, and coffee ice cream.

CREOLE COFFEE: Dark roasted, finely ground coffee brewed with about 20—or up to 40—percent chicory, a plant that's related to the dandelion, and dried, roasted, and ground as a coffee substitute or stretcher. It's a New Orleans and French specialty, slightly bitter, almost peppery. Chicory has no caffeine, is cheaper than coffee, and adds lots of body, darkness, and flavor.

Flavor coffee with an ounce of your favorite liqueur: Anisette, crème de menthe, crème de cacao, Cointreau, Grand Marnier, Kahlua, brandy, cognac, even vanilla extract (only about 1 teaspoon). An ounce of tawny port or muscatel in a cup of cold, double-strength coffee, poured over cubes, slightly sweetened, and topped with a strip of orange peel is a delicious and refreshing summer drink.

CAFÉ ROYALE: Put a sugar cube in a teaspoon, fill with cognac, ignite, and drop into a cup of hot coffee.

CAFÉ VIENNOISE: Add a jigger of rum and a dollop of whipped cream per cup of coffee.

CAFÉ

are wet. Once this water has dripped through, add the rest, also with a circular motion. When that's down, the coffee is done. Remove filter and grinds, and pour.

This method produces superb coffee. It's quick and easy and can be done one cup at a time, too. Keep the pot on a hot plate or over low heat while it's brewing, so the coffee stays hot. Just before serving, give the coffee a quick stir, to distribute the flavor evenly.

If you swear you can't even boil water, then the *electric filter-drip coffee-maker* is for you. The method is basically the same as the filter-cone method, combined with two heating elements—one to get the water to the proper temperature and one to keep the coffee warm once it has dripped. All you have to do is measure the cold water and fine-grind coffee and push the On button. Even a child can do it.

The Bunn, Braun, and Wigomat electric filter-drip pots make excellent coffee. Zabar's sells all three, plus a variety of others. Unfortunately, some of the many models available—which Zabar's doesn't sell—are a waste of money. Some are no good unless you make a full pot; in others, the heated water drips smack down into the center of the grinds, leaving the rest barely damp. The Bunn and the Braun have several sprays that hit the grinds from all angles and wet them evenly. And the coffee is terrific.

A word of warning: No matter what the manufacturer says, always use the standard measures, as you would for any coffeemaker: two level tablespoons of coffee per six ounces of water.

OTHER METHODS

Using a *vacuum pot* requires a reasonable amount of coordination and manual dexterity; it's not for the jelly-fingered.

The regular-grind coffee is put in the top half of a two-part pot. Water is boiled in the lower bowl; then the upper bowl, with its filter and stem and holding the coffee, is put in place and twisted closed. Over low heat, the water in the bottom starts rising by steam pressure and wetting the grinds. After about a minute, when all the water is in the upper bowl, the whole thing is removed from the heat; this causes a vacuum in the bottom bowl, which pulls the coffee down through the filter. Actually, it's more difficult to describe than to do, but it is still a messy process, and one that requires precise timing and careful handling.

A bit easier, and picturesque, too, is the *plunger pot*. This is a tall cylinder, into which regular-grind coffee and water are measured. After the coffee has steeped for about four to five minutes, a plunger is pushed down into the cylinder, forcing the water through the grinds. You almost always get some grinds in your cup, but a lot of people seem to like coffee that way.

There are many ways to brew coffee without a coffee-pot. Probably one of the oldest methods is *open-pot*, or *camp coffee*. All you do is boil a measured amount of water in a pan, add the regular-grind coffee, and let it brew for four to five minutes. You can strain it or add a little cold water, or an egg shell to help settle the grinds. It takes a little practice to get it right, and the coffee can be pretty gritty toward the bottom of the cup; but this method is particularly handy if you happen to have only coffee, water, and a pot of some kind.

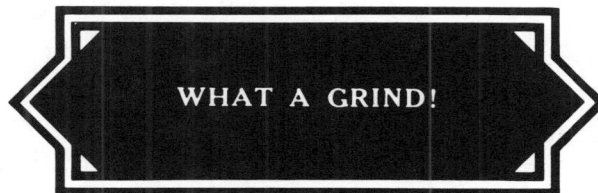

WHAT A GRIND!

Zabar's will grind your coffee beans for any brewing method. Its grinder is marked not merely "Coarse," "Medium," "Fine," but with the kind of pot or brew: "Melitta," "Chemex," "Espresso," "Turkish," and so on, to make sure you get exactly the grind you need. But it does recommend grinding the beans at home as you need them, for the very best and freshest cup of coffee.

There are dozens of grinders, manual and electric, at all prices. Also, many blenders and food processors will grind coffee beans.

Most inexpensive *electric grinders* do their work with a set of small blades that look a little like a propeller and actually chop the beans rather than grind them. These are best when you're grinding fine; they are sometimes uneven for coarser grinds. All you have to do is push a button, twist the cover, or press down on the top and wait. Use these only for coffee beans, get a separate grinder for spices, nuts, or other dried foods.

Zabar's has a large selection of electric grinders—by Braun, Bosch, Norelco, Waring, Kitchenaid, and

CARING FOR COFFEE

The care and attention Saul Zabar gives to the selection, storage, roasting, and ultimate sale of his coffees is unmatched. His suggestions for getting the most out of any coffee you buy, by mail or in person, are: First, don't buy too much at a time; second, keep whole beans in the freezer and take out only as much as you need to grind per potful.

"Oxygen is the culprit," Saul says. "As soon as coffee is exposed to air, it starts to lose the particular characteristics you chose it for in the first place."

In the freezer, beans in an airtight container will keep at least two months. Ground coffee will last a couple of weeks frozen and, despite all claims to the contrary, no more than a couple of days in the refrigerator.

Melitta. The Spong *hand-grinder* from England and the Kitchenaid and Braun Aromatic electric grinders work on a different principle: They have two opposing grooved steel discs, one that turns and one that remains stationary, grinding the beans between them. This method produces the most uniform ground coffee all the time; adjusting the space between the discs regulates the fineness.

Zabar's itself has a house-brand grinder. And that's a story in itself. Murray Klein was underselling everybody with his price on the *Salton coffee mill*: $18.95 all over town; $9.95 at Zabar's. All of a sudden, just before the Christmas rush, and probably because of the price cutting, Salton had no more coffee mills for Zabar's; the demand had mysteriously exceeded the supply. Fight-or-die Klein was not to be thwarted. He went straight to the source—Krups, the German manufacturer of the Salton machine—and placed an order. The coffee mills were a little larger and had Zabar's name on them; otherwise, they were exactly the same as the Salton. The first 10,000 were sold before the next order had been shipped, and Zabar's was well on its way to becoming one of the largest importer/retailers of coffee grinders in New York. Zabar's sells almost 10,000 of its own coffee mills a year, one-third of its total sales of grinders.

CAFÉ AU LAIT, CAFÉ CON LECHE, OR CAFFÉ LATTE

Pour equal parts of strong, hot fresh coffee and hot milk into cups simultaneously from opposite sides. That's all there is to it.

CIOCCOLATA

Pour equal parts of hot espresso and hot chocolate into cups. Top with whipped cream and grated orange peel.

CAFFÉ LATTE

Per serving, stir 1 teaspoon chocolate syrup into a tall glass filled ¾ full with hot double-strength coffee or espresso. Top with a scoop of vanilla ice cream, and pour on 1 ounce of crème de menthe.

MEXICAN COFFEE

Per serving, put 1 teaspoon chocolate syrup into ½ cup strong, hot coffee. Top with whipped creamed that has been sweetened with a little sugar and mixed with nutmeg and cinnamon.

BAGGING IT!

"We did quite a lot of research on our coffee bag," Saul Zabar boasts. "That's very unusual for any store. It's our attempt to help keep our coffee as fresh as possible once it leaves the store."

The bag is specially made for Zabar's. It has three layers: The innermost is Saran, coated to retain freshness and to keep out humidity. "We recommend freezing coffee, and this Saran lining is particularly suited for freezing," Saul explains. The middle layer is kraft paper (strong, usually brown, paper), for structural stability; the outer coated, calendered layer is for appearance and printability.

"The bag gives coffee maximum protection and shelf life," Saul points out. "The bag itself costs between fifteen and twenty cents—as opposed to about two cents for a regular paper bag."

Special bags don't stop with coffee. The bread bag is also a Zabar's exclusive. According to Stanley Zabar, it's specially coated to keep bread fresh longer, and it costs about five times as much as a normal brown-paper bag.

WHAT'S IN A BLEND?

Saul Zabar has nothing against blending coffee, but he's not in favor of the customer's doing it. Most people don't really know what they're doing and wind up canceling out the distinctive flavors of select coffees.

"Putting two [or more] coffees together generally degrades the overall tastes," Saul declares. "You obliterate the character of the individual coffee."

Zabar's sells its own *house blend*, a carefully chosen combination of Central American coffees—which ones depend on what's available.

The most Saul Zabar recommends is blending a dark-roast coffee with a lighter one.

"You're dealing with very good coffees, selected for their very specific characteristics, and they don't need tampering."

Most commercial coffees are blends. When coffee was introduced into Europe, there was only one kind, which came from Arabia, with the botanical name *Coffea arabica*. It wasn't until the nineteenth century, and the introduction of more sophisticated equipment

ICED IRISH COFFEE

2 cups cold double-strength coffee
8 teaspoons superfine sugar
2 ounces (¼ cup) Irish whisky
1 cup soft whipped cream

Put ½ cup coffee in each of 4 glasses. Add 2 teaspoons sugar to each, and stir to dissolve. Add 1 ounce whisky to each (more to taste). Fill glasses with ice cubes, and top with whipped cream.
Serves 4.
(For hot Irish Coffee, just eliminate the ice cubes.)

to roast and brew coffee, that someone figured out that blending *arabica* from different areas or from different plantations in the same area—each coffee chosen for its special qualities—could be an overall improvement.

Unless a particular brand of coffee is claimed to be 100 percent pure something or other, commercial coffees are blends of various coffees to achieve the consistency the coffees are known for. More than 100 kinds of coffee are imported into the United States. Weather conditions, harvesting methods, the length of time the green beans stand between picking and roasting can affect the coffee's quality. So it's not unusual for large coffee producers to combine several varieties, to make sure coffee from vacuum-packed cans always tastes exactly the same. Another important factor is cost. Blending a good high-priced coffee with a cheaper but still decent bean often helps keep the price of a can of coffee as consistent as its taste.

THE OLDTIME APPETIZERS

ZABAR'S®

A GOURMET & EPICUREAN EMPORIUM   SMOKED FISH
STURGEON   FRESH CAVIARS   GOURMET COOKWARE
GIFT BASKETS   CATERING   SUN-THURS TILL 7:30 PM
FRI TILL 10 PM   SAT TILL 12 PM

WHOLE GRAIN BREADS
IMPORTED CHEESE
BEAN COFFEE

COFFEE INFORMATION

Keep ground and bean coffee in freezer, not refrigerator. Store in saran-lined Zabar coffee bag. Ground coffee fades in 3 days and bean coffee within 10 days. Coffee will stay fresh in freezer for at least 2 months.

Easiest and most consistent brew method is "drip brewing" with Melitta, Chemex, Tricolator, etc. We like Melitta best. Percolated coffee can be very good if the perk time is carefully controlled to about 7 minutes on a low flame with gentle perking. Electric perks are difficult to control. Electric drip brewers, such as Melitta #130, Wigomat, and Braun are excellent. They use less coffee (finely ground), and produce a superior cup. Norelco is also recommended (use regular grind). Coffee ground just prior to brewing adds to cup quality. The simpler the grinder the better for ease of cleaning. We like the small Braun, Krups, Avia, small Salton, Moulinex, etc.

We advise against blending Zabar coffees with the exception of adding French-Italian or Vienna. Blending generally degrades the character of the individual coffees and the blended product is usually less satisfactory.

Zabar coffees are the best available from Jamaica, Central America, Africa, Indonesia, etc. We import directly most of our coffees, and do *all* our own roasting. Coffees will taste different at various times of the year depending upon season, crop changes, roast variation, etc. We want you to be satisfied. Tell us if for any reason you are not pleased.

CURRENT COFFEES LISTED IN GROUPS OF SIMILAR CHARACTER

Jamaica Blue Mountain	A rare and superb coffee, fine flavor and full body.
Jamaica High Mt. Supreme	Excellent coffee. Delicious flavor and body.
Colombia Blend Costa Rica Blend Zabar's Blend	Central American coffees of excellent character.
Maragogipe Guatemala (Giant Bean)	Mild interesting flavor. Typical Guatemala character.
Hawaiian Kona	Mild sweet lovely coffee.
Kenya AA Kenya Peaberry Mocha Style Blend	Delightful lively acidity. Full body.
Mocha Java Blend	Genuine Javas blended with Mocha-like coffees for a good well-balanced cup.
Decaffeinated Blend	Carefully processed before roasting to produce a delicious cup with less than .05% caffeine.
Vienna Roast	Fine coffees roasted to a mild espresso character.
French-Italian Roast	Full Espresso
Decaf. Espresso	Medium espresso, made from our decaf blend.

Zabar's is the exclusive importer of Jamaica Blue Mountain coffee for the eastern United States and the exclusive importer and roaster for Jamaica High Mountain in the entire U.S.A. We import enough for our own use only, and do not wholesale this coffee to *anyone*. BEWARE OF FRAUD .

We mail our coffee (5-pound minimum order) anywhere in the continental United States. Coffee is shipped U.P.S., so please provide a street address and ZIP code, *not* a post office box number. Payment can be made by credit card or check.

Our coffee can be shipped in the bean or ground to your specifications. Coffee in the bean keeps fresh for several months if kept in the freezer. We also mail all coffee makers and grinders.

Coffee is shipped on Wednesday mornings, so we recommend that your order be placed by Tuesday morning to assure a prompt shipment.

BROADWAY AT 80TH STREET   NEWYORK NEWYORK 10024   787-2000

AS PHONY AS A POUND OF JAMAICA BLUE MOUNTAIN COFFEE

Of all the coffees Zabar's sells, by far the best—and the most talked about—is *Jamaica Blue Mountain*. It's full-bodied and savory; acidy, with a rare, fine flavor and superb taste. The kind coffee dreams are made of.

It's expensive (currently, $5.98 a pound) and it isn't always available. You can get it at only one place on the entire East Coast—Zabar's. Any so-called Jamaica Blue Mountain sold elsewhere (except as noted below) is phony.

Jamaica is not one of the world's largest coffee-producing countries; it exports only about 12,000 bags a year, and the amount of Jamaica Blue Mountain is a minuscule 1,000 bags or so. Less than 5 percent of this prize gets to the United States; the bulk of it goes to Japan, where it sells, retail, for about $10 a pound. "Bags," by the way, is just a convenient term. Jamaica Blue Mountain is the only coffee still shipped in barrels, the way coffee used to be. All other coffees come in burlap sacks.

Only Zabar's in New York and B. C. Ireland in San Francisco import Jamaica Blue Mountain. Zabar's—and only Zabar's—also gets a small amount of *Jamaica High Mountain Supreme*, a fine high-grown coffee, slightly less exclusive than Blue Mountain.

NOT THE REAL MC COY

A couple of years ago, Jamaica Blue Mountain seemed to be available everywhere. Lots of it, and at high but not outrageous prices. This struck coffee pros as odd, because there was far more Blue Mountain for sale than had ever been shipped to this country. Confusion reigned. People were drinking what they thought was Jamaica Blue Mountain—and paying dearly for it.

In fact, if the coffee did not come directly from Zabar's or from one of the West Coast shops supplied by B. C. Ireland, it could have been almost anything. No matter what the shopkeeper chose to call it or how much he charged, it was an out-and-out rip-off.

The truth was, as careful investigation proved, that not one coffee bean from Jamaica, much less from its Blue Mountain plantations, was found among any lot bearing its name. Not anywhere—except, of course, at Zabar's. And the scandal erupted. Several "important

COFFEE IN A BAG

They laughed when John and Charles Arbuckle decided that people *would* buy freshly roasted ground coffee that had been packed, while still warm, into paper bags holding a pound. But the brothers Arbuckle were right, and by 1873, they were distributing their prepackaged Ariosa brand of coffee all over the United States.

When a machine for vacuum-packing foods was patented in 1898, Hills Brothers Coffee, a San Francisco-based company, found to its surprise that coffee packed this way would hold onto its flavor and freshness indefinitely. In 1900, the first vacuum-packed cans of coffee made their debut. The hissing sound when a can was opened and the aroma of freshly ground coffee quickly became part of the American way.

retail coffee stores'' are still trying to live down the embarrassment of having been caught.

That's when Zabar's took the regally impressive

letter of authorization from the Jamaica Coffee Industry Board, blew it up to poster size, and hung it right over the coffee department for all to see. And to put a stop to everyone else's claims.

Real Jamaica Blue Mountain and High Mountain Supreme *are* available at Zabar's. They are sold in the store, and small amounts are sent by mail to regular customers and to no one else. Caveat emptor!

THE KONA COFFEE STORY

Kona coffee, from Hawaii, is truly a superb brew, according to the experts. Unfortunately, it's hard to get.

The Superior Coffee Company of Chicago buys the entire crop from the Hawaiian coffee cooperatives. This company roasts it, grinds it, vacuum-packs it, and sells it mostly to restaurants and a few select distributors. Just within the last two years or so, Superior has begun selling roasted beans to a chosen group of coffee brokers. Superior sells green Kona beans only to Zabar's.

kona coffee association
P.O. Box 766
Captain Cook, Hawaii 96704

January 29, 1976

To whom it may concern:

We, the growers of Kona Coffee are very proud of our product. We work hard to maintain the standard of Kona as one of the finest gourmet coffees in the world. Genuine Kona Coffee is only grown on the slopes of Mauna Loa mountain, in the District of Kona, on the island of Hawaii. All Kona is grown by members of our Association.

Since November of 1969, all of the Kona grown has been sold and delivered to Superior Tea and Coffee Company. We know that Superior has resold less than 5% of each annual crop of green Kona Coffee to reputable, well established processors.

Therefore, it is upsetting to our Association to learn that many roasters and retailers are falsely advertising other products as Kona. Such misrepresentation harms the reputation of our product and misleads consumers.

We strongly urge all those wishing to purchase genuine Kona Coffee to investigate their source, so they may be assured of the product's authenticity. We recommend that they contact Superior to either purchase Kona or to verify that the product they purchase from another source is, in fact, genuine Kona Coffee.

We are proud to be associated with Superior Tea and Coffee Company and intend to continue our relationship in future years.

Sincerely,

Sotero Bailado

Sotero Bailado
President

kona coffee association
P.O. Box 766
Captain Cook, Hawaii 96704

May 14, 1976

Mr. Saul Zabar
Zabar's
Broadway at 80th Street
New York City, New York   10024

Dear Mr. Zabar:

The Kona Coffee Association, the organization
of all growers of Kona Coffee, maintains careful records on the distribution of Kona
coffee. We do this to safeguard the integrity
of our product.

We have checked on the distribution of the
1975/76 green coffee crop. To date, Zabar's
has been the only company on the east coast
to have purchased authentic green Kona
coffee from the 1975/76 crop.

Sincerely,

Sotero Bailado
President

"We do our own roasting," says Saul Zabar. "We totally control it, so it's done properly. Since we never have stock for more than ten days, it's always fresh. And since we buy it green, we are assured of its authenticity."

Kona has a distinctly delicious aroma, a full-bodied, lively taste. It's worth a splurge.

ESPRESSO

Espresso is not a variety of coffee bean. It's the roast and the particular way of brewing that make espresso what it is—a way of life.

At its very best, espresso is rich, nearly syrupy, and has the slightly burnt-bitter flavor common to all dark-roast coffees. It's traditionally made quickly, one cup at a time, in machines that look like museum pieces and sound like pinball machines. They were intended for cafés, not for home use, which helps explain their size and complexity. Basically, with high steam pressure, they force water through tightly packed, very finely ground coffee. The result is strong and concentrated coffee, usually drunk in small cups.

To soften the taste, steamed milk is sometimes added, usually heated and foamed by the same pressure mechanism as the coffee itself. A mixture of equal amounts of milk, espresso, and foamed milk is called *cappuccino* in Italy and *café crème* in France. *Caffè latte* (French *café au lait* and Spanish *café con leche*) has equal amounts of espresso and hot milk, poured simultaneously from opposite sides of the cup. There are endless variations of espresso with hot milk, at least one for every country where espresso is drunk.

Zabar's has an espresso-maker for everyone, at every price, and at every level of sophistication—from the simplest stove-top, turn-over type to the $1,000 super-duper, 100-cup-an-hour, imported Swiss Olympia deluxe model.

The least complicated are the stove-top pots like the *Moka*. Finely ground espresso-roast coffee is put in a basket, which is placed on a pot filled with water. A second pot, with a handle and a spout, is put on top, open end down. The whole thing is placed on the stove, and when the water is boiling, it's flipped over so the top pot is at the bottom; water seeps down through the grinds.

The *Vesuviana* is similar, but the basket for the grinds clamps on separately, and the pot that catches the coffee is a separate piece.

Neither the Moka nor the Vesuviana can steam milk. For just this reason, Zabar's sells the *Pulcinella* stove-top milk steamer. It's great fun to use. Not only does it steam milk, but it can make a dynamite-hot chocolate, hot buttered rum, or hot apple cider.

At the next level are the real espresso-makers. The *Vesubio* is the one stove-top espresso-cappuccino model at Zabar's; it's the closest nonelectric version of the café-type machines.

The *Pavoni* is a nice, manageable size, all chrome and equipped with the requisite number of valves, handles, knobs, and buttons. It has its own heating element and a pull-down lever that forces the water through the grinds at great speed—espresso! (The Pavoni and the Vesubio have separate spouts for steamed milk.)

On to the big time! Zabar's is the sole importer of Switzerland's *Olympia* espresso-cappuccino-makers, in four exciting, noisy and light-up versions.

The *Cremina*, in chrome, steel, brass, and four colors of enamel, has an 18-cup demitasse capacity and has a special tube for cappuccino. The *New York Times* named it the #1 espresso-maker in a recent survey. The *Club* model is a larger version of the Cremina, with a 40-cup demitasse capacity. Bigger yet and fully automatic and push-button—no levers or handles to pull—is the *Caffarex*, a restaurant-quality machine that has an unlimited capacity, since it can be filled again and again while it's working. Finally, the *Superclub*, also automatic, can make 100 cups an hour. It may be a bit extravagant for the average kitchen, but it's a pleasure to use.

All the electric Olympia machines are a gas! Push a button, pull a lever, and the room is filled with horrific noises—hissing, clanking, whooshing, humming—the

COFFEE ICE (GRANITA DI CAFFÉ)

About ½ cup sugar
2 cups hot espresso
1 teaspoon almond extract
½ cup heavy cream, whipped

Dissolve sugar in espresso (don't make it too sweet; it should taste like espresso). Cool slightly, and add almond extract (never add any extract to very hot liquid; it would dissipate the flavor quickly). Pour into ice-cube tray (with divider removed), and freeze about 15 minutes

Stir to break up any ice crystals on sides of tray, and return to freezer for fifteen minutes. Repeat freezing and stirring twice. Then freeze until almost firm.

Remove from tray; place in chilled bowl, and beat until mushy, but still nice and thick. Return to freezer, and freeze until firm. (Don't let it get rock hard; it should be firm, but spoonable and grainy.) Top each serving with whipped cream.
Serves 4.

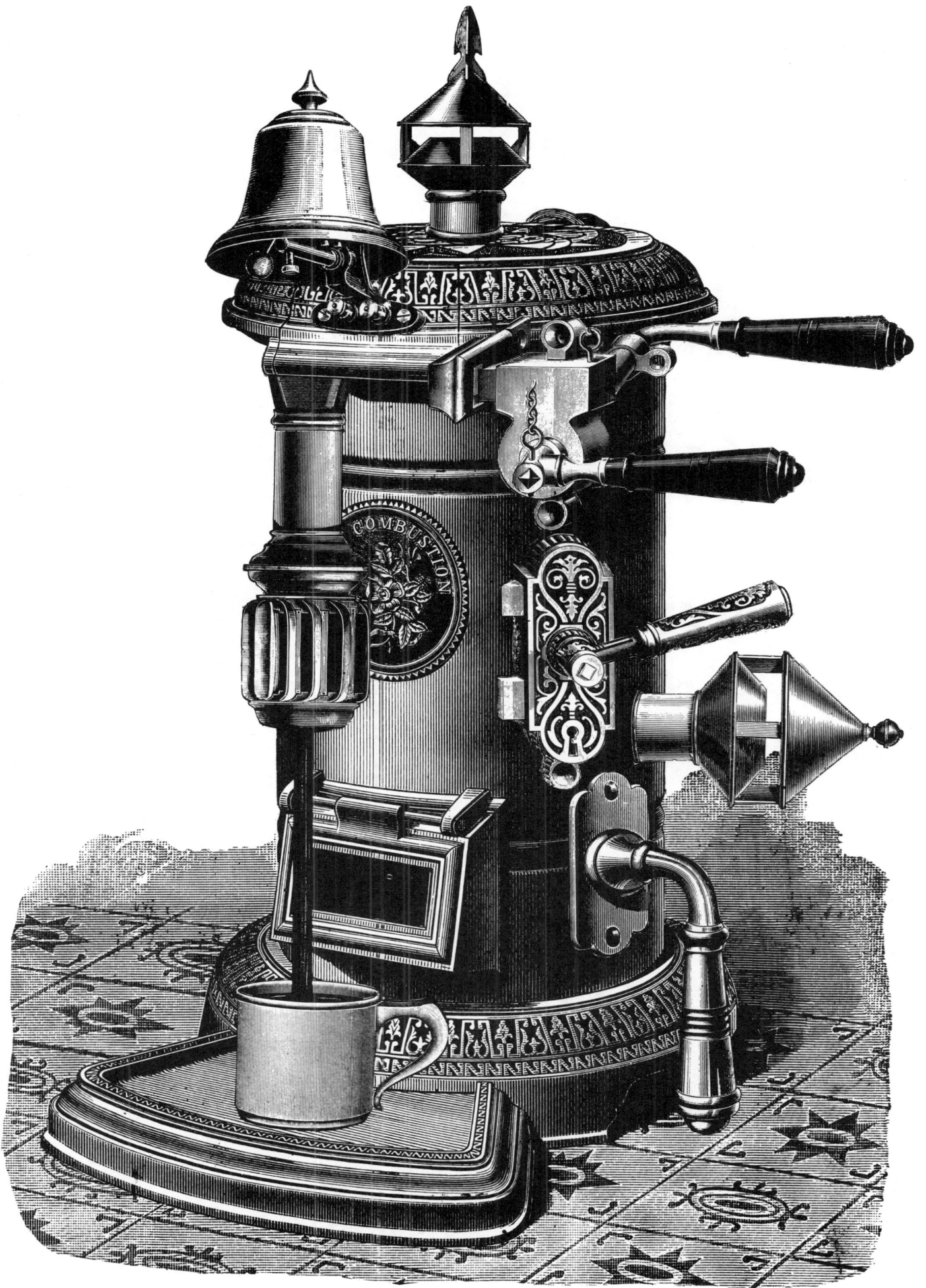

very same sounds that make an espresso machine in a café a show all by itself. And if espresso is not on the menu, all the Olympias can send steamed milk into a pot of cocoa for the best hot chocolate you've ever tasted.

MIDDLE-EASTERN COFFEE

Arabs like their coffee "as black as the devil, hot as hell, and sweet as love." (To which Talleyrand added, "And as pure as an angel.") It's easy for them to be so specific; they've been roasting, brewing, and drinking coffee that way for thousands of years.

Turkish, Greek, Armenian, Egyptian, and Arabian coffees are one and the same. All are boiled two or three times, and the most important part of the coffee, no matter what it's called, is the *kaimaki*, the thin head of froth that tops the dark, sweet, syrupy brew.

You can make Middle Eastern coffee in an ordinary saucepan, although purists prefer the *briki* or *ibrik*, a tall, cylindrical pot with a long handle. Zabar's has these pots in brass, copper, and enamel, in various sizes.

For each demitasse of coffee, a teaspoon of very fine, almost powdery coffee, most often French or Italian roast, a teaspoon of sugar, and a demitasse cup of water are put into the *ibrik* and brought to a boil over a low heat. The *kamaiki* will look as if it's about to overflow; but once taken off the heat, the brew settles down. It's brought to a boil at least once more, preferably twice. Only then is the coffee poured into demitasse cups—very carefully so that each is topped with a head of foam.

WHY COFFEE KEEPS YOU AWAKE

Medical claims for coffee are as old as the beans themselves. It has been said to cure gout, scurvy, migraine, and dropsy—or to cause leprosy and impotence. It has been prescribed as a sleeping potion, a stimulant, an aphrodisiac, and a depressant.

Coffee was the true wonder drug, for better or worse. Scientists noted that it affected people differently: Two cups might give someone a severe case of coffee nerves; 10 cups might not trouble another person at all. The true culprit, they discovered, was not the coffee, but one of its components, caffeine.

One cup of coffee has about 100 mgs. (milligrams) of caffeine, the same as does a 12-ounce bottle of Coke.

A chocolate bar has about 80 mgs.; a cup of tea, 70. Enough, in all cases, to be mildly stimulating.

DECAFFEINATED COFFEE

If caffeine is a problem the answer is decaffeinated coffee. The decaffeinating process removes 97 percent of the caffeine from green coffee beans, yet alters the taste and characteristics of the coffee itself very little.

It may come as a surprise to some Zabar's customers that beans can be bought decaffeinated. The process was invented in Germany in the early 1900s by Dr. Ludwig Roselius. He named his discovery "sanka," from the French *sans caféine*. The process is still being used. The beans are steamed for a short period to soften them, then brought in contact with a solvent that absorbs caffeine and some of the oils and waxes. The solvent is then removed by evaporation. No measurable solvent residue remains on the beans. A new Swiss water process for decaffeinating coffee, that involves no solvents, has recently been introduced. At Zabar's, you can get your decaf either way.

What happens to all the caffeine that's removed? It's sold to pharmaceutical houses or to soft drink manufacturers who use it in Coca Cola and other popular drinks.

The difference between coffee you make from decaffeinated beans and from vacuum-packed decaffeinated ground coffee is extraordinary. The popular brands, such as Sanka, Brim, and so on, taste like coffee-flavored hot water, with a definite chemical aftertaste and are very inferior to coffee made from Zabar's freshly roasted and ground decaffeinated beans.

135

Tea

"If the stranger say unto thee
That he thirsteth,
Give him a cup of tea."
Confucius

Tea drinkers are a world apart. They disdain other hot beverages and preach the virtues of tea as being good for mind and body. Each pot is artfully brewed, as if tea were a treasure, and at Zabar's it may well be. The world's finest teas are sold loose; the best pre-packaged teas are well represented.

Whether you're planning a formal tea ceremony or a simple pot of tea for friends, the choices are enormous and beguiling. Scented and flavored teas fill the air with jasmine and spices; fine black teas and heady oolongs promise delicious brews to come.

Teapots; teakettles; tea eggs, balls, and spoons; infusers of steel, chrome, wire mesh, and even bamboo are all there—everything to make you want to take tea and see.

It was when life was still a simple pleasure that man discovered tea and changed the course of history.

The Chinese emperor Shen Nung was known throughout China as the Divine Healer. By 2737 B.C., he had invented a simple plow, stumbled upon the medicinal benefits of certain plants, and was teaching his people about agriculture and cultivation. And then he discovered tea when some leaves from a shrub accidentally fell into a pot of boiling water. The delicate aroma so impressed the emperor that he drank the brew; the lovely flavor the leaves had added turned serendipity into habit.

Over the centuries, the Chinese drank tea for its curative powers rather than for refreshment. But once they began to cultivate it seriously, it became an important social and status drink. By the 1640s, when foreign dignitaries and missionaries began to visit China freely and tasted tea for the first time, there was no doubt that tea was the drink for everyone, from aristocrats to peasants.

The Japanese like to tell of a Buddhist monk named Daruma, who left India to preach in China. He promised not to sleep for nine years and devote himself to prayer. He couldn't do it! He fell asleep during meditation, and when he awoke, he tore off his eyelids in despair. Where they fell, tea plants grew. He picked the leaves, brewed them, drank the infusion, and was so refreshed that he was able to start praying again and complete his vigil. He took tea leaves to Japan, where tea's miraculous properties soon became equated with Japanese Buddhism.

THE TEA CEREMONY

The Chinese introduced tea to the Japanese in the sixth century, along with Buddhism, art, and civilization. But tea drinking and growing in Japan began in earnest only hundreds of years later when the way to China was opened. And along that way traveled the newest rage from the south, Zen Buddhism, and its accompanying tea ritual.

This was an art form as well as a religious exercise, and the Japanese quickly adopted and adapted it. The Zen ceremony appealed to the Japanese sense of austerity and simplicity and, in its most spiritual sense, was considered a step on the path to enlightenment.

According to formal rules set down in the sixteenth century, the tea ceremony is beautifully choreographed, with a subtle yet exhaustive attention to detail. Every move has its place; none is so showy as to overpower another. Each participant has his role: The host, humble and self-effacing, prepares tea as if it might be the only time he will do so; it must be, therefore, perfect. The guests are admiring, accepting, never critical.

Even the design of the teahouse is part of the drama; it represents the purity of a Zen monastery. The long path to the teahouse allows each guest to leave the outside world behind; the low doorway to the tea room itself assures that each person who enters will stoop in a gesture of humility.

The ceremony has undergone very few changes since then; it's performed in Japan today much as it was by the original Zen masters.

TEA AROUND THE WORLD

Tea in India has its legends, too, remarkably similar to those of the Japanese. However, tea has grown wild in northeastern India, in the area known as Assam, and has probably been drunk or eaten there for centuries. The British made that discovery in the eighteenth century, but refused to believe it. They insisted that the native plant was not tea but camellia (which does belong to the tea family), and so brought in Chinese tea plants and Chinese laborers to cultivate them. It took the British a century to recognize their mistake and agree that the Indian tea would be a fine, exportable crop. Now India is the largest tea-producing country in the world; it is followed by its neighbor Sri Lanka.

The Dutch introduced tea to the Western world in the middle of the seventeenth century. But not easily. Although the Dutch aristocracy took to it immediately, doctors in Germany were attacking it, and the French both opposed it and praised it—mostly opposed. Some physicians believed that tea could cure any ill; others thought it might be fatal. But once a tea-drinking physician called it the "divine herb" and likened it to nectar and ambrosia, the French were off and running. Anything worthy of that description was certainly going to be *très chic* very soon.

The British, meanwhile, were heralding tea as a

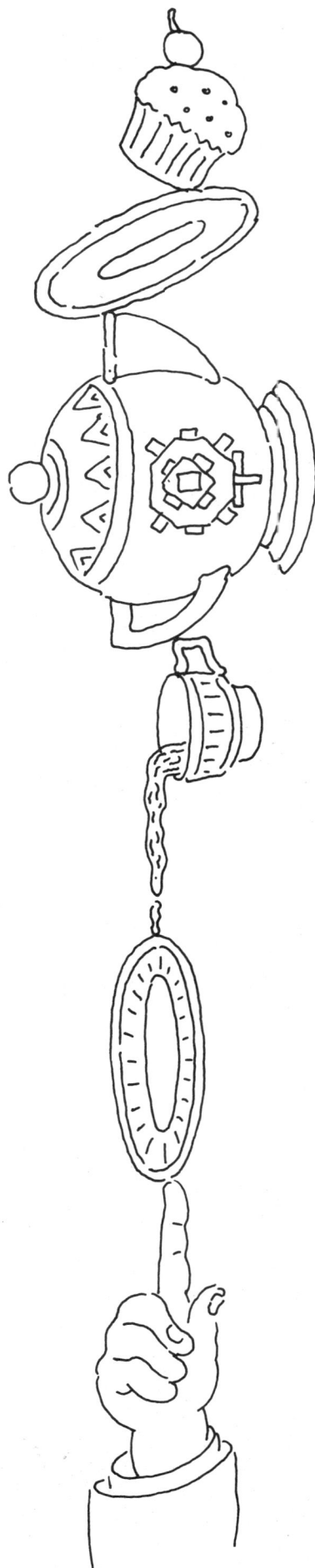

health drink, especially in the coffeehouses. It was prohibitively expensive (about $50 a pound in 1660 versus $15 a pound in 1978) and heavily taxed (as much as 200 percent of the price), so it isn't surprising that an anti-tea bandwagon was dominated by economists who thought it obstructed industry by making men indolent and prone to miss work; scholars who considered it too costly for the lower classes, although they were buying it anyway; and social reformers who claimed it made men immoral, since the women hired by wealthy aristocrats as tea blenders were, more often than not, their mistresses.

Between the king and his taxes, the philosophers and their diatribes, it was only natural that wholesale smuggling of tea became a way of life. Smuggled tea was cheaper—no taxes—and to lower the price even further, it was sometimes cut with gunpowder or sawdust, or other leaves were substituted for the real thing. Used tea leaves were even dried and sold as fresh, which did give some credence to the claim that tea was bad for your health.

All this didn't seem to matter very much. Whether it was, as one pundit put it, because of tea's "persistent availability and continued promotion" or because it made a drink of delicious taste and freshness, by the 1800s Britain was a nation of tea drinkers.

That the United States is second only to Britain in tea imports these days and that Americans drink about 40 billion cups of tea a day are quite remarkable facts, considering all the hot water tea has been in over the years.

Early tea drinkers easily might have quashed future plans for the beverage. They were treated to a brew that had been harshly boiled and was acridly just this side of unappetizing. It was served unadorned by

AFTERNOON TEA

The nineteenth century in England was a time of excesses, and dining well and fully was certainly one of them. The habit among the upper classes was to have an enormous breakfast and an equally large meal in the evening. Lunch, if any, was usually just a snack, because the servants were traditionally given the afternoons off and the ladies of the manor could hardly be expected to fend for themselves.

The Duke of Bedford's wife, Anna, a trend setter among her peers if ever there was one, couldn't hold out from breakfast to dinner, and as soon as her staff returned to duty at five, she called for tea and cakes to help her get through the remaining hours until the evening meal.

Had Anna had more will power, the custom of afternoon tea might never have seen the light of day.

milk or sugar, and sometimes just the leaves, plain or mixed with butter, were offered for eating.

Things got somewhat better when the Dutch brought tea to New Amsterdam in 1650. They brewed it with great pomp and ceremony, as they had at home. When New Amsterdam became New York in 1664, the British added their own tea-drinking habits. Elegance and refinement were stressed, and tea gardens, similar to those in London, soon attracted the most fashionable folk in the area. Tea became easily the most popular drink in the colonies.

A century later, no American patriot would be caught dead drinking tea. It had become the focal point of a disagreement between king and Colonies that ended in the Revolutionary War. The Boston Tea Party in 1773 was only the first in a series of protests that lasted until independence was achieved.

THE WHAT AND WHERE OF TEA

Tea is the queen of beverages, and only water is drunk in greater quantity. From seed to cup, tea is a treasure, cultivated with great care and reverence.

The tea plant is an evergreen shrub that grows best in the tropics and subtropics. It loves warm, wet days, but will flourish almost anywhere. Tea grown at higher, cooler altitudes, in fact, is often considered to be the finest, much the same as rare, high-grown coffees are.

Nearly 70 percent of the tea imported into the United States comes from India, Sri Lanka, and East Africa. The rest comes from China, Africa, Indonesia, Japan, and Argentina. Zabar's, says Murray Klein, has the very best examples from all the tea-producing countries in the world.

PLUCKING

Tea is still picked by hand. Picking is a delicate and painstaking process, much too fine for machines. The pluckers, mostly women, take only the top two leaves and the bud and gently toss them into baskets balanced on their heads or backs. The women are amazingly fast and dextrous. An experienced plucker gathers 40 pounds of leaves and buds a day—enough to make 10 pounds of tea.

PROCESSING

Processing is a three- or four-step operation: *Withering* removes as much moisture as possible from the leaves. The leaves are spread on racks. In dry climates, they're left to wither naturally; where it's humid, hot, dry air is circulated by fans. *Rolling* breaks up the cell structure and releases the natural juices and fragrances. *Fermentation* exposes the leaves to air, to absorb oxygen and change their color from green to copper or black. (Green teas do not go

THE ACCIDENT OF THE TEA BAG

A New York tea-and-coffee merchant named Thomas Sullivan was the first to realize the expensive folly of sending out the customary taster's samples of tea in costly tins and chests—as they had been sent out for years. He had several small silk bags made, and he filled each with a portion of tea.

His customers thought he intended them to brew the tea right in the little bags, and they did. They were delighted with the convenient, premeasured, prestrained system for making perfect tea, and orders began pouring in—not just for tea, but for tea packed in those little silk bags. Today, more than half the tea drunk in this country is made with tea bags. Silk, on the other hand, is no longer used.

through this process; coloring teas are only slightly fermented.) Finally, *drying* or *firing* stops any further oxidation and dries the leaves evenly.

TYPECASTING

There are only three classes of tea: black, oolong, and green. All are grown on the same bushes; it's the processing that gives them their distinguishing characteristics. Within each classification, there are dozens of varieties, of course, usually named for the areas where they are grown.

BLACK TEA: Almost all (97 percent) of the tea drunk in the United States is black tea, called that because the full processing treatment, from withering to firing, turns the leaves black. Keemun, Darjeeling, Souchong, and Lipton's are black teas. They have a rich, strong flavor and mellow aroma.

OOLONG: This tea is lightly withered, rolled, and only partially fermented before being fired. The leaves are half black and half copper-colored, and produce a tea that is rich and fruity.

GREEN TEA: Completely unfermented. The leaves are steamed or heated rather than withered, then rolled and dried. Because the tea is not exposed to air and oxidation does not take place, the leaves remain green. Green tea is light and clear, with a delicate, but extremely flavorful taste.

Orange pekoe is a grade of black tea with long, thin, whole leaves, taken from the top of the plant. *Plain pekoe* has leaves that are shorter and not as wiry. *Pekoe Souchong* denotes a rounded leaf.

These are *leaf grades*, made up of the larger leaves left after the broken grades have been sorted out. They need a longer brewing time to reach optimum flavor and color.

Broken grades are the smaller and broken leaves—about 80 percent of the crop. They need less brewing time, and the result is a stronger, darker tea. They are the choice grades in most of the world, especially in the United States, where they are the essential tea for tea bags.

The smallest particles left are graded *dust* and are mostly used for blending with larger grades.

Green teas are graded differently—according to leaf size *and* the style of drying. Gunpowder tea, for example, is made from small leaves rolled into pellets.

MAKING THE PERFECT POT OF TEA

Like making good coffee, brewing good tea isn't terribly difficult if you follow the four golden rules advanced by the experts at Zabar's. They're easy to follow, guaranteed foolproof, and precise enough for even a novice to master.

1. Use a teapot. Rinse it with hot water, to preheat it before adding tea and water.
2. Use fresh, cold water, brought to a rolling boil. Reheated water or hot tap water would taste flat.
3. Measure the tea into the pot: one teaspoon measure per six ounces of water.

The best way is to put the tea leaves directly into the pot. But if you don't care for tea floating around in your cup, the next best thing is to use a tea ball or tea

SUN TEA

1 quart cold water
10 tea bags

Time and energy. Two precious commodities there's never enough of. To save a little of both, especially if you're not in a hurry for your tea, take a nice, bright summer morning. Fill a jar with one quart of cold water and add the 10 tea bags—string and tags removed, so they don't leave an aftertaste.

Place it outside in the sun, and go on about your day. Come back in about 6 hours—just when a cold glass of iced tea is exactly what you need. Squeeze the tea bags against the side of the jar, and toss them on the compost heap. The tea will be perfectly brewed. Just pour it over ice, add lemon and sugar to taste, and drink up. That's all there is to it.

142

egg. They're usually aluminum, sometimes ceramic or bamboo, perforated, spherical or egg-shaped "tea bags" on a chain. Fill ball or egg with tea, one teaspoon per cup; remember that tea leaves expand when wet, so never fill it to the top. Then place it in the teapot.

4. Pour boiling water over the tea in the teapot. Cover, and time it—three to six minutes, depending on the tea. Color is not a reliable indication of strength, so don't overbrew. Some teas—green tea, for example—are light-colored even at full strength. Don't underbrew, either; if you like your tea weak, add plain hot water after it has steeped.

A second potful from the same leaves is not recommended. Weaker, less flavorful tea would result, with few of the lovely, fragrant attractions of a freshly brewed pot of tea.

A few words about tea bags: If you prefer to use them, follow the rules for brewing loose tea. Don't just dunk a tea bag in a cup of hot water until you think the color is right. Put the bags, tags removed, into the preheated teapot, and brew as carefully as you would loose tea, using one bag per cup, boiling water, and patience.

Two words about instant tea: Forget it! Even if it does make up about 25 percent of the tea sold in this country each year.

TEA AT ZABAR'S

Right next to the coffee department, surrounded by all sorts of wonderful tea-brewing paraphernalia, are the teas. Loose teas, displayed invitingly in airtight canisters, tantalize and tempt the senses. Teas from Russia, India, Sri Lanka, Africa, Formosa; each has its own style and grace, its own loyal followers, who wouldn't dream of drinking anything else. According to Murray Klein, tea is more and more popular on the Upper West Side, especially with so many fine ones to choose from.

DRAGON WELL: The rarest of China's green teas, light and clear, sweet and delicate, grown in Chekiang province near a legendary spring called Dragon Well. It's the most famous and one of the great teas of the world.

EARL GREY: A flavored (with oil of bergamot, a pungent, highly scented herb, used by American Colonists instead of tea during the Revolutionary War) black-tea blend. The original recipe is said to have been given by a Chinese mandarin to an ambassador of the British prime minister, Earl Grey, in 1830.

ENGLISH BREAKFAST: The most popular tea at Zabar's. A black tea, traditionally China Keemun, it is said to

TEA ICE CREAM

A deliciously different treat for ice-cream lovers. Try making it with English Breakfast Tea.

3 cups milk
3 cups heavy cream
4½ tablespoons loose tea
2 cups sugar
4 egg yolks, beaten
¼ teaspoon salt
1 teaspoon grated lemon or orange rind

Heat half the milk and half the cream in a double-boiler top until scalded. Remove from heat, and add tea. Let steep for about 6 minutes.

Add sugar, egg yolks, and salt; cook over boiling water, stirring constantly, until thick. Strain out tea leaves, and let cool slightly.

Add remaining milk and cream and the rind. Let cool thoroughly, then freeze in ice-cream machine, following manufacturer's directions.
Makes ½ gallon.

ICED TEA

The first thing astronaut John Glenn asked for when he returned to earth was a glass of iced tea, confirming the fact that a blast into space can work up a terrible thirst.

Before 1904, no one had even dreamed of drinking tea any way but hot. When Richard Blechynden, the English representative of a tea-export group, visited the Louisiana Purchase Exposition in St. Louis, he inadvertently changed the tea-drinking habits of a nation. He was there to introduce the black teas of Ceylon and India to Americans, who were accustomed to only the fragrant green teas of China.

But he hadn't counted on the weather, which was so oppressive and sultry that no one was interested in drinking hot tea. Fair goers headed to wherever iced drinks were being served. Blechynden was an inventive fellow, and he poured his hot tea into tall glasses filled with ice and called it iced tea. By the time the fair was over, his was the most popular cold drink in St. Louis and was well on its way to becoming the national summertime drink in the United States. More than 18 billion glasses of iced tea are drunk in this country every year, all because of a heat wave in 1904.

be the best of the black teas in China. It got its name because the addition of milk (an English breakfast habit) brings out its distinctive perfume. "Don't use cream," it is advised. "It destroys the smooth, winy flavor and aroma of the tea."

LAPSANG SOUCHONG: An acquired taste for most people, but the tea is big with Zabar's Chinese-food freaks. It's a black tea with a distinctly smoky flavor, from China's Fukien province.

FORMOSA OOLONG: This is reputed to be the very best oolong tea available anywhere. It is deliciously aromatic and richly flavorful, and it is picked only once a year.

DARJEELING: Indian black tea—some say the finest and most delicately flavored in the world—grown at high elevations in the foothills of the Himalayas. It has a superb aroma and subtle flavor—the champagne of teas.

ASSAM: More tea comes from Assam than from anywhere else in India. The black tea of this area is strong and flavorful and makes a brisk, pungent cup. As the Indians put it: "If strength is your weakness, Assam is just your cup of tea."

KEEMUN: China black tea, the best produced. It has a terrific aroma and rich taste, like vintage wine, and has one of the best keeping powers of all tea. A good bracer in the morning, a nice pick-me-up in the afternoon.

JASMINE: A green tea combined with jasmine blossoms for delicate fragrance and taste. It makes an elegant and distinctive brew that, after years of experimentation with other scents, has proved to be the best.

CEYLON: Blends from the best estates in high growing areas. These are strong, rich black teas, flavorful and aromatic.

RUSSIAN: Mostly grown in Georgia, near the Black Sea, Russian teas are light and not terribly strong, but delightful to sip. Brewed at full strength in a samovar or a teapot, it's a prime example of one of Zabar's most unusual tea offerings.

Buying in bulk may not be your cup of tea, and Zabar's carries one of the largest selections of *tinned teas*, loose and in bags, to be found anywhere: the finest imported teas from Twinings, Jackson's of Piccadilly, Bigelow, and Wagner's; McGrath's Original Irish Tea; Constant Comment, a spiced tea rich with cinnamon and orange peel; and several delicate green teas from China.

For the increasing number of tea drinkers who prefer *herbal brews*, no problem. Zabar's has them. A complete line of Celestial Seasonings from the exotic Red Zinger to the soothing Lemon Mist. And peppermint, comfrey, camomile, sassafras—nearly everything that grows—from Pompadour and Fixmille.

When Mo Siegel started Celestial Seasonings in 1970, it was with divine inspiration—and within two years, his Red Zinger tea was in the most fashionable cups in the country. Nine years later, herbal teas that don't remind you of boiled crabgrass, and a one-big-happy-family-type of operation in Boulder, Colorado make Celestial Seasonings a multi-million dollar success story, still growing by leaps and bounds.

RED ZINGER: A fruity, spirited drink that accounts for at least 30 percent of Celestial Seasonings' sales, and 90 percent of its reputation, made up of rosehips, hibiscus flowers, lemon grass, peppermint, orange peel, wild cherry bark, and wintergreen. It's full of Vitamin C, and great hot or iced.

LEMON MIST: Light and airy, and wonderfully refreshing, a combination of lemon grass, lemon verbena, spearmint, blackberry, rosehips, comfrey, alfalfa, red clover, orange and lemon peel, eucalyptus, and bergamot oil.

SLEEPYTIME: A soothing, comforting bedtime tea, with chamomile flowers, spearmint, tilea, passion flowers, lemon grass, raspberry, orange, hawthorne, and rosebuds.

MO'S 24: Mo Siegel's favorite, made up, obviously, of 24 different herbs and flowers, including, spearmint, hibiscus, comfrey, chamomile, catnip, yarrow, and blueberry.

ROASTAROMA: A mixture of grain and spice, that satisfies like coffee, with no caffeine. It's made with crystal malt, roasted barley, carrots, chicory, cassia, star anise, and allspice.

PELICAN PUNCH: A children's tea made of crystal malt, peppermint, carrot, blackberry, licorice, and vanilla and almond extracts.

MATTE ORANGE SPICE: "The perfect companion for those times when energy is low and the day is long," Mo Siegel says. Made up of Brazilian roasted and green matte (the dried leaves of a South American evergreen, the major drink in South America and Russia, with a robust, stimulating flavor), sweet Spanish orange peel, Mexican lemon grass, orange blossoms and leaves, cinnamon, cloves, ginger, and star anise.

SPEARMINT, PEPPERMINT, and CHAMOMILE TEAS: Pure herbs, delicious and refreshing, good for what ails you.

MELLOW MINT: A smooth and invigorating combination of alfalfa, peppermint, papaya, comfrey, and licorice.

MORNING THUNDER: Mo Siegel's answer to coffee—lots of caffeine (54 percent more than coffee), but made of black teas and roasted and green matte.

MATTE CHICORY: Brazilian green and roasted matte and chicory, a good pick-me-up.

EMPEROR'S CHOICE: The first of Celestial Seasonings' non-herbal teas, although the black teas are mixed with cassia, ginseng, orange peel, rosehips, ginger root, lovage, peony root, and licorice. A strong, flavorful brew.

ROSEHIPS and LEMON VERBENA TEAS: Just the herbs, full of Vitamin C and light, delicious teas.

BREAD
PASTRY
PASTA

The Staff of Life

"There's only one thing wrong with Zabar's. They don't have Hershey Bars."
Anon.

BY BREAD ALONE

At 6:00 every morning, when most New Yorkers are fast asleep and dreaming pleasant dreams, Zabar's doors are opening and closing with determined regularity and fresh, hot bread.

Between 6:00 and 8:00, about 20 bakeries deliver goods, some still hot to the touch. Trays and bags of breads, rolls, bagels, croissants, and brioches are quickly stacked on the empty shelves. What's left when the store closes each night is returned or thrown out. Very little is either. Each week, out of Zabar's and into the mouths of New Yorkers go 10,000 croissants and brioches, more than 3,000 pounds of rye bread, and tons of assorted other breads and rolls. Hardly anything is ever left over.

The first delivery of the day is usually by Victory Bakers, with its still-warm *rye* and *pumpernickel*. Victory rye is something special. It's liberally sprinkled with caraway seeds and Polish *chernishkas*, tiny black roasted seeds that taste somewhere between pepper and caraway. This is truly a seeded rye, chewy and crunchy. It's especially good for sandwiches, as it doesn't get soggy.

Hot on their heels is Orwasher's, with its special *raisin pumpernickel*, so heavy with raisins that it's like dessert. With sweet butter or cream cheese, it's luscious—provided you make it home with any left. Orwasher's also supplies a *handmade rye*, not as popular as the regular rye, because it doesn't look as pretty; but 40 to 50 pounds of it are snapped up each week by knowing customers, who love its thick crust and tangy flavor. It's better in thick slices than thin, cut by hand rather than machine. The secret of Orwasher's bread is that it's baked in what is probably one of the only—not to mention the largest—brick hearth ovens in New York. It's the same oven Louis Orwasher's grandfather put in around 1900, and the last time it broke down, Louis had to import a repairman from Ohio to fix it.

From Moishe's Bakery come more *pumpernickel*—the best, according to Murray Klein—dark and moist; *challah's*; and good, old-fashioned, *European-style corn bread*, dense and chewy, with the thickest crust this side of the Urals. These, too, should be cut by hand, into chunks rather than slices, to be savored just as they are. The challah is great fresh; but when it's a few days old, it makes the best French toast ever.

"We sell more *croissants* than any other single store in New York," Murray Klein boasts, as boxes and boxes of the freshly baked, melt-in-your-mouth wonders are delivered. And the *brioches*. Egg-rich, golden-brown, delicious. It isn't any wonder that when the

BETTER BREAD THAN DEAD (OR, WHY ARABS DON'T EAT MATZOH)

Egyptian tomb paintings glorified life for those who were leaving it, and the growing, harvesting, and grinding of grain for bread-making was a common theme.

One of the stories of the time tells of a baker who had mixed his bread batter and forgotten about it. By the next time he looked, it had risen to twice its size, and the baker was panic-stricken. He couldn't just throw it out, because the Pharaoh's penalty for anyone found wasting food was public beheading. The baker didn't know quite what to do with it, so he threw out half of it and mixed some new batter into what was left. When that doubled in bulk once again, he decided he might as well bake it this time. The resulting crusty brown loaf was presented to the Pharaoh as a special gift from the baker, and unleavened bread was soon a thing of the past.

store opens each morning, customers line up to get their breakfasts.

Baguettes and *rolls* come next, followed by *Sicilian* and *Italian whole-wheat breads*. *Baguette* is French for baton, and indeed, the loaves are thin (about two and a half inches in diameter) and long, as long as two feet. The *flutes* are wider, about four inches around, and the *ficelle* is the skinniest French bread. (*Ficelle* is French for string.) For the most part, the only difference between French and Italian bread is the shape —the French is longer and thinner. But depending on the bakery, there can be differences among Italian breads. *Sicilian bread* is usually kneaded longer and harder and topped with sesame seeds. It comes in a variety of shapes—S's, braids, and hourglasses. *Neopolitan-style bread* is softer and is round or flat or shaped like a log. No matter the shape, all have a light, crunchy crust and a porous interior—which makes them perfect sponges for soaking up sauce and gravy. Split lengthwise, they hold a hero sandwich together better than any other bread.

Swirls of light and dark make the next *rye bread* fancy and festive; it looks particularly pretty on a buffet table.

Three kinds of *pita bread*, Middle Eastern in origin, (white, whole-wheat, and sesame) give a whole new dimension to sandwich-making. The breads are hollow, so by opening them up and filling them with almost

anything—tuna or egg salad; shredded lettuce, to-matoes, cucumbers, even meatballs or veal parmigiana —you have a nice, self-contained little package that doesn't leak.

The *sourdough breads* at Zabar's are a real treat. They may be long or round, white-flour or whole-grain, light and dense at the same time, with the character-istic sourish tang. According to legend, sourdough came to light in Egypt about 5,000 years ago. Air-borne yeasts—actually bacteria—became mixed with flour and water and then fermented. The mixture was kept alive and bubbling and was constantly replen-ished as portions were removed for baking. Although Columbus brought sourdough starter to North Amer-ica, the thought of sourdough bread now conjures up visions of pioneers, prospectors, and the mining camps of the Gold Rush era.

As the morning passes, more keeps trickling in: *Greek bread*, *Russian pumpernickel*, black or golden, *Irish soda bread*, *health bread*, *onion rye*, and a *white bread* that has absolutely no relationship to the kind that is supposed to build strong bodies, but rather is fine-grained and firm, slices without crumbling, and has, as Murray Klein puts it, soul.

Then come the *bagels*, which New Yorkers haven't been able to do without since the first Polish and Aus-trian Jews brought them to the United States around the turn of the century. It was actually a Viennese baker, it's said, who invented the idea of baking bread shaped like a stirrup (*beugel* or *bügel* in German). They are not light-and-crisp confections, but chewy and almost tough, and they tend to sit like a lump in your stomach—and well they should. Their outside is thick and crusty, their inside doughy. Bagels require a goodly amount of chewing, but that's the way they taste best—replete with the flavor of malt and yeast.

SAUSAGE BREAD

This one is one you won't find at Zabar's; it's too perishable.

1 cup milk
¼ cup warm water
1 package active dry yeast
½ cup unsalted butter, melted
1 teaspoon salt
2 tablespoons sugar
4 to 5 sifted cups flour
1 egg
½ pound pepperoni, sliced thin
Melted butter or salad oil

Scald milk; set aside to cool to lukewarm. In warm water, dissolve yeast; add milk, ½ cup melted butter, the salt, sugar, 2 cups of the flour, and the egg, and beat well. Stir in enough more flour to make a stiff dough. (You may need up to 5 cups.) Knead on a floured board for 8 to 10 minutes, until smooth and elastic. Place dough in a greased bowl; turn it over to grease top. Cover, and let rise until doubled in bulk—takes about 1 hour.

Punch down; remove from bowl. Cut in half. Roll each half into an 8- by 10-inch rectangle. Spread half the pepperoni slices on each, and, from the short side, roll up like a jelly roll. Seal edges. Brush with melted butter or oil; place on greased baking sheet, and cover with a damp cloth. Let rise until doubled again—takes about 45 minutes to 1 hour.

Meanwhile, preheat oven to 350°F. When loaves have doubled, bake for 45 minutes to 1 hour, until golden and a loaf sounds hollow when tapped.
Makes 2 loaves.

Variation: Known in N.J. as "Sandy's De-light": Instead of pepperoni, use an equiva-lent amount of cooked Italian hot sausage, sautéed with ½ cup chopped onions, ½ cup chopped green pepper, and 2 to 4 cloves of minced garlic.

(Bagels do come sprinkled with onions, salt, garlic, sesame seeds, raisins and cinnamon.) Days old, bagels are more like rocks than bread. Sprinkle them with a little water, and put them in a 350°F. oven for ten minutes, and they're as good as new.

"Bakers come from all over—New York, Philadelphia, Canada—to sell to Zabar's, because once we approve of them, it's like gold," Murray Klein says.

Take Joe Spiekerman, for instance. For a long time, he was after Klein to sell his *Swiss peasant bread*, but it was too expensive, even for Zabar's. But Joe was persistent, and enough people at the store, including Klein, liked it, so they took it on. That was a wise choice. Spiekerman's Swiss peasant bread and *peasant pumpernickel* have become a New York status symbol; no longer does one merely serve bread, one brings out the Spiekerman's. What makes it so good are the natural ingredients and especially the loving care with which it's baked. The breads are round and crusty, with a plump inside that doesn't even need butter it's so tasty. Zabar's sells close to 3,000 loaves of Spiekerman's breads a week.

Zabar's could easily cram other varieties onto its shelves, but it doesn't, and for one good reason. Despite the hordes of possibilities, most of them simply don't measure up to Zabar's standards.

"Everything we select is the best," says Klein. "We don't have a lot of room, so we have to sell out everything. People come from blocks away just to buy bread, so ours has to be better than just good to make them want to come so far."

Bread is such a big seller at Zabar's that out-of-towners often stop on their way to the airport to buy

SLICING A BAGEL

There are two ways to do this (actually three if you count the wrong way), and which works better depends on how dextrous the slicer is.

Method I: Lay the bagel flat on a breadboard. Cover the entire thing with one hand, and with the knife in the other hand, slice through, parallel to the board.

Method II: Stand the bagel on its side, and hold it at the top between thumb and forefinger. Carefully, starting at the top, with the knife resting on the bagel but under your fingers, slice away. Be sure the rest of your hand is out of the way of the blade. Zabar's sells a plastic bagel slicer that holds the bagel in this position for you.

Wrong way: On the palm of your hand. It's too risky.

a dozen assorted loaves to take home and freeze. All bread tastes better fresh, obviously; but frozen bread will last about three months before it dries out and loses its original flavor. Freeze only fresh bread, wrapped tightly in aluminum foil. It can be cut into sections, because once it has thawed, it should be eaten immediately. Put frozen bread, still wrapped, in the oven (375°F.) for about 15 minutes; then remove the foil, and heat for five minutes, to crisp the crust. You can thaw it first by letting it stand, still in

IRISH SODA BREAD

This is just like the one at Zabar's.

3 ounces unsalted butter, softened
2 eggs
4 cups flour
1 tablespoon baking powder
1 teaspoon salt
1 cup buttermilk or milk
2 teaspoons caraway seeds
½ cup raisins or currants

Preheat oven to 400°F.

Mix the ingredients in the order listed in a large bowl with a wooden spoon. Mix for five minutes. Divide dough in half, and put each half into an ungreased 8-inch baking dish. Sprinkle a little flour on each loaf, and slash a cross in the top of each. Bake 30 minutes. *Makes 2 loaves.*

its wrapping, at room temperature for two to three hours. Frozen sliced bread can be put right in the toaster.

Stale bread needn't be a total loss. You can try to freshen it by putting it into a damp paper bag, closing the bag tightly, and heating it in a 425°F. oven for five minutes; or by sprinkling it with water, wrapping it in foil, and heating it the same way. Heating it, unwrapped, in the top of a double-boiler top over boiling water for five minutes will work, too.

If it won't freshen, use it for bread crumbs, croutons, or French toast. Any bread is all right used this way. Rye and pumpernickel crumbs are great coatings for fried foods; whole-wheat crumbs and cubes make bread pudding and stuffing for poultry notably original. If all else fails, feed the stale bread to the birds.

NOT BY BREAD ALONE

For anyone with a sweet tooth, Zabar's is paradise. Cakes and confections abound; suppliers range from the best commercial producers to the newly divorced woman around the corner who's starting a business.

Honey-dripping *baklava* and *trigona* (triangular, pistachio-nut-and-honey pastries) come from Poseidon Confectionery, the best Greek bakery in New York—some say this side of Athens. *Russian coffeecake* is an incredibly delicious treat, chock-full of nuts,

raisins, and dried fruit and baked especially for Zabar's. *Carrot cake* comes from Levana and Guidos; and little mini-loaves of *sweet breads, tannies* (butterscotch brownies), *fudgies,* and *coffeecakes* from Tootie's Goodies. *Swedish bow-ties,* doused in confectioners' sugar; *ruggelach* (heavenly Jewish cream-cheese pastries filled with nuts, raisins, and cinnamon); Barbara's *chocolate-chip* and *oatmeal-raisin cookies,* big and chewy and all natural; Famous Amos' famous chocolate-chip and pecan delights; Magic Mommy *brownies* (no additives, no preservatives); *Scandinavian tosca* and kringle (confectioner's-sugar drenched fried cookies) from Brooklyn's Little Sweden bakers; *cherry, cheese,* and *apple strudel* from Mrs. Herbst—a breath-taking and weight-gaining multitude of sins, fresh and tempting, with a come hither appeal that only the strongest-willed can resist. Leave it to Zabar's to find "Rennie's Chocolate Cake"—absolutely the best chocolate cake in New York City, possibly even the whole country. It's rich and moist, melts in your mouth, and is amazingly light. No additives, no preservatives, just pure chocolate and deliciousness.

CHEESECAKE

Some like it creamy, some like it Italian-style (made with ricotta and candied fruits), some like it light and airy, but nobody doesn't like cheesecake. Zabar's gets it from the best cheesecake-makers in the metropolitan area.

From S & S and Cheesecake Elegante come cheesecakes to make your heart stop, the lightest, cheesiest, yummiest possible. All very different, and all very fattening.

When cheesecake seems a bit too much, there's an equally delicious, but much less caloric solution. From the country that brought you Amaretto, the wonderful Italian, almond-flavored liqueur, come *Amaretti di Saronno*. These are hard, crunchy macaroons, sprinkled with little crystals of sugar, and they are definitely habit forming. They come in beautiful tin canisters—bright red—in three sizes. As it says on the canister: "Excellent when eaten alone. Can be used to enhance gourmet dishes. Delightful when taken with ice cream or coffee." Bet you can't eat just one.

A PASSION FOR PASTA

There's nothing like fresh pasta made from durum wheat, hard and full of gluten and proteins that keep the starch from breaking down while the pasta cooks, and Zabar's fresh pasta offers just this. Pasta is simply flour and water or eggs mixed into a dough, kneaded, stretched thin, and cut into shapes by hand or machine. Zabar's features egg, spinach, whole wheat, and tomato pastas, from the thinnest (Cappelini d'Angelo) to the widest (lasagna), cut fresh before your eyes. Cheese or meat-filled ravioli, canneloni, manicotti, stuffed shells, cappaletti, and totellini are ready and waiting for sauce and stove. (Zabar's pasta can be put into an airtight plastic bag

and stored in the refrigerator for a few days or frozen for a few months.)

Fresh pasta is quick and easy to cook—and even easier to overcook, so pay attention to what you're doing.

In a large pot, bring three quarts of water per half pound of pasta to a rapid boil. Add a tablespoon or two of olive oil, to prevent the pasta from sticking together, and as much salt. Gently lower the pasta into the water; bring back to the boil, and stir to separate the pieces. Cook only until the pasta is *al dente*—the exact time depends on its size and shape and whether it's fresh or packaged. How do you know? Zabar's will give you a full set of instructions and serving suggestions, or lift a strand or piece out of the water, and bite into it; it should be firm and resistant to the teeth. Drain and serve.

How much uncooked pasta to use is really a question of who's eating and when. As a side dish, you might figure about four people to a pound (sparse, but pasta is filling). As a main course, allow one third of a pound if the sauce is particularly rich and heavy or full of meat and sausages. If it's neither, figure about half a pound per person. The next best thing to fresh pasta is good imported Italian pasta, light golden tan in color, whole, smooth, glossy, never crumbly or splintery.

DeCecco brand truly comes close to the flavor and texture of fresh pasta, and Zabar's carries it happily. Unlike some American brands, which are not as *buoni* as they claim and fall apart in your mouth or even before, DeCecco pasta stays perfectly *al dente*, just the way it should.

Pasta comes in dozens of shapes and sizes: long and thin, such as spaghetti, and perfect for thick sauces and grated cheeses; twisted shapes, such as fusilli; hollow ones like macaroni, which absorb more sauce and are richer; big hollow ones—rigatoni and cannelloni—which are perfect for stuffing. Below are the packaged pastas you'll most likely be able to find.

PACKAGED PASTAS

ANELLI: Rings. *Anellini* are little rings, and *anellini rigati* are little rings with grooves or ridges. Perfect for soup.

CANNELLONI: Large, hollow tubes. Usually stuffed with ricotta cheese mixed with spinach, ham and spices, or ground chicken or veal.

CAPELLINI: Very fine, rounded (like spaghetti), usually in nests. Sometimes called angel's hair. Nice with delicate sauces.

COLORINI: Kid stuff. Macaroni with vegetable coloring.

CONCHIGLIE: Shells. Plain or grooved, large or small. Used in soups, with tomato sauce and cheese; jumbo size for stuffing.

FARFALLE: Butterflies. Bow-shaped egg pasta, for light sauces.

FETTUCINI: Flat, thin noodles, white or flavored and colored with spinach. Great with cream sauces because they stick to the surface.

FUSILLI: Twisted spaghetti, used the same way. *Fusilli bucati* is thin, twisted, hollow macaroni.

LASAGNE: Wide, flat noodles, sometimes rippled. Used for layering with sauce and filling.

LINGUINI: Narrow, flat spaghetti. Goes best with tomato or wine sauces and especially clam sauce.

MACARONI: Short, curved, hollow pasta tubes; elbow macaroni is semicircular. Both absorb sauce. Macaroni and cheese is always a classic; it's great with any pasta sauce.

MANICOTTI: Large tubes. Usually served stuffed, like cannelloni.

MEZZE ZITI: Large, tubular macaroni, long like spaghetti. Can be stuffed, used for macaroni and cheese, or just sauced.

ORZO: Looks like rice; tastes like pasta. Use in soups or as a substitute for rice.

RIGATONI: Large, hollow tubes, ridged. Nice with pesto (green garlic) sauce.

RUOTE: Wheels. That's what they look like, with hubs, spokes, and ribs. *Rotelle* are small wheels. Drenched in tomato sauce, they're both big favorites with kids.

SPAGHETTI: Long rods, of different thicknesses, indicated by numbers, from very thin to thick. Takes well to heavy sauces, especially tomato.

TAGLIATELLI: Ribbons, similar to fettucini, but narrower.

TORTIGLIONI: Short twists.

VERMICELLI: This means little worms in Italian. Very thin spaghetti.

155

ROOM AT THE TOP

Housewares

"It's a miserable place to shop, with or without the numbers and the pushing and the shoving. But it's worth it in the end, and Zabar's is the only place I'll put up with it."

Peter Nero

Who would have thought that the fourth-biggest-selling area in Zabar's would be, of all places, the ceiling? It was all Murray Klein's idea. When there was not another inch of room on the floor for a box or a basket or a crate or a display of some new housewares item, and what was on the highest shelves was simply gathering dust, Klein said, "Let's hang it from the ceiling." It was a brilliant idea.

Absolutely dazzling copper from France is one of the first things that hits the eye. Heavy-duty, tin-lined, hammered or smooth-finished, the copperware comes in every conceivable shape and form: pots, pans, ramekins, molds, bowls, fish poachers, soup tureens, ladles, teapots, snail dishes, au gratins, butter warmers, utensil sets, pot racks, and more. And at much lower prices than you could hope to expect.

"We used to carry Portuguese copperware," Klein says. "It's cheaper, but it falls apart, so we stopped, and went directly to France to get the best."

And that's not the half of it. Strainers, colanders, mixing bowls, whisks, spoons, woks, corkscrews, milk pitchers, sponges, dish towels, potholders, lemon peelers, fruit pitters, crêpe pans, tea balls, butter curlers, rolling pins, garlic presses, bagel cutters, thermometers, scales, salad spinners, timers, juicers, aprons, steamers, cheese graters, mortars and pestles, and much, much, much more hang suspended from S-hooks all over the ceiling. What's too heavy or too bulky to hang is piled behind the cheese display or wherever there's a little room. Pasta makers, food processors, yogurt makers, electric flour sifters, cookbooks, even paper plates. Whatever you might possibly need or want to make your kitchen complete. You can spend as little as 20 cents on a French sponge (it looks like a piece of cardboard; put it in water, and it fills and expands—magic!) or as much as $1,000 on the spectacular Cremina SuperClub espresso machine.

All this is Murray Klein's pride and joy. He has literally filled the store—the ceiling, that is—with every possible kitchenware item he has ever heard of. And as soon as something new is invented, it's there, too. (All *New York* magazine had to do was mention that a specific glass coffee carafe was the best designed, most functional ever made, and within 24 hours, it was at Zabar's.)

It's a full-scale, nothing-missing, Utopian extravaganza; thousands and thousands of enticing excuses for slaving over a hot stove.

POTS AND PANS

A good cook is only as good as his pots and pans. And Zabar's has gone out of its way to offer the best of the best: well-balanced, high-quality, brand-name equipment—at discount prices, too.

There are several choices of material. While *copper* is the serious chef's first choice—because it's unequivocally the best conductor of heat—it's also usually the most expensive and the most difficult to take care of. Copper pots must be lined—with tin, sterling silver, or stainless steel—if you're going to cook in them, and all of Zabar's are. They are, without a doubt, beautiful to look at hanging from a pot rack, but they probably are a lot less practical than other choices.

Aluminum, for example, is an excellent conductor of heat, and strong, too. But it does need watching, because food can burn or stick to the bottom (porcelain-enamel-coated aluminum eliminates the sticking problem, but the coating can chip), and it does discolor some high-acid foods, such as spinach. However, it's a very good choice, and Zabar's carries thirty items of the Leyse line of professional heavy-gauge-aluminum cookware, as well as a full selection of French Mauviel, black-coated Calphalon, and others.

Old-fashioned *cast iron* conducts heat slowly but evenly. It's heavy, and if you drop cast-iron cookware on a hard surface, it may break, but when it is kept properly seasoned and oiled, it's a joy to cook with—nothing sticks. Porcelain-enamel-coated cast iron, like Copco and Le Creuset, is good-looking—both brands come in dazzling colors—and unlike regular cast iron, it doesn't rust. The coating does, however, occasionally chip or crack, and because the pans are coated, they are less efficient heat conductors than naked cast-iron cookware. They are all extremely heavy, and many people find them uncomfortable to handle.

Stainless steel is strong and easy to clean, but not a great conductor of heat for cooking unless it has a copper or heavy-duty-aluminum bottom or a three-ply inner core of copper or aluminum. Zabar's imported Norwegian stainless steel is heavyweight, with a perfect sandwich layer of aluminum on the bottom.

Nonstick cookware is coated with plastic so foods won't stick. It's lightweight, attractive, and, at Zabar's, imported from France.

FIVE KITCHEN CHOTCHKAS YOU MAY NOT BE ABLE TO LIVE WITHOUT

Egg piercer: Makes a tiny hole in the shell of a raw egg.
Cherry pitter: Also works on plums.
Butter slicer: Perfect little pats every time.
Mincing rocker: Looks like a toy; minces parsley with a rocking motion.
Dripless tea ball: Comes with its own little saucer.

Of course, you can also cook in *glass, ceramic, porcelain, earthenware,* or *stoneware,* all of which are better at retaining heat than distributing it evenly. They will crack or break if exposed to sudden temperature changes, and unless they are specifically labeled flameproof, they cannot be used over direct heat. Flameproof cookware, on the other hand, can be used on top of gas stoves, but isn't very efficient on electric ranges. If a pot is labeled ovenproof or heatproof, it should not be placed over direct heat, but used only in the oven. And always use a trivet at the table; hot pots melt plastic and burn wood.

KNIVES

Just as important as the right pots and pans are the right knives—not just with a properly sharpened blade, but with a comfortable, well-fitting handle and a good tang (the part of the blade that fits inside the handle).

First the blade. Carbon or stainless steel? Stainless doesn't rust. Carbon steel does rust and pit, but some chefs prefer them.

The handle should fit your hand comfortably and preferably be made of wood, so it won't get slippery and hard to grasp. The tang, in a good knife, should be attached to the handle with rivets, not glue, so it won't loosen with washing and use.

Zabar's carries a complete line of Sabatier carbon and stainless steel knives. They are beautifully balanced, ebony- or plastic-handled, and come in a wide variety of sizes. You could easily make do with two basic knives: a chef's knife for chopping and a paring knife for slicing. That's just for openers, however. As you become more proficient, you can add anything from cleavers to clam knives.

THE FOOD PROCESSOR FRACAS

From the minute Craig Claiborne first mentioned the Cuisinart food processor, cooks all over the country had to have one. It became a timesaving, lifesaving kitchen necessity, despite its high price tag.

To Zabar's Murray Klein, it was just another imported machine he could sell in the store.

1975. Cuisinart was the "in" appliance, at the very top of everyone's "must have" list. Murray Klein put one in the window priced at $149—a full 25-percent discount, as everywhere else it cost $200.

Some Zabar's customers who had paid full price for

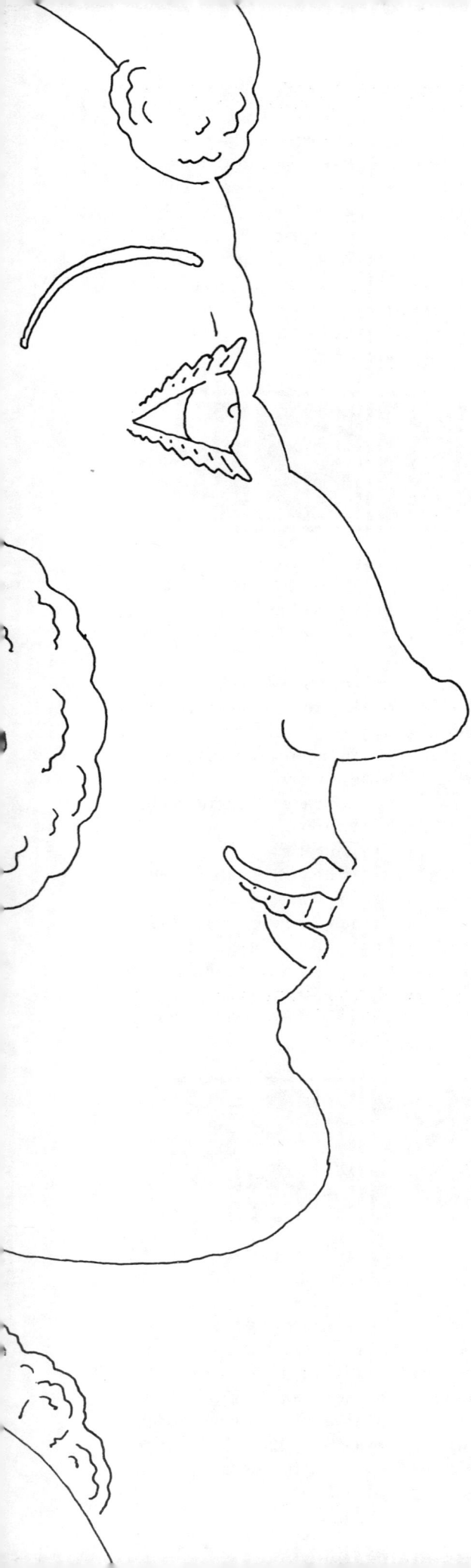

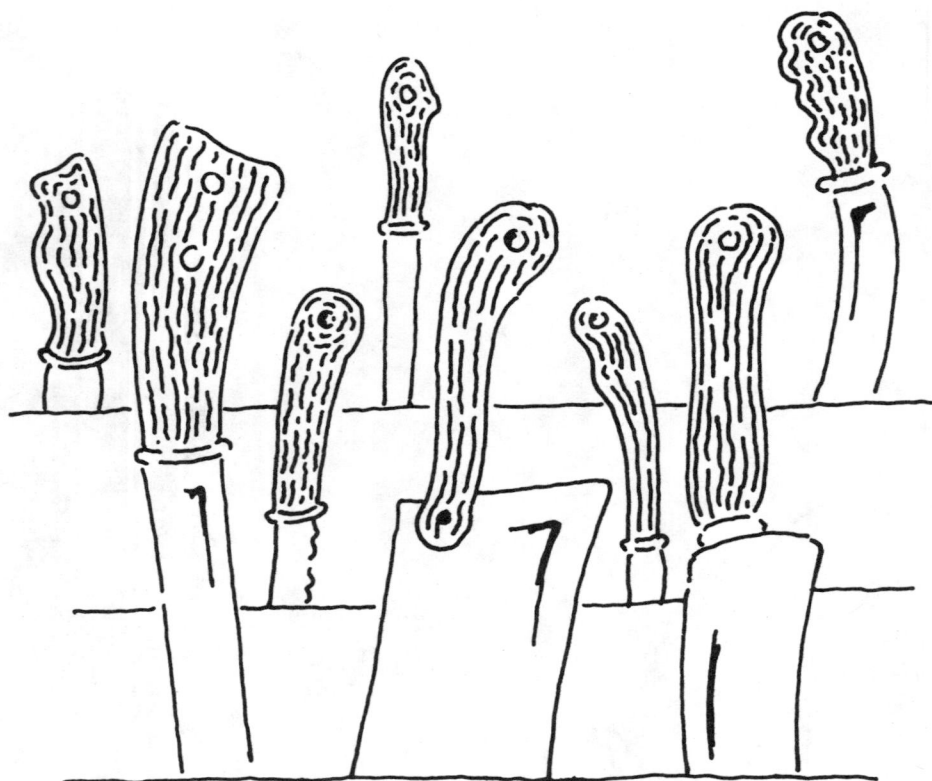

CHEF'S KNIFE (Also called the Cook's Knife): It is the most basic, most necessary knife in any kitchen, primarily for chopping. They are available with blades from 7 to 13 inches long, rigid, tapered blades, slightly curved for balance.

PARING KNIFE: This is actually a scaled-down version of the chef's knife, with the blade 3 to 7 inches long, tapered and firm, but without the pronounced curve of the chef's knife. Use it for paring, slicing, taking pits out of fruit, and so on.

BREAD KNIFE: Great for getting through crusts; the serrated edge of a good bread knife should not be used to saw heavily, but as a means to reaching the delicate insides of a crusty loaf.

FRUIT/VEGETABLE KNIFE: They may or may not be serrated, but the blades are usually no more than 4 inches long, and rather pointed, making them perfect for slicing everything from lemons and tomatoes to sausages.

BUTCHER KNIFE: This is not for chopping, but for cutting raw meat. The blades are 10 to 12 inches long, and curved like a scimitar.

BONING KNIFE: The blades of these knives may be rigid for large jobs, or flexible for smaller ones. It has a narrow, pointed blade from 6 to 11 inches long.

CARVING KNIFE: For cooked meats, to get perfect slices, a good carving knife will have a thin, slightly flexible blade, straight and to the point.

FROZEN FOOD KNIFE: This is almost a saw, a strong, tooth-bladed knife, just perfect for cutting through frozen foods.

GRAPEFRUIT KNIFE: A sharp, serrated edge on a thin, pointed blade (some grapefruit knives are almost concave), great for separating grapefruit sections from their skin.

CLEAVER: A wide, heavy blade, just made for cutting through bones, lobsters, and even for chopping onions, parsley, ginger, garlic, and so on.

FISH KNIFE: An all-purpose fish knife is usually serrated on one side (for scaling), sharply honed on the other, for slicing and cutting, with a sharp point that will open clams and peel and devein shrimp.

their machines at Bloomingdale's were understandably upset. They complained to Bloomingdale's. Bloomies complained to Cuisinart. And Cuisinart told Zabar's to cut it out, or else.

Murray Klein took the machine out of the window, but he wasn't about to change his price. It stayed right at $149. And suddenly, no more Cuisinarts were available for Zabar's. The manufacturer refused to sell the store a single one.

That's all Murray Klein needed to hear. He's a man who loves a good fight, and this one looked as if it would be a corker. Like a squirrel hoarding nuts against the winter, Klein set out to gather Cuisinarts from a nationwide network of small stores. One from here, three from there, half a dozen from someplace else. It took some doing, but he managed to round up 200 in dribs and drabs, and he joyfully informed the Sales & Bargains editor of *New York* magazine that Zabar's now had Cuisinarts for $135. One to a customer, please. Murray Klein had decided to teach Cuisinart a lesson they would never forget. You don't mess around with Klein.

By noon, day one of the sale, all 200 had been sold and more than 900 rain checks given out. You couldn't keep people away. One man flew in especially from Washington, D. C., for a Cuisinart. He bought one, ran out of the store, changed his clothes at a friend's place, and got right back in line to buy a second. By the time he was ready to try this a third time, there weren't any left.

ENTER THE LAW

Discounting the Cuisinart and making headlines weren't quite enough. It was time to really go into action.

Stanley Zabar had seen a newspaper account about a Connecticut lawyer who had successfully sued the Ford Motor Company on behalf of an auto-parts dealer who had been selling Ford parts below list price until the company stopped filling his orders. Stanley wanted this lawyer on Zabar's side, and he got him. Not only was he delighted to represent Zabar's, but he was a long-time customer.

In May, 1976, Zabar's sued Cuisinart and Bloomingdale's for restraint of trade. The lawyer asked for $5 million in damages. And more important, for Cuisinarts.

After 18 months of haggling, fighting, and refusing to give in, the suit was settled out of court. Zabar's got its food processors, plus the right to sell them at any price. Zabar's customers, who had waited patiently to redeem their rain checks, got not only their Cuisinarts, but a bonus—a coffee mill and five pounds of beans. And Murray Klein began to collect more Cuisinarts, ready for the next battle if there was to be one, a gleem of retribution in his snapping green eyes.

ONCE MORE INTO THE FRAY

He'd do it all over again.

"Why not?" he asks. "No one can dictate prices

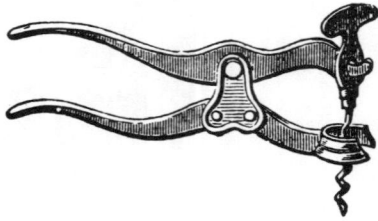

to me. I can sell the machine for whatever I want. If I want to give away Cuisinarts for free, that's no one else's business but mine."

Besides, he likes·to make waves. "There's always something to fight over, and this I know for sure, if I ever give up without a fight, I might as well die—and quick."

Zabar's is still selling Cuisinarts for the lowest price in town—when it can get them. Despite all the publicity and the lawsuit, the machines are still not easy for Zabar's to come by. But that doesn't really seem to matter. Zabar's isn't pushing them, anyway. Instead, it's promoting the Sanyo processor, which sells for about $70 and which Zabar's feels is a fantastic machine (Zabar's sold almost 10,000 American Food Processors in the first two months the store carried them, but manufacturing changes didn't meet with Murray Klein's approval, so he stopped selling them.)

"You have a friend with a Cuisinart?" Klein asks a skeptical customer. "Take a Sanyo home and compare them. If you don't like it, bring it back, and I'll give you back your money."

LABELS FOR LESS

There's nothing Murray Klein likes better than taking pages from the latest Bloomingdale's housewares catalog, blowing them up to poster size, and putting them in Zabar's window, with his prices right beside theirs. Zabar's prices usually are in the neighborhood of 30 percent lower than Bloomingdale's—or anyone else's, for that matter. For exactly the same items, with all tags, labels, warranties, guarantees, and what-have-yous intact—and prominently displayed.

This upsets a lot of people: Small retailers who think that maybe manufacturers won't sell to them either, as they haven't sold to Zabar's in the past; large retailers who don't cotton to the idea that they're being undersold and that their ads are doing double duty; and wholesalers and importers who have to listen to the complaints of their biggest customers.

Murray Klein doesn't care. "I have to give them a hard time," he says. "I have to straighten them out or they'll choke me. I'm not going to let them get away with anything."

Cuisinart was just one of the battles Murray has fought. Salton "ran out" of coffee grinders when Za-

bar's started selling them about half price; Jena glass, famous for a unique teapot, mysteriously couldn't fill a Christmas order; Romertoff just didn't have any more clay cookers to send to Zabar's.

Undaunted, Klein assumed his familiar fighting stance. He went directly to the German manufacturer of the Salton grinder and ordered 10,000 of his own. And eventually sold twice that many. He called on his small retailers all over the country and offered them 10 to 15 percent over wholesale to order Jena teapots and Romertoff cookers for him. They did. And he paid the extra postage, as well. And never raised Zabar's prices.

It's more than getting even, it's a way of life for Murray Klein. It isn't the money (he has more than enough; "I could live on a dollar a day," he says) or simply turning over merchandise—"Just to sell? That's nothing. If that's all there was to it, I would leave." It's the constant challenge, the fights, the triumph over the Establishment that keep him going. The satisfaction that comes from doing something.

TUNE IN NEXT WEEK . . .

Zabar's is like a museum that's constantly changing its exhibits. Just as soon as you figure out where everything is—bingo—it's new, different, and terribly exciting.

Just a year ago, the Zabar's Wares Fare Annex, one store away from the main emporium, opened with a flourish.

Now, even that's changed. Today, it's a sinfully tempting pastry counter and a European-style, stand-up espresso and cappuccino bar. Copperware still hangs from the ceiling, and steel shelving still holds pots, pans, and housewares in neat rows. But the bulk of the annex has given way to a far better idea—"Delice La Cote Basque," the very finest, most delectable pastry confections ever, from New York's undisputed heaven-on-earth French patisserie. Just a few steps away is coffee, Zabar's finest, made in the exclusively Zabar's Cremina Espresso machines. It was Murray Klein's latest brainstorm; one more turn-around through the evolving door that is Zabar's.

Actually, it's all part of a master expansion plan, and by the time it's fully realized, you'll be able to walk through a Zabar's that's made up of several individual shops—a little like Paris' Fauchon—all tied together by old-fashioned wood, brick, and rounded glass exteriors.

The only thing Zabar's won't ever change is their commitment to "the best quality at the best price."

The Zabar's of this very minute is only a part of what is still to come.

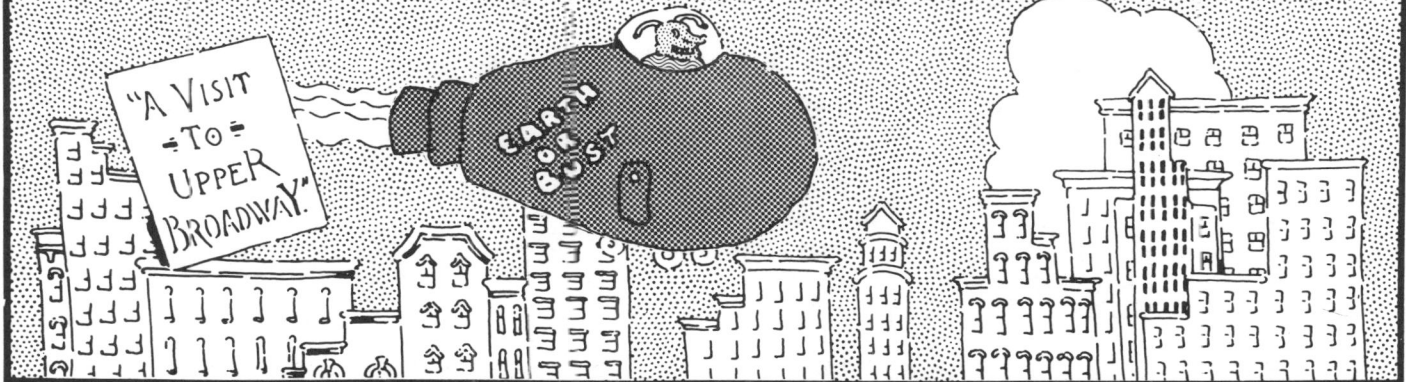

FROM APPLE CORERS TO
ZABAGLIONE MOLDS

Zabar's is dazzling—and sometimes expensive. But the budget-conscious can have a field day with the housewares; some prices range from downright cheap to truly inexpensive.

COFFEE MILLS AND GRINDERS
Braun mini-grinder KSM1
Braun mini-grinder KSM11
Braun Aromatic KMM1
Norelco grinder
Waring grinder
Kitchenaid grinder
Zabar's KM75 (by Krups)
Zabar's Z75 (by Philips)
Krups Grindmaster
Bosch K3
Bosch K4
Spong hand grinder (small)
Melitta Beanery

COFFEEMAKERS

Electric Filter Drip
Bunn-o-matic
Krups Coffee Plus
Wigomat 14, 161, 120
Bosch
Melitta 1-cup Personal Coffeemaker

Non-Electric Filter Drip
Melitta Glass, 6-cup, 8-cup, 12-cup
Melitta Porcelain, 4-cup, (101)
Melitta Coffee Warmer
Chemex with wooden collar, 3-cup,
    6-cup, 8-cup, 13-cup
Chemex Coffee Warmer

Paper Filters
Melitta Filters—all sizes, e.g.,
    PA6-100
Chemex filters—FP-1 or FP-2
Tricolator filters—FX10
Tricolator filters—FX12
Bunn basket filters, pack of 100
Cleaning kits for all automatic drip
    coffeemakers

COOKWARE

Clay Cookers
Romertopf clay pot cookers
    (unglazed): No. 109, No. 111,
    No. 113, No. 114 (for fish)
Parchment paper
Claypot Cookbook

*Heavy Gauge Aluminum Cookware
    by Leyse*
Leyse professional aluminum cook-
    ware line, over thirty items
    including:
3-quart covered sauté pan
7- and 8-inch omelet pans
8-quart savory cooker
Asparagus steamer
10-quart stock pot

16-quart stock pot
3-quart double boiler
1½-quart covered saucepan
4½-quart covered saucepan

*French Heavy Gauge Tin-Lined
    Copper*
    Zabar's now features New York's
largest and finest collection of
French copper cookware, from the
factories of Mauviel, Havard, Dela-
lande, and Lefèvre. Our prices are
the lowest anywhere for heavy gauge,
tin-lined pieces, both hammered and
and smooth-finished polished copper. Choose from stock pots, Fon-
dues, sauté pans, frying pans,
saucepans, paella pans, oval or
round au gratins, oval fryers, snail
dishes, butter melters, utensil sets,
pot racks, fish poachers, double
boilers, charlotte molds, fish molds,
soup tureens, preserve basins, za-
bagliones, flambé, ladles, colanders,
and more.
18-cm cover with brass handle
20-cm zabaglione
14-cm covered charlotte mold
8-cm butter melter with iron handle
16-cm oval casserole with lid
24-cm round casserole with lid
40-cm paella pan
20-cm pomme anna saucepan with
    lid
18-cm saucepan with brass handle
32-cm covered sauté pan with two
    handles
20-cm splayed sauté pan
22-cm round frying pan
40-cm oval frying pan

Enamelled Cast Iron Cookware
Full line of Le Creuset in open stock
Full line of Copco enamel as well
    as cast aluminum in open stock
T-FAL skillets and baking pans

Imported Stainless Steel Cookware
Zabar's imports the Norwegian
    Polaris line of 18/8 stainless steel
    cooking utensils, pots, pans, and
    kettles. For example: 2⅔-pint
    teakettle with copper bottom
16-cm round covered casserole with
    wood handles

Do-It-Yourself
Salton original yogurt maker
Salton ice cream maker (1C-4)

Soda Syphons
ISI one-quart glass and wire mesh

syphons, available in silver or
black
ISI CO_2 capsules

Pasta Machines
HOAN or Ampia hand-operated
    chrome steel
Bialetti electric machine, with many
    rollers

Food Processors
Sanyo Food Factory: rated as being
    one of the best—pushbutton op-
    eration, variable speed, finest sur-
    gical steel blades

Hobart K5A: especially good for
    mixing dough—classic design,
    stainless steel and enamel, 5-quart
    bowl, balloon whisk, dough hook,
    mixing blade. Hobart's top-of-the-
    line for home use
Norelco Food Processor
Waring Food Processor
Moulinex La Machine
Moulinex La Machine, Deluxe Model
Vitamix model 3600 mixer-blender-
    juicer
Large assortment of books relating
    to food processor cooking

Juicers and Extractors
Braun MP50 Juice Extractor
Sanyo Juicer Extractor, with auto-
    matic pulp ejector, multiple
    speeds
Sanyo Citrus Juicer
Sanyo Extract-a-Blend (combina-
    tion juice extractor and juicer
    blender)
Orbis battery-operated juicer
Zyliss hand juicer

Fish Poachers
16-inch stainless steel poacher
12-inch French heavy steel, tinned

Omelet Pans
Full stock of omelet pans including
    traditional French steel pans,
    aluminum, cast aluminum, enamel
    on cast iron, as well as crêpe pans
    in either steel or enamel

Woks
14-inch traditional steel wok with
    ring and cover
Deluxe set: wok, ring, cover,
    utensils, book
Electric Wok
Electric Tempure Cooker

Meat Slicer
Collapsible electric slicing machine
by Krups

Steamers
Collapsible stainless steel vegetable
steamer with lift ring
Tournus French Couscousier

KITCHEN THINGS

Cheese Slicers & Graters
Wide range of cheese implements including knives, cutters, planes,
wire cutting blocks, Swedish steel
bell graters, Mouli graters, Copco
graters
Robinson cutter-plane with riveted
rosewood handle
Robinson plane with lucite handle
Stainless bell grater

Fondue Sets
Many models in copper, steel,
enamel, ceramic, with or without
stands and burners
From Spring, hammered copper
2-quart fondue with wrought iron
stand and tray, wooden handles
We stock fondue forks, fondue
mixes, fondue fuel, and sterno

Teapots and Teakettles
Glazed stoneware by Otagiri
Terra Cotta with insert by Otagiri
Jena glass teapot with insert
Jena glass Teatime pot
Jena glass Teatime warmer
Jena glass tea glass with handle
Jena glass saucer
Gailstyn 4-cup enamel teapots
(4 colors)
Revere 3-quart whistling kettle,
stainless steel with copper bottom
English 3-quart copper kettle with
coil bottom, for gas stoves
Copper kettles by Benjamin &
Medwin, 2-quart
Copco Teakettle in enamel or cast
aluminum
See a wide assortment of steel,
chrome, wire mesh, and bamboo
tea balls and spoon infusers

Stoneware
We have Zanesville's Peddlarware
mixing bowls, baking dishes,
onion soup bowls, and covered
casseroles in bisque and chocolate
brown glazed stoneware

Salad Bowls
A variety of wooden salad bowls,
utensils, and serving bowls, e.g.,
10-inch teak bowl by Kalmar

Peppermills
Peugeot 4-inch walnut or blond
Peugeot 10-inch walnut
Copco lucite mill
Swinger lucite mill
Perfex cast aluminum with side
loading port
Large assortment of pepper mill and
salt shaker sets in wood, silver,
copper, pewter, etc. by Wm.

Bounds, Dudley, Kebow, Olde
Thompson

Salt Mills
Marlux
Copco
Swinger
Peugeot 4-inch walnut salt shaker
(matches pepper mill)
Marlux wooden nutmeg grinders

Cookbooks
We carry the entire Time-Life
Cookbooks of the World series.
Wide range of paperback titles
dealing with cheese, coffee and
tea, wok cookery, claypot cooking,
food processors, etc.

CUTLERY

Full line of Sabatier carbon and
stainless steel knives, sharpening
steels, cleavers, carving forks,
starter sets, steak knives, and
specialties
9-inch stainless steel carver
8-inch stainless steel chef knife
5-inch stainless steel boning knife
4-inch stainless steel parer
Bread knife
Knife sharpener
Tomato knife
Clam knife with rosewood handle
4-inch full tang stainless steel
paring knife, with brass riveted
wood handle

KITCHEN GADGETS

We stock a wide variety of gadgets
and small utensils for the kitchen,
including radish cutters, apple
corers, nutmeg graters, natural
compressed sponges, snail tongs,
snail forks, nutcrackers, vegetable
peelers, egg separators, bagel
cutters, egg piercers, corkscrews,
lobster picks, cherry pitters, flour
sifters, potbrushes, full-o-suds
scouring brushes, pizza cutters,
measuring cups, measuring
spoons, cookie cutters, basting
brushes, quiche pans, spatulas,
cake servers, egg slicers, ladles,
scoops, rolling pins, pastry bags,
spreaders, springform pans,
coquille shells, snail shells, loaf
pans, shishkebab skewers, asbestos
pads, flametamers, meat tender-
izers, meat grinders, nylon
basters, potholders, salad driers,
rotating food choppers, mincing
rockers, melon ballers, butter
curlers, french-fry cutters, garlic
presses, garlic baskets, corn-
holders, slaw cutters, swingaway
openers, over-the-sink cutting
boards, bamboo serving trays,
honey dippers, mortars and
pestles, steam pudding molds,
soufflé dishes, ramekins, cow
creamers, lemon strippers, tooth-
picks, chopholders, and hundreds
of other items.

KITCHEN ACCESSORIES

Zyliss or Triumph salad spinner
Zyliss garlic press
Zyliss lemon press
Zyliss hand juicer

Kitchen Scales
French and West German scales by
Terraillon, Soehnle, Bila, Eva
Terraillon BA2000 2-kilo
Soehnle 2-kilo collapsible
Bil 2-kilo
Kitchen timers by HOAN and
Terraillon

Glazed Stoneware Mugs
Large variety of designs by Otagiri

Ice Cream Scoops
Italian chromed steel automatic
scoops in three sizes
Zeroll scoop with antifreeze handle

Kitchen Thermometers
Full range of Taylor thermometers
for every need—candy, deep fry,
oven, instant reading, meat, etc.
Deluxe instant reading thermom-
eter can be used in microwave
ovens

Cutting Boards
Joyce Chen lucite cutting boards,
small, medium, large, pastry slab

Pot Racks
Wrought iron half-moon racks
Taylor & Ng wall and hanging
wooden stainless steel racks, e.g.,
36-inch wood wall rack

Colanders
Copper colander with stainless steel
liner, 9- or 12-inch
Stainless steel colander, 9- or 13-inch
Aluminum colander, 12-inch or
10-inch with long handle
8-inch enamel colanders, assorted
colors
15-inch extra large heavy aluminum
chef model

Whisks
Large assortment of whips and
whisks, tin, wood handles, stainless steel, etc.
15-inch balloon whisk, wood handle
13-inch stainless steel whip

Strainers and Sieves
Full range, 3-inch strainer with
plastic handle to Italian stainless
steel 7-inch sieve to extra fine
boullion strainers

Mixing Bowls
Solid copper bowls for the stiffest,
highest beaten egg whites: 8-inch,
10-inch, or 12-inch diameter
3-piece stainless steel mixing bowl
set

ZABAR'S VERY OWN FUN-TO-WEAR
T-SHIRTS!
Didn't we say Zabar's has everything! Bright white combed
cottons set off with zippy orange
letters. The whole family will get
a kick out of them.

A Catered Affair

"Every time I walk by, I have to stop inside just to inhale."
Gael Greene

When you absolutely can't stand the idea of whipping together another intimate little brunch for 10 or a celebration dinner for 100 or 1,000, Zabar's will handle it.

The catering service is a natural extension of the store. And a highly successful one. By Labor Day, for instance, Zabar's is usually booked for more than it can handle on New Year's Eve, and a year in advance is not too soon to put in a bid.

"Catering is a success," Murray Klein says. "I made the price so attractive that if you had twenty people and you bought the food yourself, it would cost about the same. And it wouldn't be as attractive. I give people a price they can't refuse."

Klein's given a new meaning to "breakfast-in-bed" with his catering philosophy. For $75.00, Zabar's will deliver a sumptuous Sunday morning fantasy for two: caviar and sour cream, bagels and cream cheese, goat cheese, juice and pastry. Less extravagant feasts can be had starting at $21.50. All you have to do is call. Picnics, too, can be catered with a little advance notice.

His philosophy is simple. "Most caterers think that people get drunk at parties and don't know what they're eating, anyway. We don't feel that way. Whatever we send is the best from Zabar's. Besides, I would say, conservatively, that for every party of twenty we cater, we get four new customers who never heard of Zabar's before."

The catering operation is at least a four-man job. Klein always supervises and selects the food; sometimes he'll even cut bagels and slice fish. Nothing leaves the store without his okay, and his careful attention shows. There is always one fish to rearrange, one slice of roast beef to move, one pickle to add.

Since he's been running the catering show, he likes to say there have been virtually no complaints. When pressed, he'll admit there have been a few, but not many, and each is considered legit. Even the one from the hostess who ordered for 20 and 30 showed up, and she ran out of food.

MURRAY KNOWS BEST

"Customers take what I tell them to take," he says. "If I think they're wrong, I don't take the order.

"I had a run-in with a man, the head of a very big real-estate company. He came with his chauffeur and started to tell me what he wanted. I told him to leave it all to me, and if he didn't like it, he didn't have to pay for it.

"Right away he wanted to see Stanley Zabar. The boss. He thought I just worked here. But Stanley told him to listen to me or go someplace else."

Stanley and Saul Zabar don't interfere with Murray Klein. Especially about catering. They don't know much about it, so whatever Murray says, they back him up 100 percent. In this case, the man finally gave in and let Murray Klein make up the order the way he wanted to. But he did have his wife call Zabar's and make some discreet inquiries.

It's even more important for Murray Klein than for his customers that everything be superb. And he's so very sure of what he's doing that he rarely asks for a deposit on a party order. "You trust me to make you a party. I trust you. If you don't want the food, you can always leave it here." That never has happened.

When his son Roger was bar mitzvahed, Klein naturally had several tables of Zabar's finest at the synagogue for the traditional after-services kiddush. They were beautiful. Whole whitefish, plump and large, boned and put back together, sitting proudly on wooden boards with silver heads and tails. Platters of smoked salmon, sturgeon, pickled herring; scallion cream cheese, bagels, rolls, cakes, cookies, and, of course, a braided challah. Simple, but magnificent, less designed to feed people than to let the congregation taste and share in the Kleins' happiness. It was easy. Bar mitzvahs catered by Zabar's are a regular New York happening.

When a young dentist approached Klein one afternoon and said, "I want to throw a party for about a thousand. What do I do?" Klein was truly in his element.

First the food. A Zabar's smorgasbord that included a little bit of everything. About 250 pounds of assorted smoked fish—carp, lox, salmon, sable, whitefish. Another 250 pounds of deli meats—roast beef, corned beef, pastrami, ham, and tongue. Salads—coleslaw, potato salad, baked-salmon, lobster, chopped-liver. About a dozen trays of relishes—pickles, olives, sauerkraut, sour tomatoes, and peppers—maybe 200 pounds altogether. Fifty loaves of bread—rye, pumpernickel, raisin pumpernickel—and 50 dozen bagels, bialys, and small rolls. About 100 pounds of cheese—whole wheels of Brie, Jarlsberg, Cheddars, Swiss, and, of course, plain and scallion cream cheese. Zabar's also supplied the butter, mustard, mayonnaise, ketchup, and several beautifully arranged platters of fresh fruit. Not to mention 100 pounds of Russian coffeecake and assorted cookies, 15 pounds of Zabar's Special Blend coffee, two pounds of tea, ten pounds of sugar, four gallons of milk, and a dozen lemons.

Enough to feed an army. The choices, with the dentist's approval, of course, were Murray Klein's. He met with no opposition. And there was still more.

The accouterments: chairs, tables, coffee urns, and so on. If Zabar's couldn't supply them, Klein knew who could. Zabar's doesn't get involved in that end of the catering business, but can recommend places that specialize. Wine and liquor? Klein did the computations and came up with the numbers and the best places to get the beverages. He and the host decided on beer and wine, about 30 cases of each. Soft drinks, too. Beverages wouldn't run out. Plates, napkins, cups, eating utensils—all paper or plastic, to keep things easy. There wasn't anything Klein didn't think of. Right down to the salt and pepper.

About two weeks before the party, Klein went to see the hall and what he'd have to work with. He suggested arranging the food on two levels, to ease the crush of 1,000 invited guests plus the inevitable extras. With four bar areas, to leave room for strolling musicians.

The real work for Zabar's started the morning of the party. The catering staff began setting up the platters—about 100 of them for just the sliced fish and meats (separately, of course). The whitefish was fileted and sliced, then put back together on boards;

shiny, golden, and beautiful. The whole breads were sliced by machine; the bagels, bialys, and rolls by hand —mostly by Murray Klein himself. These would go into baskets at the hall, the cheeses on cutting boards, the salads and condiments in bowls. As each platter was finished, it was wrapped and refrigerated. By four that afternoon, everything was in the truck and on its way.

It was perfect. Platter after platter of food that seemed to come from an endless kitchen. More than enough of everything, despite uninvited guests. A bash for 1,000, and Murray Klein and Zabar's handled it as effortlessly as if it had been a quiet little dinner for a dozen.

DOING IT YOURSELF

That's how Zabar's does it. Unless you happen to have a staff of four, doing it yourself will be difficult, obviously, but it needn't be overwhelming.

First of all, know your limits. A meal for a thousand people requires a caterer; 25 or 50 can be manageable.

Buffets are the easiest way to serve a lot of people with the least confusion and effort. In fact, *buffet* is what the French call a meal served on boards to coach travelers on a train. They ate standing up—on the run, as it were. The buffet grew into a much more elaborate production as restaurants adopted the principle, to provide customers an opportunity to see everything offered.

According to Murray Klein, there are some general rules that can help you do your own catering.

MEAT: "Figure on about a quarter pound per person. It doesn't sound like enough, but there will be other food." (Professional caterers think in terms of about 12 ounces [¾ pound] of protein foods per guest. This total includes meat, fish, and cheese.)

CHEESE: Two ounces (⅛ pound) per person. That's a lot of cheese to buy, and just a conservative estimate. A wheel of Brie weighs about 3 pounds, a wheel of Jarlsberg about 20. Cheddars can go from a pound to 20; a large wheel of Swiss weighs around 200. The more people you have, the simpler the choices should be.

FISH: Murray Klein calculates about 6 ounces per guest, enough for two hefty sandwiches. (Except for lox, or smoked salmon—2 ounces per person is plenty.)

CAVIAR: This is tricky, because you can't be precise. If you buy the best, 1 to 2 ounces per guest lets even big eaters go overboard. Cheaper caviar can be mixed with sour cream or cream cheese, to stretch it considerably.

BREAD: You can get about 20 thin slices from a 1-pound loaf. But who likes thin bread? Figure on five people per loaf, and at least one roll, bagel, or bialy per person if there's bread, too.

BUTTER, MAYONNAISE, MUSTARD: More is always better here. Leftover butter can be frozen if it hasn't been at room temperature too long. If you slice the butter beforehand, you can get 32 big pats to the pound.

SALAD: Here Klein goes back to his quarter-pound-per-person. That's subjective, though. Some people love potato salad and hate coleslaw, and vice versa. Everybody loves chopped liver.

PÂTÉ: From a pound of pâté, you can get about 20 half-inch-thick slices. One slice per guest may sound skimpy, but good pâté is rich and filling.

COFFEE: A pound will make 40 cups. A pound of tea will easily serve 100. When you make tea in quantity, pour a quart of boiling water over ¼ pound of tea. Steep for 5 minutes; strain, and dilute—1 part brewed tea to 8 parts of fresh boiling water.

MILK, CREAM, AND SUGAR: About ½ pound of sugar and a pint of cream will be plenty for 25 cups of coffee. For tea, serve the same amount of sugar cubes—they're more elegant—and always milk (about 1 ½ cups per 25 cups of tea). Two lemons will provide about 20 thin slices.

DESSERT: A gallon of ice cream will serve 25 people. And ¼ pound of cake per person is one way to figure it. If you preslice the cake, figuring will be easier. A 9-inch layer cake can be cut into 12 slices; a 9-inch pie into 8 wedges—small ones, perhaps, but then a guest sampling each pie will look less gluttonous. About 5 pounds of cookies should do for 25 people. For fruit salad, figure on 6 servings per quart. Chocolate mousse? Half-cup servings are large enough.

ALCOHOL: The amount to serve depends on your guests. But the wine and liquor people recommend the following: six 4-ounce glasses of wine per bottle; two ounces of spirits (scotch, rye, gin, vodka, rum, etc.) per drink; twelve drinks from a fifth, sixteen from a quart. Count on at least two drinks per person, no matter what the beverage.

CANAPÉS, HORS D'OEUVRES, AND TIDBITS: There's a difference, you know. Canapé means sofa in French, which is why canapés usually have a bread or pastry base. They accompany drinks. Hors d'oeuvres are most often served alone, with bread and crackers. Cocktail tidbits—chunks of wurst or cheese, and so on—are more filling than either, but also less fashionable. Figure about six per person.

These are just the basics, and you can put them together almost any way you choose. You have to know your guests and their eating proclivities—as well as your own concept of what's enough—to make even a simple buffet a success.

DELI BUFFET FOR 12

4 pounds (1 pound each of 4 kinds) cold cuts—
corned beef, pastrami, tongue, roast beef,
turkey, ham, salami, etc.
2 pounds coleslaw
2 pounds potato salad
1½ pounds chopped liver
3 loaves rye bread, or 2 dozen rolls
6 large sour pickles, quartered lengthwise
4 sour tomatoes, quartered
4 pickled peppers, hot or sweet, quartered
or cut in eighths
½ pound ripe black olives

Don't forget mustard, mayonnaise, butter,
ketchup, salt, and pepper. Add crackers for the
chopped liver.

DELI BUFFET FOR 30

8 dozen assorted hot hors d'oeuvres—miniature
quiches, meat pies, egg rolls, cheese puffs,
pigs in blankets; all are available frozen
1 12-pound roast turkey, carved and put back
on frame
7 pounds assorted cold cuts
5 pounds coleslaw
5 pounds potato salad
3 pounds chopped liver, or 2 pounds pâté
1 or 2 loaves party rye bread—tiny loaves
just right for chopped liver
3 loaves rye bread, or 5 dozen assorted small rolls
2 dozen sour pickles, sour tomatoes, and
pickled peppers, all quartered
½ pound ripe black olives
½ pound green olives

SUNDAY BRUNCH FOR 8

1½ dozen (more or less) bagels and bialys
1 pound scallion cream cheese
1 pound plain cream cheese
½ pound lox
1 pound Nova Scotia salmon
½ pound smoked sable
½ pound baked salmon, or 1 pound baked-salmon salad
1 large smoked whitefish—about 2 to 3 pounds
1 pound pickled herring in cream sauce
1½ pounds coleslaw
2 pounds potato salad
2 large Bermuda onions, sliced
3 or 4 fresh tomatoes, sliced
½ pound Swiss cheese, sliced

PICNIC FOR 2

½ pound spinach pâté
½ pound hickory-smoked ham
½ pound Lebanon bologna
1 loaf Swiss peasant bread
1 small goat cheese, such as Banon or Montrachet
½ pound Russian coffeecake
2 fresh apples or pears, halved, spread with Pommery mustard, topped with a slice of Gruyère or Jarlsberg and a slice of cervelat
Wine—a nice light, dry white or a young Beaujolais

BACHELOR'S DINNER, I

Appetizer: Gravad lax or cold poached salmon
Entrée: Zabar's baked, stuffed chicken breast or lemon-garlic chicken
Salad: Asparagus spears or artichoke hearts
Dessert: Brie; fresh pear
Wine: Light, dry white—Graves, or Sauvignon Blanc

BACHELOR'S DINNER, II

Appetizer: Marinated mushrooms
Entrée: Texas Barbecue shell steak
Salad: Three-bean
Dessert: Russian coffeecake
Wine: Full-bodied red—Barolo, perhaps

BACHELOR'S DINNER, III

Appetizer: Antipasto salad
Entrée: Baked salmon, with lettuce, sliced tomato, onion, and cucumber on the side
Dessert: Cheesecake
Wine: Chablis or Pinot Blanc

EASY 10-MINUTE DINNER FOR 2

4 "Specials" frankfurters or knockwurst
½ pound Zabar's baked beans
½ pound sauerkraut

Heat sausages and beans together until hot. Serve sauerkraut, cold or heated, as desired.

HEARTY BRITISH BREAKFAST FOR 2

Porridge (oatmeal, made according to directions on box)
Kedgeree (1 cup cooked rice mixed with freshened finnan haddie, heated in melted butter, seasoned with cayenne pepper and curry powder, and topped with sieved hard-cooked eggs)
4 eggs, scrambled with bacon or ham (2-3 slices per person) or sausages (2-3 per person)
Fried bread (slices of white bread quickly seared in bacon drippings)
Grilled tomatoes and mushrooms
Scones, oatmeal cakes, or Irish soda bread
Butter, jam, marmalade
Tea or coffee

Instead of kedgeree, you might serve finnan haddie or kippers. Simmer 2 slices finnan haddie in ½ cup milk (or enough to cover), ¼ cup chopped onion, and ½ teaspoon peppercorns for 10 minutes; top with mustard cream sauce. Or dot 2 or 4 kippers with butter; sprinkle with lemon juice; broil until just brown.

DUCK À L'ORANGE PDQ

This takes about 15 minutes from start to finish, and is so good that you can take all the credit.

ORANGE SAUCE:

1 tablespoon red wine vinegar
1 tablespoon dark brown sugar
½ cup beef stock
½ teaspoon cornstarch
1 tablespoon grated orange rind
¼ cup orange juice
1 teaspoon lemon juice
2 tablespoons Cointreau or Curaçao
1 tablespoon unsalted butter

1 Zabar's roast duck, quartered
Orange sections

Make Orange Sauce: In a saucepan, carefully cook vinegar and sugar until caramel-colored. Add beef stock and cornstarch, stirring to make sure no lumps form; cook, stirring until thickened and clear. Add remaining sauce ingredients; simmer, uncovered, 5 minutes. Taste, and correct seasonings if necessary.

Put duck in a shallow roasting pan, and pour sauce over it. Broil about 5 inches from heat, until sauce glazes. Before serving, garnish with orange sections.
Serves 4.

The trick to a good smorgasbord is eye appeal. In Denmark, the term means open-face sandwiches; in Sweden, a platterful of cold meats, salads, cheeses, smoked fish, and lots of herring.

½ pound marinated herring
½ pound herring in wine sauce
½ pound smoked salmon
½ pound cooked baby shrimp
½ pound smoked eel
½ pound caviar
1 pound boiled ham
1 pound roast beef
1 pound smoked tongue
½ pound pâté
1 disc Camembert
½ pound Roquefort or Danablu
½ pound herring salad
½ pound crabmeat salad
½ pound cucumber salad
½ pound 3-bean salad
½ pound beet-and-onion salad
½ pound marinated mushrooms
1 loaf rye bread
1 loaf pumpernickel

Garnishes:
Hard-cooked-egg slices, lemon slices, chopped chives, bacon, anchovies, tomato slices, onion slices, horseradish, mayonnaise, butter, mustard.

Open-Faced Sandwiches:
Pumpernickel, buttered and topped with marinated herring, herring in wine sauce (both cut in strips), and herring salad.
Pumpernickel, buttered and topped with a slice each of pâté, ham, and smoked tongue.
Pumpernickel, buttered and topped with hard-cooked-egg slices, caviar, and mayonnaise, or with egg, smoked eel, and chopped chives.
Pumpernickel, buttered and topped with roast-beef and ham slices, asparagus tips, and mayonnaise.
Rye bread, buttered and topped with pâté, bacon, tomato slices, and horseradish.

EASY-TO-MAKE CANAPÉS AND HORS D'OEUVRES

Stuff pitted green olives with softened Cheddar cheese; wrap in bacon, and broil until bacon is crisp.

Top rounds of black bread with soft pâté; sprinkle with chopped pistachio nuts and chopped black olives.

Stuff cherry tomatoes with softened cream cheese that has been thinned with a little milk.

Peel and halve Anjou pears; wrap in thin slices of smoked beef.

Spread sesame bread sticks with Boursin cheese (or wrap in Swiss cheese), and wrap with prosciutto.

Trim all crusts from an unsliced loaf of whole-wheat bread. Slice lengthwise. Butter each slice, and add a layer of smoked salmon and a sprinkle of lemon juice and black pepper. From short end, roll up like a jelly roll; chill. Slice before serving.

Mix 4 ounces lumpfish caviar with 1 cup sour cream, 1 teaspoon lemon juice, and ½ pound scallion cream cheese. Spread on toast rounds or cracker.

Cheese Logs: Mix plain or scallion cream cheese, Roquefort or Cheddar, and seasonings to taste—such as Worcestershire sauce, cognac, garlic, Tabasco, grated onion, chopped olives. Roll mixture into logs; chill. Then roll in chopped chives, peanuts, or almonds, or in sesame seeds.

Cheese Spread: Use equal parts shredded Gruyère, crumbled Camembert, crumbled Gorgonzola, and softened scallion cream cheese. Beat with electric mixer until creamy. Sprinkle with paprika; chill. Spread on crackers or in celery stalks.

A CATERED AFFAIR

A HERO'S WELCOME
AND HOW
TO GET ONE

In New York, they're called heroes; in New England, grinders or submarines; poor boys or hoagies in the South. The French and Italians usually just split bread and fill it up with whatever's available. In the States, there's always dry sausage, other meat, cheese, roasted peppers, anchovies, and olives. Truly, the best part of these sandwiches is stuffing them with whatever you like best.

Start with bread—the long Italian loaves are best—split in half lengthwise. Spread with butter, mustard, mayonnaise, or even all three.

SAUSAGE:
Genoa Piccolo salami
Zabar's Love and Garlic salami
Toscano salami
Cervelat
Kielbasa
Mortadella
Capocollo

OTHER MEATS:
Hickory-smoked ham
Prosciutto
Pancetta
Black Forest ham
Smoked turkey
Roast beef
Lachschinken
Smithfield ham

CHEESE:
Swiss
Provolone
Muenster
Mozzarella
Bel Paese
Gruyère, plain or smoked
Jarlsberg
Fontina

Once you've got the sausage, meat, and cheese down, you need a salady topping. Shredded lettuce, onion and tomato are the usual; but chopped sweet or hot peppers, coleslaw, marinated asparagus spears, marinated mushrooms could be nice.

There are no hard-and-fast rules. Build your hero any way you want to, in absolutely any order. Sprinkle the whole thing with a little oil and vinegar and salt and pepper; top with other bread half, and dig in. And have plenty of napkins at the ready.

ZAKUSKA FOR 12—A RUSSIAN-STYLE ANTIPASTO

¾ *pound pâté, sliced thin*
6 to 12 ounces caviar
3 pounds smoked salmon, sliced very thin
1 pound smoked turkey
1 pound Virginia ham
1 pound prosciutto
1 pound cucumber salad
½ *pound chopped-herring salad*
1 pound spicy eggplant salad
1 pound asparagus vinaigrette
½ *pound Greek olives*
1 loaf Russian black bread
1 loaf rye bread
1 loaf French bread, sliced and toasted
  (for pâté and caviar)

This traditional Russian assortment goes with, naturally, icy-cold vodka.

CREAM-CHEESE
KISSES

1 package (10) refrigerator biscuits
¼ pound Zabar's scallion cream cheese

Preheat oven to 350°F.

Separate biscuits (each should easily come apart into 3 sections; you should have 30 rounds of dough). Put about ½ teaspoon cheese in center of each round; bring dough up around cheese, to form a kiss. Brush with lightly beaten egg white, if desired.

Bake 10 to 12 minutes, until golden-brown. *Makes 30 kisses.*

CHEESE-AND-ASPARAGUS
CANAPÉS

2 tablespoons butter
4 slices white bread, toasted
¼ pound pancetta
12 marinated asparagus spears, drained
4 slices Edam cheese
Chopped parsley

Butter toasted bread. On each slice, place a layer of pancetta, 3 asparagus spears, and a cheese slice. Broil until cheese is melted and bubbly. Sprinkle with parsley. Cut into thirds, if desired. *Makes 4 large or 12 small canapés.*

LOBSTER WITH CAVIAR SAUCE

4 pounds cleaned, cooked lobster or crabmeat
1 cup mayonnaise
1 cup sour cream
2 teaspoons grated lemon peel
2 tablespoons lemon juice
1 tablespoon grated onion
1 tablespoon chili sauce
Salt and freshly ground pepper, to taste
Dash Tabasco
½ cup salmon caviar

Put lobster or crabmeat in a serving bowl. Combine all other ingredients except caviar, and mix well. Swirl in caviar, but don't mix too well—it should look pretty. Pour over shellfish, and chill.

SPECIAL SUPPER FOR 16

Pâté maison with French bread (1 to 1½ pounds pâté; 1 loaf bread)
Lobster with Caviar Sauce (below)
Swiss Salad (below)
Chocolate mousse or cheesecake (2 quarts mousse; 1 large cake)

SWISS SALAD

½ pound marinated mushrooms
½ pound drained artichoke hearts
½ pound drained hearts of palm
4 hard-cooked eggs, chopped
3 tablespoons drained, chopped capers
1 cup diced Swiss cheese
2 cups diced celery
5 cups cooked, peeled, sliced potatoes
1 cup diced fennel
¼ cup mayonnaise
5 tablespoons white-wine vinegar
1 cup olive oil

In a serving bowl, combine all ingredients except last three. Blend mayonnaise, vinegar, and oil. Pour over vegetables, and chill.

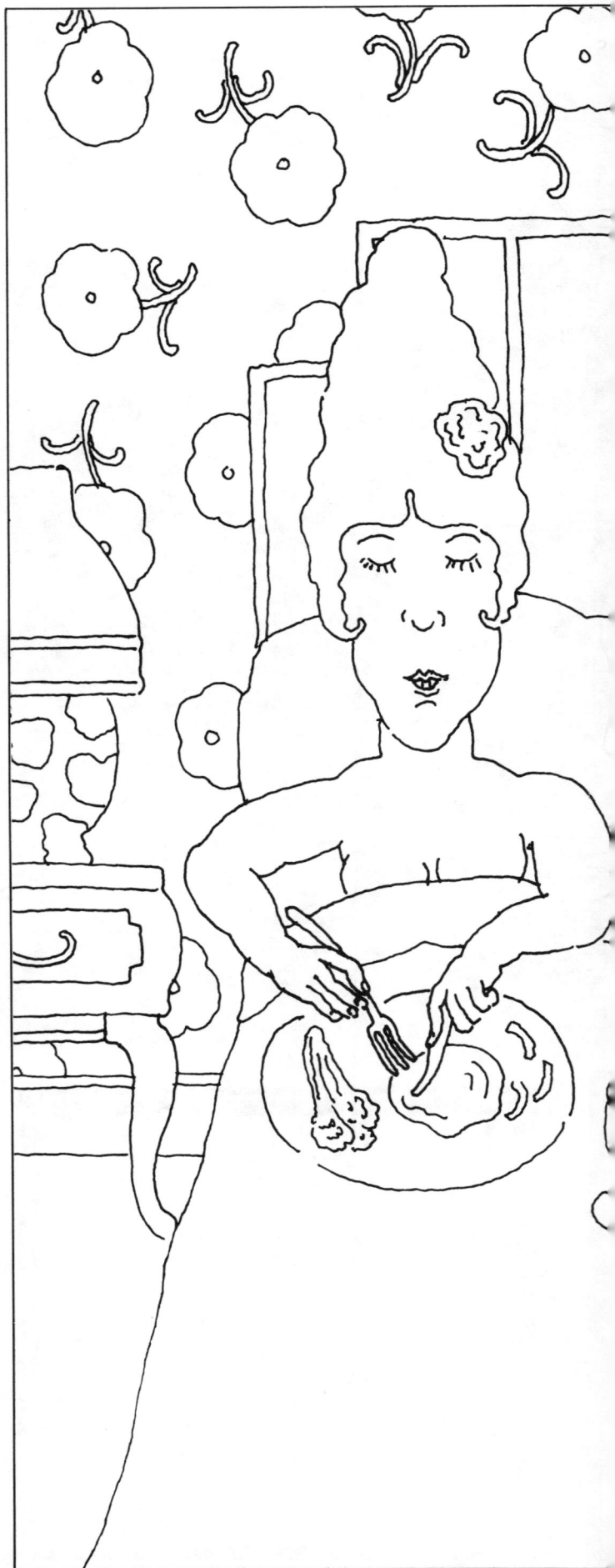

THE CHEESE BOARD

Some general rules: Figure on between 3½ and 4 ounces of cheese (total) per person, with 3 or 4 varieties of cheese. Always try to include one soft, one semi-soft, one blue, and one fresh or goat cheese, and be sure to have at least one of them well-known and well-liked (such as Emmenthal, Gruyère, or Cheddar) for the less adventurous. Mild cheeses deserve mild breads and crackers—French and Italian loaves, water biscuits, etc. The stronger cheeses can handle a more flavorful assortment of breads and crackers—ryes and pumpernickels, rye crackers, etc. Some sample cheese boards follow:

Boursault
Camembert
Gouda
Danablu
Baguettes,
Pumpernickel,
English water
biscuits

Bel Paese
Emmenthal
Brie
Münster
Brown bread,
Creme crackers,
Swedish flatbread

Cheddar
Banon
Gorgonzola
L'Explorateur
Peasant bread,
Water biscuits

Appenzel
Roquefort
Danish Tybo
Carré de l'Est
Sour-dough rye,
Challah,
Water biscuits

Jarlsberg
Chabichou
Bleu de Bresse
Reblochon
Rye crackers,
Pumpernickel,
French bread

Gjetost
Neufchatel
Stilton
Havarti
Digestif biscuits,
Italian bread

Montrachet
Cantal
Edam
Vacherin
French bread,
Water biscuits

Fontina
Provolone
Gorgonzola
Bel Paese
Italian bread, what else?

Longhorn Cheddar
Tilsit
Limburger
Petit Suisse
Italian or French bread,
Rye crackers,
Cream crackers

Colby
Saga
Gruyère
Port du Salut
Pumpernickel or
black bread,
Flatbread

THE ZABAR'S GUIDE
TO WEIGHT LOSS
WHILE STUFFING
YOUR FACE

BREAD: _calories_

Bagel (1)	120
Bialy (1)	120
Challah (1 slice)	65
French (1 slice)	58
Italian (1 slice)	55
Pumpernickel (1 slice)	74
Raisin pumpernickel (1 slice)	100
Rye (1 slice)	56
White (1 slice)	62

CAVIAR:

1 ounce (regular)	74
1 ounce (pressed)	89

CHEESE:

Blue (1 ounce)	103
Brick (1 ounce)	105
Camembert (1 ounce)	84
Cheddar (1 ounce)	111
Cream (1 ounce)	105
Cream (1 tablespoon)	56
Edam (1 ounce)	105
Gouda (1 ounce)	108
Gruyère (1 ounce)	110
Monterey Jack (1 ounce)	103
Muenster (1 ounce)	100
Parmesan (1 tablespoon, grated)	29
Provolone (1 ounce)	99
Swiss (Emmenthal, 1 ounce)	104
Velveeta (1 ounce)	84
Gjetost (1 ounce)	135
Mozzarella (1 ounce, skim milk)	79
Mozzarella (1 ounce, whole milk)	96

FISH:

Eel (smoked, 4 ounces)	374
Finnan Haddie (4 ounces)	117
Haddock (smoked, 4 ounces)	117
Herring: Bloaters (4 ounces)	222
Brined (4 ounces)	247
Cream Sauce (8 ounces)	392
Kippered (4 ounces)	239
Matjes (8 ounces)	480
Pickled (4 ounces)	253
Wine Sauce (8 ounces)	360

calories

Mackerel (smoked, 4 ounces)	250
Salmon (smoked, 4 ounces)	200
Sturgeon (smoked, 4 ounces)	169
Whitefish (smoked, 4 ounces)	176

MEAT:

Bacon (Canadian, 1 slice)	58
Bacon (Canadian, 3 ounces)	185
Bacon (regular, 2 slices)	98
Bologna (4 ounces)	312
Braunschweiger (4 ounces)	364
Capocollo (4 ounces)	565
Cervelat (dry, 4 ounces)	514
Cervelat (soft, 4 ounces)	350
Frankfurters (1)	151
Knockwurst (4 ounces)	317
Ham (boiled, 4 ounces)	266
Ham (country-style, 4 ounces)	353
Corned beef (4 ounces)	424
Dried beef (4 ounces)	231
Liverwurst (fresh, 4 ounces)	350
Liverwurst (smoked, 4 ounces)	364
Mortadella (4 ounces)	358
Pastrami (4 ounces)	272
Salami (cooked, 4 ounces)	353
Salami (dry, 4 ounces)	510
Tongue (4 ounces)	181

MISCELLANEOUS:

ChowChow pickles (sweet, 4 ounces)	132
ChowChow pickles (sour, 4 ounces)	33
Chutney (Major Grey's, 1 tablespoon)	53
Honey (1 ounce)	86
Jams and preserves (1 ounce)	77
Mustard (1 ounce)	26
Olives (green, 4 medium)	15
Olives (ripe, 3 small)	15
Pâté (1 ounce)	131
Pickles: Dill, 1 large	15
Bread and butter (4 ounces)	83
Sour, 1 large	14
Potato Salad (½ cup)	167
Sauerkraut (½ cup)	21

ZABAR'S®

A GOURMET & EPICUREAN EMPORIUM　　SMOKED FISH
STURGEON　　FRESH CAVIARS　　GOURMET COOKWARE
GIFT BASKETS　　CATERING　　SUN-THURS TILL 7:30 PM
FRI TILL 10 PM　　SAT TILL 12 PM

WHOLE GRAIN BREADS
IMPORTED CHEESE
BEAN COFFEE

Catering Selections
Zabar's Cold Buffet

Prices on the following items are furnished by Zabar's on request.

ZABAR'S FAMOUS PLATTERS

MEATS: Beautifully decorated ready-to-serve trays accompanied by salad and coleslaw, pickles, mustard, and Russian Dressing, plus an assortment of sliced Zabar's bread. Your choice of four sliced meats from the following:

Roast beef	Tongue	Black Forest ham
Corned beef	Kosher salami	Pastrami
Turkey	Italian salami	Boiled ham
Virginia ham	Smoked turkey	(Swiss cheese included with hams)

SMOKED FISH: Attractively decorated trays including Nova Scotia or Scotch salmon, kippered salmon, sable, and large whitefish (boned, filleted, and presented whole), plus Greek olives, Zabar's cream cheese with scallions, plain cream cheese, sliced bagels, and pumpernickel bread.

SMORGASBORD: Accompanied by Zabar's breads and imported crackers. An order for 20 includes four choices from the following (add an additional choice for each 10 people):

Matjes herring	Imported cheeses	Crabmeat salad
Pickled herring	Chopped chicken liver	Chicken salad
Schmaltz herring	Shrimp salad	Whitefish salad
Pickled lox	Pâté maison	Baked salmon salad
Scallion cream cheese	Lobster salad	Greek salad

CHEESE: Ten to twelve imported cheeses presented in wedges on garnished platter, served with French or pumpernickel bread cut into small pieces and imported crackers. Cubed cheese platters also available. Cheeses usually available include:

French brie	Italian Fontina	Italian Bel Paese
French gourmandise	Danish blue	French Roquefort
English cheshire	French goat	French port salut
Danish tilsit	Wine cheddar	French Boursin
Norwegian Jarlsberg	German bianco	Swiss Gruyère

JUMBO SANDWICH: Your choice of any assortment of meat and/or seafood salads on rye, pumpernickel, or white bread. Sandwiches are cut in thirds and attractively arranged on garnished trays. Price includes sliced pickles, mustard, and Russian dressing on the side. Smoked fish sandwiches are also available, with price varying according to fish.

CUBED MEAT: Baked Virginia ham, Polish kielbasa and Italian salami cut into bite sized pieces, includes rye or pumpernickel bread and mustard.

FRESH IRANIAN MALLOSSAL CAVIAR: For that special occasion! Large grain Beluga or medium grain Sevruga available in 4-ounce, 7-ounce, or 14-ounce tins, or in the original 2-kilo tin.

WHOLE SMOKED NOVA SCOTIA OR SCOTCH SALMON: The entire salmon is expertly sliced and reshaped to its original form on a wood or marble fish board with silvered head and tail.

WHOLE SMOKED LARGE WHITEFISH: Boned and filleted, presented whole in the skin on a marble board.

GRAVLAX: Whole side of fresh salmon cured in a dill sauce. The entire side of salmon expertly sliced and reshaped to its original form on a wood or marble board. Average weight 1½ lbs.

WHOLE POACHED SALMON: Delicately poached in white wine, presented whole on wood or marble fish board, garnished with sliced lemons and capers. Average weight 3 to 4 pounds.

CHOPPED CHICKEN LIVER MOLD: Includes pumpernickel bread or crackers.

WHOLE PÂTÉ MAISON WITH TRUFFLES: Presented whole or cut into strips; includes sliced pumpernickel bread and imported crackers.

WHOLE TURKEYS CARVED AND REPLACED ON THE FRAME: Roasted, twelve pounds and up (weight before roasting). Smoked, approximately 12 pounds.

WHOLE BAKED VIRGINIA HAM: Approximately 12 pounds. Thinly sliced, and reassembled to its original shape on a decorated platter. Sliced Swiss cheese available at additional cost.

WHOLE HOT ROAST BEEF: Approximately 18 to 20 pounds before roasting. Cooked to your order and tenderly watched.

STANDING ROAST RIBS OF BEEF: Roasted in our Texas barbeque ovens, giving it a subtle and lightly smoked flavor. Cooked to your order. Average 4 ribs.

SHELL STEAK ROAST ROAST: Whole boneless shells of beef roasted to your order with a light smoked flavor. Average weight 8 pounds.

BRISKET OF BEEF:

Roast brisket of beef: Marinated for five days before roasting in our professional ovens. A special treat.

Our own famous barbequed brisket of beef: Roasted in our Texas barbeque ovens, giving the brisket a slightly smoky flavor.

CHICKEN BALLENTINE: A large whole boneless chicken breast is stuffed with fresh mushrooms, herbs, and rice and baked. A wonderful main course.

ZABAR'S FAT-FREE FRENCH-STYLE ROAST DUCK: Bred in the French tradition, more breast and no fat. Stuffed with fruit and vegetables, can be eaten cold. Average weight 2 pounds.

ZABAR'S FRENCH SMOKED DUCK: This no-fat duck is lightly smoked, enhancing its natural flavors. Average weight 2 pounds.

ROAST CORNISH GAME HENS: Average weight 1½ pounds. Roasted in our Texas barbeque ovens, which give these hens a delicate smoky flavor.

ROAST MILK-FED WHITE VEAL: A delicate whole roast stuffed with imported fontina, ham, and spices.

QUICHE: To be heated by the customer. Quiche Lorraine, spinach, mushroom, onion, or seafood quiches available in 4-inch and 8-inch sizes.

HOT SMORGASBORD: Sweet butter puff pastry hors d'oeuvres made especially for Zabar's, to be heated by the customer. These include:

2 dozen cocktail franks in jackets	2 dozen shrimp with sherry
2 dozen mushroom puffs	2 dozen lobster with cognac
2 dozen crabmeat puffs	1 dozen miniature quiches Lorraine

DESSERTS: Our cheesecakes, miniature danish, Danish butter cookies, as well as Famous Amos chocolate chip cookies. On Fridays, Saturdays, and Sundays, we also feature our own famous Russian-style coffee cake filled with fruits and nuts, and freshly baked strips of cherry, cheese, or apple strudel.